NEUROPSYCHOLOGY OF ART

Brain Damage, Behaviour and Cognition:
Developments in Clinical Neuropsychology
Titles in Series

Neuropsychology of Art
Neurological, cognitive, and evolutionary perspectives

Dahlia W. Zaidel

Psychology Press
Taylor & Francis Group

HOVE AND NEW YORK

First published 2005 by Psychology Press
27 Church Road, Hove, East Sussex BN3 2FA

Simultaneously published in the USA and Canada
by Psychology Press
270 Madison Avenue, New York NY 10016

Reprinted 2007

Psychology Press is an imprint of the Taylor and Francis Group, an Informa business

Typeset in Times by RefineCatch Ltd, Bungay, Suffolk
Printed and bound in Great Britain by
MPG Books Ltd, Bodmin, Cornwall
Cover design by Jim Wilkie

British Library Cataloguing in Publication Data
A catalogue record for this book is available from the British Library

Library of Congress Cataloging in Publication Data
Zaidel, Dahlia W.
   Neuropsychology of art : neurological, cognitive and evolutionary
perspectives / Dahlia W. Zaidel.—1st ed.
      p. cm.
   Includes bibliographical references and index.
   ISBN 1–84169–363–4 (hardcover)
  1. Neuropsychology. 2. Art. 3. Creative ability. 4. Cognitive
neuroscience. 5. Evolutionary psychology. I. Titles.
   QP430.Z35   2005
   612.8'2—dc22
                                                  2005011761

ISBN 978-1–84169–363–7 (hbk)

*Dedicated to the memory of
Roger W. Sperry, Nobel Laureate,
scientist and artist*

Contents

viii   *Contents*

Series preface

From being an area primarily on the periphery of mainstream behavioural and cognitive science, neuropsychology has developed in recent years into an area of central concern for a range of disciplines. We are witnessing not only a revolution in the way in which brain-behaviour-cognition relationships are viewed, but a widening of interest concerning developments in neuro-psychology on the part of a range of workers in a variety of fields. Major advances in brain-imaging techniques and the cognitive modelling of the impairments following brain damage promise a wider understanding of the nature of the representation of cognition and behaviour in the damaged and undamaged brain.

Neuropsychology is now centrally important for those working with brain-damaged people, but the very rate of expansion in the area makes it difficult to keep up with findings from the current research. The aim of the Brain Damage, Behaviour and Cognition series is to publish a wide range of books that present comprehensive and up-to-date overviews of current developments in specific areas of interest.

These books will be of particular interest to those working with the brain-damaged. It is the editors' intention that undergraduates, postgraduates, clinicians, and researchers in psychology, speech pathology and medicine will find this series a useful source of information on important current develop-ments. The authors and editors of the books in this series are experts in their respective fields, working at the forefront of contemporary research. They have produced texts that are accessible and scholarly. We thank them for their contribution and their hard work in fulfilling the aims of the series.

CC and GH
Sydney, Australia and Birmingham, UK
Series Editors

Preface

The artist's studio, regardless of its location and time in history, is a natural laboratory for neuropsychology and neuroscience. Unlike the deliberate theory-driven stimuli created in scientific laboratories for the purpose of deriving models of behavior and the mind, artists often create their works spontaneously, their productions reflecting the mind in the brain in a natural setting. Art expression is by and large unique to humans and, basically, no different from language expression in the sense that both represent diverse communication forms each with potentially infinite combinations. At the same time, neuropsychological evidence from artists with brain damage suggests that the two forms are not necessarily related, that is, language can become severely affected in a given artist following damage while art expression is only minimally or not at all affected. This in turn raises the possibility that at the dawn of human brain evolution, language and art were not that closely intertwined. In the absence of fossil and archaeological evidence to the contrary, this still remains an open question, and one that will always be difficult to resolve. In the evolutionary scheme of things art could have developed earlier than language, preceding it not because of its non-verbal format, but because of its symbolic, abstract, and communicative value; alternatively, art making and language could have emerged slowly, and in parallel, in the same evolutionary window. The emergence of both modes of communication likely relied on pre-existing biological mechanisms and neuroanatomical arrangements that supported cognitive abstraction, something that probably took millions of years to evolve.

This book is intended for neuropsychologists, neuroscientists, neurologists, psychologists, anthropologists, archaeologists, artists – advanced students, clinicians, researchers – anyone working with or who is interested in the human brain, brain damage, and the relationship between art and brain. It discusses both visual and musical arts.

There are no specific neuropsychological tests that measure the essence of art or its unique features, whereas there are numerous tests that measure neuro-components of language, and other types of cognition, and their localization in the brain. We know only a few of the equivalents of "words" and "grammar" in art although we are able to derive meaning from art without being aware of its vocabulary and syntax. In the visual arts, for instance, the vocabulary is based on forms, shapes, and patterns that are represented with angles, perspective lines, convergence, vanishing points, overlap, light–dark gradations, illusory depth, canonical views, embedding, texture, medium, colors, shadows, edges, and much more. These examples name but a few of the alphabetical primitives in the visual arts, and they do not all have ready interpretations within existing neuropsychological tools or models. Clarifying the relationship between art and brain has not been top priority in neuroscientific research, despite the enormous intellectual appeal inherent in the relationship; it is barely in its initial stages of scrutiny. Moreover, the significance of the full artistic composition, as a whole, lies in interpreting the cultural (and ecological, environmental) context in which the art is produced and is experienced. An interdisciplinary approach to the neuropsychology of art is thus essential.

The core of neuropsychology has been built from investigations of neurological patients with localized brain damage. However, neuropsychological and neurological reports of artists with brain lesions are rare, commonly not empirical, and are published by non-artists. In the majority of those published cases, little information is provided for the immediate post-damage period, to say nothing of the ensuing few months, and hardly any empirical data are provided; the reports are based predominantly on observations. With the famous artists, there may have been an incentive not to hold on to documentation of initial attempts at art production particularly when preserved art skills emerged subsequently with time. Documentation of very early works could be extremely useful and revealing for neuropsychology, even if complicated by the immediate neurophysiological reactions in the brain to the damage. The best that neuropsychologists can do with the data is be guided by existing neuropsychological principles (derived and gleaned from non-artists) that tap known components of general perception and cognition. Exploration of art following acquired neurological brain disorders in established artists, in artists with congenital brain disorders, and in artists with sensory deficits, helps build up a broad elucidation of the relationship between art and brain. All of this is attempted in this book.

Neuropsychologists have traditionally separated sensory deficits from central impairments in order to be sure that the behavior under study is due to brain rather than to sensory damage. Sensory issues that are not clarified muddy the neuropsychological picture. For this reason, clarification of any sensory deficits in artists further inform the relationship between neuropsychology, the brain and art. It is particularly important not to ignore deficits in vision and hearing in a field as little explored as this. For example, in assessing central control of visual art, eye health has to be taken into account, either explained or ruled out. Exploring the nature of art from its early beginning hundreds of thousands years ago through its development and multiformed practice, as is done in this book, enhances the potential for insights into art's neural substrates and propels the extraction of meaningful patterns. An understanding of the neuropsychology of art requires an interdisciplinary approach: combining such diverse fields as neuropsychology, neurology, and psychology with art history, anthropology, archaeology, evolutionary and biological theories means talking about some basic essentials of these fields and creating a knowledge base for the reader. In addition, society's preoccupations and expectations at the time of production are invaluable for obtaining a judicious perspective of the art. In the dawn of human evolution, habitat, climatic conditions, terrain, predators, food sources, and more, all played roles in what could be produced by way of art.

The literary and written arts are not examined in depth in this book simply because neurological cases of literary artists are exceptionally rare. They have ceased to produce (artistic works) following left hemisphere damage, and no published cases with right hemisphere damage from the literary arts are known to me. Unlike the visual and musical arts, in the production aspect of the literary arts, artists rely heavily (perhaps even principally) on the workings of the left hemisphere. Any role that the right hemisphere might have in these arts is little explored and is uncertain, largely because of paucity of relevant neurological cases. While there is continuing debate on the components of language to which the right hemisphere contributes (e.g., jokes, humor), in the normal or damaged brain, there is wide agreement on the main specialization of the left hemisphere in language functions (see end of Chapter 1 for discussion of aphasia and laterality). Consequently, for now, it is difficult to meaningfully explore the ways in which the brain damage fragments elements of literary writing and the whole cognitive and creative thinking that goes into it.

Both the visual and musical arts are explored here; more discussion is devoted to the former than to the latter. The elements that enter into artistic productions in the artist and the reactions to them by viewers are important. Questions about the neural substrates of art (neuro-components) have been a source of deep fascination in diverse and wide scholarly and scientific fields. Neurological evidence from brain-damaged artists is critical, even if such cases are relatively rare, because ultimately the damage breaks behavior into units that help shed light on the artist's brain and cognition. Extracting and distilling the post-damage artistic behavior in order to formulate a unitary theory of the neuropsychology of art can, however, be complicated by lack of uniformity in the behavior.

I discuss the visual and musical arts against the background of early human beginnings and the biological origin and significance of the practice of art, as well as the effects of brain damage on art productions by established artists. I consider, too, special groups of artists such as autistic visual savants, and dementia patients. I examine the relationship between art and functional localization in the brain, hemispheric specialization, handedness, the health status of the eye, neurocognitive abilities and the brain, stored concepts in long-term memory and experience, emotions, film (cinema), colors, talent, creativity, beauty, art history, and relevant neuropsychological issues. The bottom line in art production is talent, an elusive, ill-defined attribute, which, considering the evidence presented in this book, may be diffusely represented in the brain and thus explain preservation of skills and creativity despite neurological damage.

A major brain and behavior organizing principle in neuropsychology is hemispheric specialization. Empirical studies have supported the widely accepted notion that the two hemispheres are distinguished by characteristic cognitive and thinking computational styles: the left hemisphere, besides its main language specialization, applies a detailed, attentive, piecemeal, analytic, and logical computational approach whereas in the right hemisphere, computations are assumed to be done according to global, wholistic, or gestalt strategies. However, there is no strong evidence to support an early theory that the right hemisphere specializes in art (production or appreciation), in creativity, or in music, more than the left hemisphere. That the right is the creative and artistic hemisphere is an old notion, originally formulated only as a working hypothesis in left–right hemispheric research. The ensuing years did not support that early hypothesis. It is highly likely that both hemispheres modulate many human perceptions and expressions through functional specialization and complementarity, and this includes the multiple components of art, creativity, and emotions.

Moreover, as will become clear by reading Chapters 2 and 5, brain damage, whether unilateral or diffuse, does not lead to creation of brand new artistic styles but rather to adjustments to the motoric or sensory consequences of the damage (see introduction to Chapter 2 for artistic style definition). An artist dedicated to abstract expressionism, an art style devoid of realistic figurative forms, does not begin to depict representational forms following brain damage; pre-morbid specialization does not swing into a diametrically opposite mode of representation. Changes in techniques can and do occur, however. Artistic talent and skills remain preserved despite ravages of brain damage, regardless of laterality or etiology.

Chapter 1 is an overview; it introduces the major issues that need to be considered in discussing the neuropsychology of art and imparts a backdrop for further discussions in the following chapters. Chapter 2 describes specific established professional visual artists with acquired brain damage due to unilateral stroke, as well as art in slow neurodegenerative diseases that compromised both hemispheres. Functional compensation and reshaping of neuronal substrates contribute to post-damage production, and these reorganization issues are covered. Chapter 3 discusses vision and color perception at the level of the eye as well as the brain, and discusses the effects on art of sensory alterations in vision, and damage compromising visual processing areas in the brain. This chapter also describes eye diseases and problems in specific established artists. Chapter 4 combines discussion of autistic savants and those with fronto-temporal dementia. Highly skilled visual autistic artists demonstrate functional separation in the brain between two modes of communication, language versus art, and they contribute to an understanding of brain and art by what is absent (or severely compromised) in their art. The issue of emerging artistic productions in non-artists with dementia is discussed in terms of functional compensation, neuronal rewiring, and the serial lesion effect. Chapters 5 and 6 cover music. Chapter 5 focuses on established composers with localized brain damage and those with neurodegenerative diseases. As with the visual artists, such cases are extremely rare. Well-known composers with neurological disorders caused by syphilis and other causes are described and explored as well. Chapter 6 progresses to musical performers and amusia, and very recent findings from fMRI (functional magnetic resonance imaging) and other neuroimaging experiments designed to determine cortical localization of aspects of music listening. Chapter 7 emphasizes many known concepts from neuropsychology of perception and cognition, gleaned over the years from non-artists that enter into visual art production and art observation. The role of the right hemisphere in drawing and space perception in pictures is essential for gaining an understanding of the neuropsychology of art. Consequently, the development of illusionistic depictions of depth in the history of Western art is covered here. Chapter 8 concentrates on drawings in patients with various etiologies of brain damage and describes the syndromes of hemi-neglect and simultanagnosia. Chapter 9 is a discussion of beauty and its depiction in visual arts (including film), pleasure in art, and emotions as pertaining to art. Empirical studies of brain activity in these three areas are described, even as there is remarkable dearth of such studies. The relevance of the reward system to pleasure is argued and explored. Chapter 10 intensifies and expands the discussions in the previous chapters by reviewing issues of human brain evolution, early emergence of art, archaeological finds, and the biology of art, both visual and musical. Animal displays in mate selection strategies are juxtaposed with the display and purpose of human art, bringing in ethological observations into the discussion. The relevance of early emergence of symbolic representation to writing and pictures is also explored. Chapter 11 examines some important issues in the neuropsychology of creativity, of talent, and clues to talent from special artists (autistic savants and dementia patients). Main inferences from the lessons of art in established artists are offered in the ending sections. Chapter 12 offers conclusions and directions for future research in the neuropsychology of art. At the end of each chapter (save for Chapter 12) there is a list of further readings. A subject index and an author index are provided at the end of the book.

Ever since I first used art works as stimuli in neuropsychological experiments, I became fascinated with the mind of the artist and its underpinning in neuroanatomy (Zaidel, 1990a). Creating tests in the laboratory in order to explore behavior based on a theory is highly controlled by scientific rules and conventions so that valid, reliable, repeatable data can be obtained. René Magritte, the Belgian Surrealist painter, created art works that were similar to my laboratory-created stimuli, only they were more imaginative, and more daring in violating physical and logical rules of the real visual world. The distortions were relevant to my work at that time. Wanting to gain additional insights, I used them to supplement and enrich my research and have continued to use art works as stimuli in subsequent experiments designed to determine hemispheric roles in art (Zaidel & Kasher, 1989). Not being an artist, but a lover of art, this approach to science allowed me to enjoy and wonder about art in a scientific laboratory setting.

I would like to thank Hana Jung for preparing some of the illustrations, Christina Kyle for general assistance, Stanley Schein and Jim Thomas in my psychology department for discussions of color vision, Ross Levine for many suggestions that improved parts of the manuscript, Andrea Kosta for extensive discussions, comments, and suggestions, and Chris Code for invaluable feedback on versions of the manuscript.

Dahlia W. Zaidel
University of California, Los Angeles, 2004

1 Approaches to the neuropsychology of art

Introduction

Beginning in the mid-nineteenth century, with the establishment of a correlation between language functions and brain regions within the left cerebral hemisphere, there has been a trend in neuropsychology to link specific cognitions with discrete regions of the brain. This has largely been accomplished through studies of fractionated behavior following acquired brain injury in neurological patients. The location of the damage, together with the consequent behavioral breakdown, opened windows on mind–brain associations involving language, perception, memory, motor skills, personality, and what are generally considered to be higher cognitive functions. The components of behavior have to be defined in order to make such associations. The association between art and brain, however, has proven difficult because its components are elusive. What abilities of Michelangelo's mind went into painting the Sistine Chapel or sculpting *Moses* or the *Pietà*? What in Monet's mind controlled his water lily paintings, or in Gauguin's his *Ancestors of Tehamana* painting, or, in ancient artists, the cave walls at Lascaux and Altamira? Similarly, what were the components of Verdi's mind when he composed *Aida*? And what brain mechanisms were at work in the great plays, poems, literature, and ballets that continually remain sources of attraction and fascination? The answers to some of these challenging questions can be explored with the perspectives of neuropsychology.

While practically everyone in society, at an early age, can learn to speak and comprehend language, only a select few in modern Western society can create art with qualities that elicit pleasure and appreciation for centuries and even millennia. Because the compositions of such artists seem to incorporate special and unique abilities, their biological basis in the brain remains a challenge. Neuropsychological methods can provide only a partial view into the "neuro-map" of art. To gain further clues and insights we need to consider the life of early humans, evolution of the human brain itself as well as evidence and discussion from diverse fields such as archaeology, biology, mate selection strategies, anthropology, the fossil record, and ancient art. Abundant human art is said to have emerged between 35,000 and 45,000 years ago in

Western Europe (Bahn, 1998). The changes in the morphology of the human brain coupled with archaeological evidence of art-related relics along with the biological development of various cognitive abilities suggest that surviving ancient etchings, paintings, statues and figurines, particularly from this Western European Paleolithic period, were not sudden expressions of mind and brain. Instead, the evidence suggests that the underlying neuroanatomy and neurophysiology evolved slowly, well before that period and may have supported earlier artistic expression (McBrearty & Brooks, 2000). Figure 1.1 illustrates cave art from Western Europe dating to 30,000 years ago (Valladas et al., 2001) and Figure 1.2 illustrates much earlier beginnings of human art in Africa (McBrearty & Brooks, 2000).

Neurological disorders have been described predominantly in visual and musical artists. Very little is known about the neural substrates of art (the neuro-components) in creative writing both because there is a dearth of known writers with localized cortical damage and because language is often so seriously disrupted following left hemisphere damage (no published cases

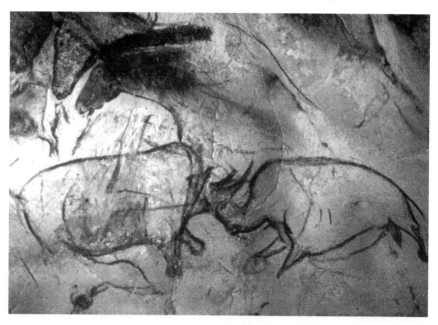

Figure 1.1 Prehistoric cave art from Western Europe (Valladas et al., 2001). This was drawn about 30,000 years ago in the Chauvet cave in Vallon-Pont-d'Arc, Ardèche, France, as determined through radiocarbon dating. On the upper left corner we can see several horses, and in the center at least one rhinoceros. It belongs to the Aurignacian period in Western Europe. This predates the better known cave art from Altamira and Lascaux, which are thought to have been painted some 12,000 to 17,000 years ago. They belong to the Magdalenian period. (Printed with permission from Nature Publishing.)

Behavioral Innovations of the Middle Stone Age in Africa

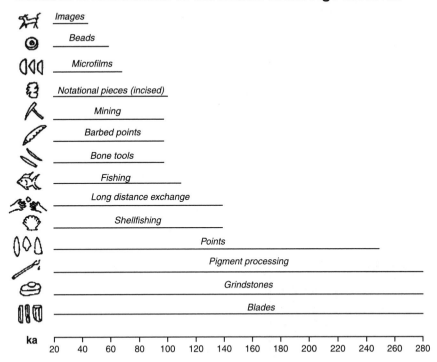

Figure 1.2 This is a summary of the emergence of art forms in Africa (McBrearty & Brooks, 2000). (Reprinted with permission from *Journal of Human Evolution*.)

of writers with right hemisphere damage are known to me) that insights into writing processes are effectively denied (Alajouanine, 1948). Consequently, the emphasis here is on individuals engaged in the visual and musical arts.

The relationship between art and the brain needs to be charted. The relationship can benefit a great deal from exploring deficits in established artists after they have sustained brain damage. Searching and documenting patterns in their artistic endeavors following the damage helps reveal aspects of the relationship, zero in on the anatomical and functional underpinning, and identify questions brought up by the patterns.

Definitions and purpose of art

What is art? Art includes paintings, sculptures, pottery, jewelry, drawings, music, dance, theater, creative writing, architecture, film (cinema, movies), photography, and many additional fields. These are but examples. The list is long. By and large there seems to be a consensus that art is a human-made creation with a social anchor that communicates ideas, concepts, meanings, and emotions, that art represents talent, skill and creativity, that it gives rise to pleasure through the elicitation of an aesthetic response, even while, for the most part, art does not seem to have a direct utilitarian purpose. At the same time, a myriad of examples of art works throughout the world complicates the imposition of clear-cut, precise, or logical boundaries on art as a category of human creation.

The wide range of possible human activities that express art is described by anthropologist Ellen Dissanayake (1988):

> Perhaps the most outstanding feature of art in primitive societies is that it is inseparable from daily life, also appearing prominently and inevitably in ceremonial observances. Its variety is as great as the kinds of lives (hunting, herding, fishing, farming) and the types of ritual practices (ceremonies to ensure success in a group venture or to encourage reunification after a group dissension; rites of passage; accompaniments to seasonal changes; memorial occasions; individual and group displays). All these may be accompanied by singing, dancing, drumming, improvisatory versification, reciting, impersonation, performance on diverse musical instruments, or invocations with a special vocabulary. Decorated objects may include masks, rattles, dance staves, ceremonial spears and poles, totem poles, costumes, ceremonial vessels, symbols of chiefly power, human skulls; and objects of use such as head rests or stools, paddles, dilly bags, pipes and spear-throwers, calabashes, baskets, fabric and garments, mats, pottery, toys, canoes, weapons, shields; transport lorry interiors and exteriors; cattle; manioc cakes and yams; or house walls, doors, and window frames. Songs may be used to settle legal disputes or to extol warriors as well as for lullabies and the expression of high spirits. A large part of the environment may be rearranged and shaped for initiation or funeral rites; theatrical displays may go on for hours or days. There may be painting on a variety of surfaces (ground, rock, wood, cloth); piling up of stones or pieces of roasted and decorated pork; considered display of garden produce; body ornamentation (tattooing, oiling, painting). Many of these occasions for art have counterparts in the modern developing world.
>
> (Dissanayake, 1988, pp. 44–45)

As this description shows, art can be many things. We in Westernized societies typically think of art as something viewed in museums or seen in the theater or heard in a concert hall or read in a book. By comparison, the list of artistic expressions provided by Dissanayake demonstrates the motivation, need, and drive as well as the capability that humans possess to create boundless expressions of art. Language, the prime example of the human mind, is characterized by its combinatorial power and infinite potential to create units of meanings through vocabulary and syntax. In this regard, art and language share the same cognitive underpinning. Art can be infinitely combinatorial too. It should thus not be surprising that the art of many human societies is nearly limitless in creativity and skill.

Multiple components of art and brain damage in established artists

How are we to understand the neuroanatomical and neurophysiological underpinnings of all of these artistic expressions? A unified behavioral expression represents a complex conglomerate that is more than the sum of its parts, with several brain regions simultaneously involved in its execution. Art production is not alone in this regard. Mere observations of psychological phenomena or theorizing alone are not sufficient to uncover the components of complex behaviors, abilities, and talents. At the same time, the ability to create art is just as susceptible to breakdown and fractionation following brain damage as other behaviors are, which suggests that some of its units and mechanisms can be unmasked. Similarly, sensory deficits in artists, particularly with vision and hearing, can throw additional light on the final artistic product. A painting by Vincent van Gogh, for example, is a unified product, the execution of which required multiple components from diverse functional domains including visual perception, color vision, creativity, fine finger dexterity, motor control, eye–hand coordination, conceptual understanding, spatial perception, problem solving, reasoning, memory – to name but a few requirements. And, of course, it is the fusion of the elusive attribute of talent with training and expertise – the unique decision-making apparatus determining the nature of the composition, the colors, the lines, tilts, angles, and so on – that needs to be understood against the background of neuroanatomical substrates. Currently, rather than a single region, given the available data, it would appear that art is the functional realization of multiple components that engage many regions in the brain.

The perspective adopted here is that the most useful insights into the neuroanatomical underpinnings of the complex process of creating art can be gleaned from the consequences of brain damage in established professional artists, those whose works have been exhibited, appreciated, studied, sold, discussed, remembered, and admired prior to the injury. It is clear that they have artistic talent, creativity, and skills. The more localized the damage is to a specific region, the more valuable it is for reaching conclusions regarding these underpinnings. The main neuropsychological interest lies in emergence or not of alterations following the damage, and if alterations do occur, what are their causes. The cognitive underpinnings of art production and appreciation as revealed through brain damage in artists is little explored, largely because localized damage in such artists is rare. Even the cognitive underpinnings of art as studied under laboratory conditions in normal subjects with intact brains is quite complex and has yet to fully explain such important issues as talent, skill, and creativity.

It should be kept in mind that art conception and construction following the damage is the outcome of combined activity of both healthy and diseased tissue. Or viewed in another way, the work is reflection of the brain's reaction to neural irregularity (Calabresi, Centonze, Pisani, Cupini, & Bernardi, 2003; Duffau et al., 2003; Kapur, 1996; Ovsiew, 1997; Rossini, 2001). Functional reshaping of the brain consequent to damage is currently under increasing scrutiny with neuroimaging techniques, particularly with respect to language (Duffau et al., 2003). Functional reorganization is an issue that should be considered in contemplating the neural support for art (and this is discussed in the last section of Chapter 4).

Artists with sensory problems in vision or hearing highlight a main argument of this book, that art is a complex expression of experience, conceptual and memory systems, talent, skill, and creativity. Artists with seriously compromised vision due to disease, for example, are able to continue painting (see Chapter 3), while musicians with extremely poor hearing go on composing (see Chapter 5). A blind artist, Lisa Fittipaldi, untrained in art before the onset of her blindness, was nevertheless able to paint competently in color. Artists with progressive debilitating effects of Parkinsonian tremors were able to hold and control the paintbrush. The latter artists and their various conditions are discussed in Chapter 2.

Visual arts, perception, and neuropsychology

Neurological patients with damage to either the left or the right hemispheres are often required in the clinical or laboratory to interpret, manipulate, organize, arrange, match, or name pictures. Indeed, using pictures in neuropsychological testing is a widespread practice. Inferred function from the outcome of these tests is useful to explorations of the neuroanatomical underpinnings of the visual arts. The pictures may depict realistic objects or simple geometrical shapes. Damage to either hemisphere does not necessarily result in apictoria (the inability to derive meaning from *any* type of pictorial material). Behavioral impairments may also be seen depending on the nature of the task. Similarly, damage to either hemisphere does not obliterate the ability to draw some basic, common visual percepts. The laterality of the damage may, however, affect the characteristics of the drawings as well as the depiction of depth.

Production of art works recruits activity of several brain regions and their functions. The list includes planning, motor control, hand–eye coordination, the hippocampal formation, memory, long-term memory, concepts, semantic knowledge of the world, emotional circuitry, the parietal lobes, the control of meaning and space, global and detailed perception, disembedding strategies, sustained attention, and other widespread neuronal networks. Put another way, the arts exemplify neuropsychology in action. Realistic depictions of, for example, nature scenes, still lifes, animals, human figures and faces, all require spatial cognition; such figures can also be depicted in abstract forms. Both the right hemisphere and the detailed, analytic, and sustained attention of the left hemisphere are simultaneously involved in the production of visual art. In the visual arts, the tilt, angle, size, shape, form, height, or depth of the elements in relation to each other constitute the theme of a picture. In a rare case of an artist drawing a portrait while his eye and hand movements were being monitored by a specialized tracking device, it was found that, rather than starting with a global contour of the visual model – something associated with the right hemisphere and its cognitive style – the artist, Humphrey Ocean, nearly always began with a detail first, working his way from the inside outwards (Miall & Tchalenko, 2001). The attention to local details is precisely the cognitive style associated with the left hemisphere. A similar observation was made regarding the drawing approach of Nadia and EC, two autistic savant artists with exceptional graphic abilities for depicting realistic figures (see Chapter 4); they started with the details within the containing form and proceeded from there to complete the contour frame (Mottron & Belleville, 1995; Mottron, Limoges, & Jelenic, 2003). This strategy demonstrates that both hemispheres concurrently play significant roles in the production of visual art.

Sometimes, to achieve a particular effect, artists, in their depictions, violate the rules of natural physical space. It is the left hemisphere that specializes in processing incongruous combinations of reality (Zaidel, 1988a; Zaidel & Kasher, 1989). The best known genre where realistic objects, or their parts, are juxtaposed incongruously so as to violate physical rules of reality is that of the artist René Magritte, and other artists in the school of Surrealism; prior to that school, artists such as Manet and Cézanne experimented with established notions of spatial relationships. Figure 1.3 provides examples of Magritte's work. In Asian and ancient Egyptian art we find abundant examples of an absence of three-dimensional representations. Viewers find such art pleasing despite its incongruities and disregard for depictions of natural physical laws. The society in which the ancient artists of Egypt depicted flat worlds devoid of linear and convergent perspective is the same society that built magnificent three-dimensional architectural structures, the plans for which had to require excellent three-dimensional visualization and spatial cognition. Similarly, viewers of abstract art find it pleasing and meaningful. Thus, illusionary depth and the physical rules of spatial relationships may be ignored in the practice of art.

Color, art, and neuropsychology

An enormous amount of visual art is in black and white. Consider the sketches, engravings, etchings, lithographs, and illustrations of Rembrandt, Leonardo da Vinci, and Michelangelo, films by Fellini and by Bergman, pottery and marble sculptures by Bernini and Michelangelo, buildings by Frank Lloyd Wright, the ancient Egyptian pyramids, the Taj Mahal, and so forth. Consider, too, the fact that there have always been color-blind artists as

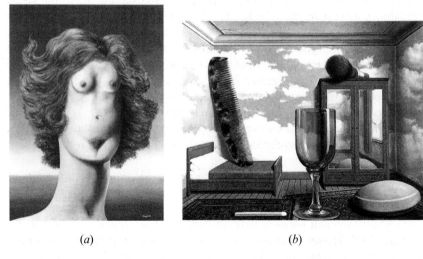

(a)   (b)

Figure 1.3 a, b Paintings by René Magritte (1898–1967), a Belgian member of the
Surrealist art movement. He painted deviations from reality in highly
systematic and deliberate manner (Gablik, 1985). His real-world forms,
figures, and shapes all have depth, they do not appear flat, they seem to
be highly realistic, and they have the visual quality of a photograph in
some sense. This is true regardless of whether the details are part of a
body or part of a landscape scene. The realism of the individual parts
that make up a whole in his paintings is greater compared to the other
artists. And he makes full use of a single light source to create a shadow
such as we would see in the physical world. It seems always to be the
case in Magritte's work that individual forms are depicted according to
physical and logical rules of nature, and what are altered in his paintings are their relationships to each other. What is truly creative is his
treatment of juxtaposition of the details in the composition as a whole
entity. It takes an exceptional intellectual ability to rise above the known
physical rules of nature. **1.3 a** *The Rape*, painted in 1934, and **1.3 b**
Personal Items, painted in 1952. © 2003 C. Hercovici, Brussels / Artists
Rights Society (ARS), New York.

well as established artists who are nearly blind (see Chapter 3). We do not
necessarily need to think of color and art in the same mental instance when
attempting to analyze variables that enter into the brain's artistic processes.
Colors do indeed have an evocative effect on human perception, appreciation,
and existence, and they have considerable meaning in nature, too; without a
doubt their incorporation adds to the complexity, abstraction, and beauty of
the final product. Colors display yet another feature of artistic talent; they
provide an additional layer indicative of the artist's subtle understanding.
Some exceptionally skilled autistic savant artists, such as Nadia and EC,
rarely incorporate colors into their graphic productions, suggesting that a
special artistic cognition is required for the application of color to works of
art (see Chapter 4).

Rather than the eye, it is the mind that largely shapes displays of the visual field into coherent forms. The health of the eye, however, may impact the entire composition. What constitute visual forms are features such as line orientation, tilt, edges, boundaries, and contrast. Their unification into a meaningful whole is under cortical control. Given normal perception, the meaning of forms is then derived from long-term memory where experience and formal learning accumulated from infancy onward are stored. Indeed, new perception is driven by long-term memory and aided by attentional mechanisms searching for known forms in a constant, active manner (Zaidel, 1994). Most cognitive psychologists would say that reality is constructed in the mind of the perceiver (Kalat, 2002).

Acquired brain damage can impair the perceptual process and the attainment of meaning from visual percepts. This may lead to visual agnosia (the loss of knowledge of previously known things and thus the loss of meaning), a condition in which patients have an irregular understanding of the world (Farah, 1990). However, across individuals, an unusual perception does not necessarily stem from an identifiable agnosic disorder; there may be variability in the mechanisms of perception and the attainment of precept meaning in the first place. Artists' creations reflect their unique perceptions of the world, while non-artist viewers frequently do not comprehend, appreciate, or identify with those depictions. Perhaps it is a unique neuroanatomical arrangement of their perceptual and meaning-association mechanisms together with talent that allows artists to produce works of beauty that fascinate and inspire.

Music and the brain

Musical sounds fade away in thin air and disappear without a trace unless recorded by human-made machines or written in a notational system designed to represent the sounds. We do not have records of musical or linguistic sounds produced by ancient humans and cannot easily trace the acoustic arts with respect to their relationship to the evolution and development of the brain. However, we do have evidence, unearthed by archaeologists in Slovenia and France, of ancient musical instruments – flutes – believed to be 30,000 and 53,000 years old (Gray, Krause, Atema, Payne, Krumhansl, & Baptista, 2001; Tramo, 2001). Neanderthal people, who preceded anatomically modern Homo sapiens in Europe, created flutes from bear and deer bones (see Chapter 10). With the visual arts, on the other hand, there are numerous actual examples of created works from prehistoric times to the present.

Accumulating evidence on music and brain supports the notion of a wide spectrum of activated brain regions and response to music, in both musicians and non-musicians (discussed in detail in Chapters 5 and 6). Consequently, there is no strong support for a hemispheric laterality or specialization for musical composition; evidence from brain-damaged composers suggests the likely involvement of both hemispheres. In non-musicians, the left hemisphere is maximally involved in perception of timing and rhythm while the right hemisphere specializes in pitch and timbre perception. But neuroimaging studies of music are revealing subtleties in ongoing research (Popescu, Otsuka, & Ioannides, 2004)

Art, creativity, and the brain

The creative process is traditionally associated with artists, but scientists in fact need to be just as creative, as do medical doctors to successfully diagnose and manage their patients, economists and mathematicians in their theories and solutions, teachers to educate their difficult students and stimulate their bright students, politicians to shape resolutions and win elections, avoid or end wars, and improve the lives of their constituents, and business people to expand their profits. Because creativity is more obvious in art than other fields, we have come to commonly associate the two terms. However, the neuroanatomical and neurophysiological underpinnings of artistic creativity need not be wholly different from creativity in other human endeavors.

Given talent, neurochemicals in the brain can influence artistic expression. The role of neurotransmitters in shaping creative art might be gleaned from considering special neurological cases where newly administered medication heralds artistic output; such a case, a person suffering from Parkinson's disease, is described in Chapter 11. We should also consider that people in the middle of a major depressive episode, a period when levels of the neurotransmitter serotonin are particularly low, are not creative or productive. Creativity is expressed when the episode is over, or even prior to the episode. But there would have to be talent and predisposition to art, in its various formats, in the first place. Random imbalance in neurotransmitters is not a prerequisite for artistic or any other creative expression. Upheaval or lability in mood in artists can have its origin in mechanisms related to attachment whereby a psychological sense of loss with the work's completion is followed by neurotransmitter imbalance and the concomitant mood lability.

Artists are so creative at times that their works predate formal scientific discoveries (Shlain, 1991). Indeed, visual artists have often inspired scientists to view their research projects with a fresh perspective. Unbound by the rigid rules of controlled empirical investigations, successful artists are free to let their minds soar, and this, in combination with their talent and intellect, enables them to produce highly original works. Ultimately, art in all its formats – literature, poetry, music, paintings, film, sculpture, dance, theater, or photography – reflects the mind of its creator, whether he or she has a normal brain or is an autistic savant, a person with fronto-temporal dementia, a patient who had unilateral stroke, or an exceptional artist such as Picasso. The artist's studio, whatever and wherever it is, is where the workings of the creative mind are continuously tested. The benefit of understanding art from a neuropsychological perspective is no different from the benefit of understanding foreign languages, physics, biology, neuroscience, medicine, mathematics, or financial investing. In particular, by studying accomplished artists with brain damage or with various sensory deficits, we stand to gain insight into the elusive issue of artistic talent and its representation in the brain (see Chapter 11).

After all, art is not merely an expression of talent, expertise, and creativity. It is limited and constrained by genetic and biological inheritance, by what the mind is occupied with at the time of creation, and by the artist's cultural context, education, training, and social affiliation. All else being equal, art, given its creation by an artist with a normal brain, depicts that artist's era, what is important, talked about, discussed, believed, and known by the existing society. Indeed, as Bahn (1998) points out, in agreement with Dissanayake (1988), what we in the West classify as art is, in many other cultures, considered a mere extension of cultural, religious, and experiential events. An example of the latter is the aboriginal Australian attitude toward their own rock and shelter paintings, carvings, baskets, mats and other similar productions; other examples can be found among the many Native American tribes. The most important lesson regarding art work from ancient, prehistoric times is that its original intended meaning eludes us but not its aesthetic appeal. This suggests that there is disassociation between the meaning and the aesthetics of art, implying that the latter has a stronger biological basis than the former.

Beginnings of human art

Neuropsychological understanding of art must consider early artistic expressions in the course of human evolution (discussed in Chapter 10). The early art forms provide windows of further insights. An underlying assumption concerning the beginnings is that biological mechanisms were in place to support cognitive abstraction; both art and language are modes of communication that rely on abstract expressions. But this need not necessarily imply that abstract art expression capability predicts linguistic expression. The artist and the viewer need to share the same neural substrates in order for abstract concepts to be communicated. Some ancient creations consist of only a few engraved lines grouped to form a simple pattern while others are complex and detailed depictions; similarly, some incorporate colors while others do not. A few of these ancient works continue to elicit strong aesthetic responses even now. Prehistoric surviving art rarely depicts stories in scenes, emphasizing instead individual objects such as animals, faces, hands, single dots, figurines, or geometrical shapes. Perhaps, however, the grouping of the individual figures meant something specific to the creating artist. Modern viewers ponder even the simplest depictions, attempting to interpret and explain them, whether accurately or not. These attempts are in themselves a fascinating endeavor for which there are no obvious neuropsychological explanations. In any case, art is meant for human consumption, to be understood and interpreted by observers whose minds are equally shaped by the brain that houses them.

The fact that the practice of art is ubiquitous in all human societies supports the notion of the common origin of Homo sapiens and certainly points toward shared mechanisms for brain and cognitive growth. Art gives pleasure regardless of where practiced and by whom observed, and is, in many societies, woven into every aspect of existence. European artists around the beginning of the twentieth century were greatly influenced by Polynesian and African art. The fact that they were drawn to art from non-Western cultures, incorporated their forms and designs, and, under its influence, willingly changed their own artistic style of representation, illustrates the universal communicative value of art. Unlike language, which needs to be learned in order to be understood, works of art produced by talented individuals trigger reactions in any and all viewers with no prior training required. Still, the symbolic aspect of language and of representation in art may share a common form of cognition unique to humans. Although the two forms of expression take separate routes in what they accomplish and in the effects of their communication, it can nevertheless be said that, with the possible exception of the bowerbird (an avian species known for its complex architectural marvels), only humans create art. Since only humans have elaborate syntax and a rich vocabulary in their various languages, it is only logical to assume that the communicative nature of art may have neuroanatomical underpinnings similar to those of language, as well as a common cognitive support mechanism. At present the nature of these underpinnings remains elusive.

One fascinating feature of the widespread practice of art is some running motifs in creations across distant geographical regions, so far apart that it becomes difficult to imagine the role of direct influence or necessarily shared ancestral memory. Consider the pyramids of ancient Egypt and those of the Mayas and the Aztecs – is it coincidence? Did the Mayan and Aztec peoples know of the Egyptian pyramids through legends related by ancestors who possibly originated in Asia, and perhaps heard such tales from earlier, northeast African ancestors? Anything is possible. But consider that the reasons for constructing such monuments were probably the same, a need to construct something colossal in size that had symbolic and religious significance and would serve to impress as well as demonstrate strength and power (regardless of whether or not someone was buried underneath). The cognitive processes required to conceive and execute stone constructions of such magnitude are mental properties of a natural biological evolution propelled by genetic control, selection forces, development, and growth of the brain unrelated to where the various humans lived. Human constructions in widely dispersed locations bespeak a shared brain neuroanatomy as well as common cognitive processes.

Humans and animals cannot construct anything unless their physiological reality permits it. This applies both to brain and body development. The developmental course of the brain after the anatomically modern humans emerged from Africa approximately 100,000 years ago (or maybe even sooner, according to some views, see Mithen & Reed, 2002) was predicted by its neuronal flow-chart. But actual art (symbolic, representational, and non-functional) appeared in substantial quantities in Western Europe about 35,000 to 45,000 years ago. From a purely biological perspective, it is hard to conceive that new neurotransmitters and extensive new neuronal pathways with new relay stations and projections had abruptly emerged in the brains of Homo sapiens whose art managed to survive compared to those anatomically modern humans whose art did not survive. Rather, it is more reasonable to assume that the development was gradual, evolving a type of cognition that gives rise to symbolic abstraction in art (see Chapter 10).

Possible reasons for the seemingly sudden emergence of art are speculative. In one scenario, what may have led to the emergence of abundant art may lie more in the reality of the environment in which early humans found themselves rather than in any sudden major changes in their brains. Some environments are friendlier than others, meaning that for some it may have been easier to capture and eat the kinds of foods that would further enhance the brain's biochemistry (Mirnikjoo, Brown, Kims, Marangell, Sweatt, & Weeber, 2001). Possibly, the presence of the Neanderthals (another group of early humans believed by many to be not directly related to Homo sapiens) played a pivotal role in ways not yet understood, even if not directly linked to the development of symbolic image making (Conard, Grootes, & Smith, 2004). However, with everything else being identical, the modern human brain, once formed, had to follow a common path of development and change, and it is likely that it is still evolving. All humans have language no matter where they reside geographically. The brain that supports language is the same one that gives rise to the production of art. Thus, it is not surprising that art is ubiquitous, with similar running motifs, that humans come up with similar constructions everywhere, even if separated by huge bodies of water or impassable mountains, and that they share aesthetic reactions (see Chapter 10).

Although, as stated above, anatomically modern humans in Western Europe created art in greater quantity beginning between 45,000 and 35,000 years ago, there is evidence for the practice of art predating this European period. A small volcanic stone figure, sculpted by human hands and estimated to be around 220,000 years old, was discovered in the Golan Heights of Israel. Careful examination of this figurine supports the practice of symbolic art (d'Erico & Nowell, 2000; Marshack, 1997). Predating that by 130,000 to 180,000 years are some 300 pieces of color pigments and paint-grinding instruments believed to be implements of body decoration, found in a cave in Twin Rivers, near Lusaka, Zambia. Were early hominids impressed by the colors of animals, plants, the Earth and the ever-changing skies? Did they paint their bodies in order to resemble the animals, either to appropriate their power and agility, possibly for deception, or for sheer aesthetic pleasure, or for all of those reasons and others? Humans and their immediate ancestors were creating art and using paint to represent ideas well before written language developed, although speech too existed well before writing.

Beauty in art and brain evolution

There seems to be no convincing evidence of spontaneous drawing by non-human primates or any other animal, although there is some evidence of purposeful, artful, and three-dimensional creations by some birds. The best known avian in this context is the bowerbird and its artful creations. The idea behind the creations is attraction of the female to be followed by mating (see Chapter 10). It is hard to determine if the female is attracted by some kind of a "beauty notion" in the male's creations or something else. Humans may not be the only beings responsive to beauty. Paintings, sculptures, pottery, films, and architecture – all elicit reactions through their beauty. Beauty in art plays a prominent role in attracting us to it and to enticing us to directly ornament our homes with it, listen to it, visit museums and galleries to view it, and to think of it as symbolic of our time and culture; in addition, it gives us pleasure. Even without decorations, a single architectural structure can elicit beauty reactions. Art, however, conveys a meaning independent of its beauty, and this meaning may also play a major role in attracting us to it (covered in Chapter 9).

Early humans could have been inspired by the beauty of nature and animals, or have derived pleasure from constantly being surrounded by beauty (notwithstanding the dangers that would be present in real life), at the same evolutionary period that they wanted to communicate with each other, either verbally or non-verbally, through abstract symbols. Pictorial art could have followed the practice of body decoration, which may have been inspired by the perceived beauty in animal colors and shapes. Equally plausible, the original reasons for the early steps in the direction of art creations were purely symbolic with the beauty aspect an emergent property as opposed to an element purposefully included in the artistic formula. Even now beauty may be an emergent property of the art rather than something that the artist "puts" there.

Regardless of the true reasons behind painting animals on cave walls in prehistoric Western Europe, the caves' ancient occupants could have derived an aesthetic pleasure not unlike our own as we view these "galleries" nowadays. The driving force behind the depictions may have been social and symbolic, but the pleasure of viewing symbolic objects could have been present there as well. While artistic expression is broad and apparently as limitless as language, it is nevertheless a cognitive characteristic of the human brain. The aesthetic response to art cuts across human epochs, cultures, mediums, and art styles.

Language lateralization and disorders of language (aphasia)

Clinical and empirical studies for over 150 years have consistently shown that the main language functions of speaking and comprehension, writing and reading, are specialized in the left hemisphere in the great majority of people (Saffran, 2000). Damage in the left hemisphere typically leads to different types of language disorders (aphasia). The classic functional regional map, derived largely from patients with aphasic disorders, distinguishes between speech production, Broca's area in the left inferior posterior frontal lobe, and language comprehension, Wernicke's area in the left posterior superior temporal gyrus (see Figure 1.4). Since the mid-1970s, however, this classic cortical map has expanded thanks to evidence from neuroimaging techniques and additional experimentation (Whitaker, 1996). Engagement of both cortical and subcortical regions in the whole language process is now implicated (Lieberman, 2002; Wallesch, Johannsen-Horbach, Bartels, & Herrmann, 1997), some, though limited right hemisphere involvement is seen, particularly in comprehension (Code, 1987, 1997; Zaidel, 1988b), and the role of intra-hemispheric white matter lesions is pursued (Groot et al., 2000). Moreover, the range and refinement of identified aphasic syndromes and their neuroanatomical underpinning has increased (Caplan, 1987; Whitaker & Kahn, 1994). This, together with neuroimaging, physiological recordings of the past few years (Boatman, 2004; Teismann, Soros, Manemann, Ross, Pantev, & Knecht, 2004), and neuroanatomical studies (Hutsler & Galuske, 2003) confirm that the nexus for language expression and comprehension lies in the left hemisphere (see Chapter 10 for evolutionary scenarios of human language emergence).

The current view is that a left neuronal network involving most of the perisylvian region (Figure 1.5) constitutes the crucial language processing area (Scott, Blank, Rosen, & Wise, 2000). This includes speaking, comprehending, writing, and reading. Following observations of neuroanatomical individual variability (Whitaker & Selnes, 1976), the exact boundaries of Broca's and Wernicke's areas have been re-evaluated and expanded (Blank, Scott, Murphy, Warburton, & Wise, 2002), so that it makes sense to think of a Broca's area complex and a Wernicke's area complex. Additional regions in this network have been identified: The control of speech articulation is controlled by a discrete region in the left inferior precentral gyrus, the superior tip, in the anterior insula (located deep inside the Sylvian fissure) below the frontal and temporal lobes (Dronkers, 1996). However, speech articulation dysfunction can also occur in patients with reduced blood flow in the left posterior inferior frontal gyrus and who do not have damage in the insula (Hillis, Work, Barker, Jacobs, Breese, & Maurer, 2004). Thus, Hillis and associates suggest that the orchestration of speech articulation, a complex motoric function, not only involves the Broca's area complex, it reasonably engages cortical representations of the cortical face and mouth areas (in the precentral and postcentral gyri). In other words, a network of interconnected regions in the

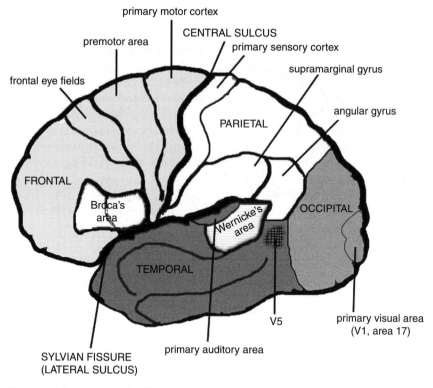

Figure 1.4 Schematic side view (lateral) of the left hemisphere showing the frontal, temporal, parietal, and occipital lobes. The right hemisphere has the same lobes, sulci, and gyri. But the main language centers are lateralized to the left hemisphere. Broca's area controls speech production and Wernicke's area controls comprehension of language. The left hemisphere specializes in the brain's main language system, including expression and comprehension, speaking, writing, and reading. Damage to the posterior region of the left frontal lobe results in Broca's aphasia, a non-fluent type in which speech is hesitant, incomplete, and lacks syntax; damage in the posterior left superior temporal gyrus results in Wernicke's aphasia, a fluent aphasia in which speech is well articulated but does not make any sense and language comprehension is absent. Damage to other regions within the left hemisphere leads to other disturbances in language.

left hemisphere is involved in speech articulation. The great variability in the size of Wernicke's area complex has been raised as well (Bogen & Bogen, 1976), and several neural subsystems within the area have been identified (Wise, Scott, Blank, Mummery, Murphy, & Warburton, 2001).

Systematic investigations of neural support for language comprehension in the right hemisphere have also been undertaken (see Friederici & Alter, 2004; Gernsbacher & Kaschak, 2003; Ullman, 2001; E. Zaidel, 1976, 1978, 1979). Aphasic disorders, their subtleties and measurements are described in detail elsewhere (for review see Saffran, 2000). The enormous literature

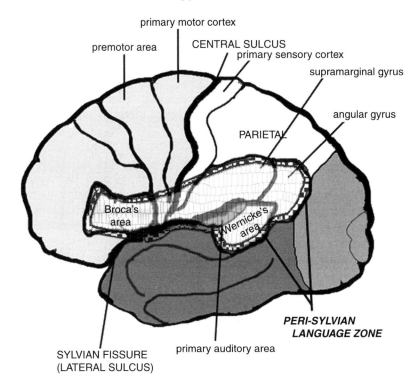

Figure 1.5 This diagrammatic lateral view of the left cortex shows the peri-Sylvian language areas in the left hemisphere. Hidden deep inside the Sylvian fissure is the insula, an area also important for language.

covering all of these findings is beyond the scope of this book (but issues of functional reorganization following unilateral damage to the left hemisphere are discussed in the second half of Chapter 4).

The arts, language, and hemispheric specialization

Art expression may have evolved parallel to language, in the same human evolutionary window, without artistic representations necessarily being the precursors to linguistic communication (see theories on evolutionary emergence of language in Chapter 10). In other words, the non-verbal or non-linguistic aspect of art does not necessarily imply "pre-language." Art reveals the mind in much the same way that language does, and the cognitive apparatus for both forms of expression may share the same neuroanatomical underpinnings, all of which could have emerged with ancient hominids some 350,000 to 400,000 years ago in Africa. The visible footprints of early language emergence could lie in the purposeful use of colors used originally perhaps for decoration or camouflage (see discussions in Chapters 9 and

10). Figure 1.4 illustrates the key language areas in the left (language) hemisphere.

Although writing, as spoken language, is specialized in the left hemisphere, there is a continuum between writing and pictures. Writing probably saw its beginnings in realistic pictorial representations that eventually evolved into formalized notational systems. The pictorial approach to non-verbal communication would seem to be the preferred mode as recently as 1000 years ago, when the Bayeux Tapestry depicting the 1066 battle of Hastings, England, was created. This is a long tale told elaborately through embroidered human figures, animals, plants, objects, and buildings, in a variety of colors and spread over seventy panels. Pictures are sometimes much more effective for conveying messages than words; the common adage that a picture is worth a thousand words is exemplified by the huge advertising billboards dotting roads and highways. Indeed, the neuropsychological impairment of simultanagnosia (the inability to derive the theme of a pictorial scene), which follows focal left hemisphere damage in the posterior temporal lobe, indicates a neuroanatomical underpinning for the interpretation of complex pictorial scenes.

Unlike language comprehension, speech, writing, and reading, functions for which there are known brain localizations, there is no neural network localization for the control of art production, no known laterality or hemispheric specialization. Nor has the lateralization of art appreciation and criticism been systematically investigated. The popular notion that art is specialized in the right cerebral hemisphere has never had a sound scientific basis. The notion originated with an early theory formulated as an initial working hypothesis pending further research. The balanced evidence has suggested otherwise. The case studies and discussions in subsequent chapters of this book illustrate that art is a "whole brain production."

Yet art is a form of communication, and in this sense it represents a "language" of sorts, albeit one with a non-verbal format. Representing figures on rocks, in caves, in cliff shelters, on canvas, in films, in musical melodies, and on the body itself – all are meant to convey specific ideas and concepts. It is representing the capacity to abstract. We may differ at times about precisely what is being conveyed, but we would more likely find common agreement precisely because of our ability to interpret abstract notions.

Talent and sensory deficits as clues to the neuropsychology of art

There is debate regarding whether artistic talent is a reflection of inherent biological capacity or the combined effects of such capacity plus guidance, training, and practice (see discussion in Chapter 11). The general issue of talent in various domains, whether it is a reflection of nature versus nurture, has been reviewed and discussed by Howe and his colleagues (Howe, Davidson, & Sloboda, 1998). Artistic talent, however, regardless of its origin, and no matter in which of the arts, is not universally endowed. In any given society throughout the world, there are only a few individuals possessing remarkable artistic talent. This would imply that talent is subserved by a specialized neuronal system whose wiring diagram is laid down from birth. The careful observations by Oliver Sacks and other researchers of skilled autistic savant artists support the notion of either a specialized neuronal system or dedicated brain regions as the neuroanatomical underpinning for some types of art production. In the group of autistic individuals, only a select few are graphically skilled artists despite their severely malfunctioning brains. What is missing in the productions of such artists, however, is what may uncover clues to the artist's mind (see Chapter 4).

The health status of the sensory organs of artists can provide extremely useful clues to each individual art's components (see Chapter 3). In the visual arts, for example, it is critical to consider the health of the artist's eyes and vision in evaluating colors and clarity of paintings, or, in the case of sculptors, the health of the arm muscles. Regardless of how experienced, talented, skilled, and creative an artist may be, the final drawing, painting, etching, sculpture, or film reflects the functioning of the eye. In the musical arts, it is similarly useful to consider a composer's level of hearing. Changes in vision or hearing can occur normally as part of the aging process or abnormally as part of a disease process, and the age at which they occur in relation to production can be extremely useful for understanding underlying brain processes.

Thus, in the search for the neurological components of art, we need to consider the following: the sensory reality of the producing artist and its influence on production; the genetics and influence of artistic talent on the final product; obvious or subtle brain damage, or alterations in the health status of the brain; the timing of these brain injuries or alterations, whether sudden or slowly encroaching; and the cultural, educational, and intellectual atmosphere present during the period of production, including early hominid evolution, and biological roots of art.

Summary

The relationship between art and the brain is somewhat elusive because the components of art have not been fully defined. Being that art is a complex behavioral expression of the human mind, it is reasonable to assume that art production is subserved by multiple brain regions. The best evidence for understanding those regions and their organization can come from established artists with focal brain damage as well as from artists with specific sensory deficits. In both the musical and visual arts there are artists with such deficits. Together, both sources point in the direction of skill preservation in the face of damage or sensory compromise. Talent in art is a critical issue. Artists with slowly evolving brain damage and those who are autistic savants are equally important for understanding the brain's underpinning of talent and neuropsychology of art. To gain insights into these issues and into art and brain, it is equally critical to consider and review evidence for the ancient origin of art. There is evidence that the origins date back to a time well before the anatomically modern human, Homo sapiens, first appeared. Its origin may be anchored in social needs and inter-personal communication and may explain why the practice of art is ubiquitous throughout the world.

Further readings

Blumenfeld, H. (2002). *Neuroanatomy through clinical cases*. Sunderland, UK: Sinauer Associates.

Bonner, J. T. (1983). *The evolution of culture in animals*. Princeton, NJ: Princeton University Press.

Brown, D. E. (1991). *Human universals*. New York: McGraw-Hill.

Buss, D. M. (1998). *Evolutionary psychology: The new science of the mind*. Upper Saddle River, NJ: Allyn & Bacon.

Caplan, D. (1987) *Neurolinguistics and linguistic aphasiology: An introduction*. Cambridge: Cambridge University Press.

Cartwright, J. (2000). *Evolution and human behavior*. Cambridge, MA: MIT Press.

Code, C. (1987). *Language, aphasia and the right hemisphere*. Chichester: John Wiley.

De Waal, F. B. M. (2002). *Tree of origin: What primate behavior can tell us about human social evolution*. Cambridge, MA: Harvard University Press.

Falk, D. (2004). *Braindance: New discoveries about human origins and brain evolution*. Gainesville, FL: University Press of Florida.

Falk, D., & Gibson, K. R. (2001). *Evolutionary anatomy of the primate cerebral cortex*. Cambridge: Cambridge University Press.

Feraud, G., York, D., Hall, C. M., Goren, N. & Schwarcz, H. P. (1983). 40Ar/39AR age limit for an Acheulian site in Israel. *Nature*, 304, 263–265.

Finger, S. (2000). *Minds behind the brain: A history of the pioneers and their discoveries*. New York: Oxford University Press.

Finger, S. (2001). *Origins of neuroscience: A history of explorations into brain function*. Oxford: Oxford University Press.

Geary, D. C. (2004). *The origin of the mind: Evolution of brain, cognition, and general intelligence*. Washington, DC: American Psychological Association.

Goldberg, E. (2001). *The executive brain: Frontal lobes and the civilized mind*. Oxford: Oxford University Press.

Gortais, B. (2003). Abstraction and art. *Philosophical Transactions of the Royal Society London, B, 358*, 1241–1249.

Hersey, G. L. (1996). *The evolution of allure: Sexual selection from the Medici Venus to the Incredible Hulk*. Cambridge, MA: MIT Press.

Hutsler, J., & Galuske, R. A. (2003). Hemispheric asymmetries in cerebral cortical networks. *Trends in Neuroscience, 26*, 429–435.

Mesulam, M.-M. (2000). *Principles of behavioral and cognitive neurology*. Oxford: Oxford University Press.

Ornstein, R. (1998). *The right mind: Making sense of the hemispheres*. Fort Washington, PA: Harvest Books.

Richerson, P. J., & Boyd, R. (2004). *Not by genes alone: How culture transformed human evolution*. Chicago: University of Chicago Press.

Swanson, L. W. (2002). *Brain architecture: Understanding the basic plan.* Oxford: Oxford University Press.

Tattersall, I. (1997). *The fossil trail: How we know what we think we know about human evolution.* Oxford: Oxford University Press.

2 The effects of brain damage in established visual artists

Introduction

Neurological cases of professional artists who have suffered known brain injury provide the richest source for understanding the components of art and the underlying neuroanatomy. While well-characterized neural and functional model systems are available in neuropsychology, very few initial steps in the establishment of art–brain models have been taken. Artists with a sudden focal brain injury, such as stroke, are ultimately the most revealing about the brain's control in art production. Similarly, exploring cases of professional artists who developed slow yet irreversible brain diseases such as Parkinson's, Alzheimer's, Lewy bodies dementia, progressive brain atrophy, or corticobasal degeneration, is equally critical for further understanding. Such cases of professional artists are exceptionally rare. Of those, most are in the visual arts. Synthesizing the available published information is hampered somewhat by several factors including, first, some of the early reports were published before the days of neuroimaging. Second, examples of artists' work are typically limited or absent altogether in some of the publications. Third, in the majority, little is known from the immediate post-damage period, a time when the brain's reaction to the damage is still "raw", to say nothing of the ensuing few months. Fourth, the reports illustrate the fact that there are no neuropsychological measures designed specifically to test deficits in art production or appreciation, not surprisingly given that the particulars in the vocabulary of art have not been thoroughly defined. Finally, not all published cases were administered standard reliable neuropsychological tests. The full range of behavioral symptoms, particularly concerning aphasia, is not always provided. The best that can be accomplished in clarifying the neuropsychology of art is to compare post-damage productions against already known neuropsychological effects.

The graphic "primitives" of art are numerous and their semiology has not been fully explored and delineated (Gortais, 2003). They can be characterized in multiple ways and their precise assessment eludes quantification. The main difficulty lies in the fact that the details in art are elements in the whole rendition, and consequently, their significance needs to be understood against the global composition. Brush strokes, for example, have a trajectory, a specific curvature, are broad or thin; influenced by granulation of the surface, flow of the paint, degree of pigment absorption, shape of the brush itself, and size of brush. Also, path of previous marks and strokes are adjusted to begin and end relative to the whole illustration. The artistic decision to place the initial mark in a specific spot on the drawing surface reflects knowledge of scaling, approximation, and context, and cannot be simply measured. Thus, the key questions in the artists described below concern preservation of skills, ability to produce art works, emergence of new expressive techniques, nature of the alterations, if any, as function of the localization and laterality of the damage, and dissociation, if any, between language impairment and art production.

In addition to the issue of skill and talent preservation, post-damage effects on art reflect not only influence of damaged tissue over healthy tissue, but also functions of healthy tissue. Both interact with each other in the production of the art. Currently, one of the actively pursued research into behavioral recovery after brain damage centers on neuroimaging and language (Knecht, 2004; Knecht et al., 2000). The general view regarding all types of behavior remains that the damage results in local reorganization of functional networks (Duffau et al., 2003). (There is discussion of functional reorganization and effects of slow brain changes in Chapter 4.)

It is important to define what is meant by art style, technique, and artistic essence in this book. Here, what is meant by *art style* is "artistic personal style": the artistic personal style is the characteristic mode of representation (genre) adopted by the artist, and practiced in the years prior to the damage. By representation is meant a type of genre as in Realism, Impressionism, Surrealism, Cubism, Abstract, and so on. For example, in the context of this book where artists with brain damage are discussed, the artistic personal style post-damage is consistent with the pre-damage style. If there are any changes post-damage, those apply to artistic techniques through which the artist depicts, represents, and expresses. It is much harder to define artistic "techniques" in this sense than to define mode of representation, because techniques consist of so many combinations of elements (see examples of graphic "primitives" above) and vary widely from artist to artist. In general, techniques are the means by which the work of art is constructed. The quality in an artist's work that remains constant is referred to here as "the artistic essence."

Art production following left hemisphere damage

Honor art student

In 1936, a neurological report describing patients with left hemisphere damage, some with aphasic disturbance, was published (Kennedy & Wolf, 1936). One of the cases was of an artist, a 19-year-old honor art student (in an art school) who suffered a sudden injury to the left fronto-parietal area, which resulted in a mild weakness of the right hand for a period of three days (the cause of the injury was not described). There were no obvious aphasic symptoms, and no verbal expressive or receptive language disturbances. However, there was a disturbance in expressive drawing. Two weeks after the injury, she was asked to draw a face. All she could produce was a circle containing two dots for the eyes, a vertical line representing the nose, and a single horizontal line for the mouth (see Figure 2.1 a). Then, she was asked to draw a picture of the American statesman Alexander Hamilton (it is not clear from the report if she had a picture in front of her or she had to draw from memory). She drew a bare outline in profile. She worked daily on this profile until she succeeded in producing a more detailed figure. Interestingly, the most glaring "error" was the disproportionately large head. At one point, she improved decidedly and was able to produce a very good three-quarter view of a normal-looking Alexander Hamilton. At the end of six months, her drawings of other figures returned to their normal artistic levels as well. Examples of the evolution of her work during that period after the damage occurred are shown in Figure 2.1 a–g. Together, they reveal that the unilateral injury interfered with execution of her artistic abilities, but only temporarily. Importantly, this case illustrates the dissociation between language and art production even with left hemisphere damage.

On the following pages:

Figure 2.1 a, b, c, d, e, f, g   A 19-year-old art student and professional artist with left hemisphere damage in the fronto-parietal region showed progressive improvement in her artistic expression in the six weeks that followed an accident (resulting in a depressed skull fracture) and surgery. The initial symptoms were expressed not in aphasia or linguistic deficits but only in right hand weakness that lasted for three days. Two weeks afterwards, she was asked to draw a face. **2.1 a** Shows her response to this request. Notice that she can write numbers better than she can draw (although number 9 was reversed). **2.1 b** Three days later she was asked to look at a picture of Alexander Hamilton and render her version on paper. Both the drawing and number writing have improved, although the drawing remains rather sketchy. There is an irrelevant circle in the area in the back of the head. The lines of the figure are angular while the numbers gain a flowing technique. **2.1 c, d, e**, and **f** all show her steady improvement in depicting Alexander Hamilton. (It is not known from the original publication if she went on to use different pictures of Hamilton in her renderings.) All this time there was no aphasia, alexia, or agraphia. Kennedy points out that this is a case of an artist in whom there was an expressive disorder but not of a linguistic nature. **2.1 g** Finally, she produced this drawing of a man's head (Kennedy & Wolf, 1936). (Reprinted with permission from Lippincott Williams & Wilkins, Medical Research.)

(a)

(b)

(c) (d)

(e)

(*f*)

January 22. '30

(*g*)

Subsequently, in 1948, Alajouanine published the first neurological report in English devoted exclusively to the effects of brain damage in several established artists (Alajouanine, 1948). The article described three artists from divergent art fields (visual art, music, and literature) who sustained brain damage in the left hemisphere that severely compromised their language abilities. The alteration in their artistic expressions varied widely.

Alajouanine's visual artist

The visual artist in Alajouanine's publication was a 52-year-old successful painter (his identity was not revealed) when the stroke occurred in the left hemisphere. Subsequently, he suffered from Wernicke-type aphasia (also known as fluent aphasia). There was no right-sided hemiplegia and this implies no involvement of the motor cortex in the left frontal lobe. Often with this aphasia, speech is fluent but can be nonsensical, made up mostly of jargon, and language comprehension is very poor or non-existent. Writing and reading are grossly affected in such patients in ways analogous to speech and comprehension. But in this case, comprehension was not severely affected. This artist had two separate strokes (time interval was not mentioned), which resulted in language impairments. He had severe anomia (word-finding difficulties) and exhibited paraphasic errors (words substituted for the ones that could not be retrieved from the mental lexicon), but with relatively better comprehension than would be expected. Both his writing and reading were quite impaired; the reading deficits suggest involvement of posterior temporal and occipital lobes. However, given the symptoms, it is possible that the damage was not extensive, and although including Wernicke's area, may have spared regions surrounding it. Alternatively, the damage may have occurred much earlier than the time when Alajouanine saw him and the acute symptoms of Wernicke's aphasia may have disappeared in the interim. However, Alajouanine observed that artistic skills remained unchanged:

> Artistic realization in our painter since his aphasia remains as perfect as before. According to connoisseurs, he has perhaps gained a more intense and acute expression. If one tries to analyze his production before and after his aphasia, one cannot find since his language deterioration any mistake in form, expression or colour interpretation ... I am of the opinion that he lays emphasis on thematic characteristics with a poetical strength, in a completely unaltered manner, and that since his illness he has even accentuated the intensity and the sharpness of his artistic realization. Moreover, his activity and production have not slowed down, and he seems to work with the same speed. Perhaps, because of new affective conditions, his works are less regular. ... Perhaps he is more prone, however, to use a previous model, or a discarded sketch.
>
> (Alajouanine, 1948, p. 235)

The last remarks are revealing; they seem to refer to a modification in creativity in that after the damage this artist used previous compositions, modifying rather than creating new designs. This case also illustrates the dissociation between language abilities and art production.

Fashion designer

Macdonald Critchley, the British neurologist, examined a multilingual fashion designer and artist who was highly regarded and successful (Critchley, 1953). He suffered a stroke in the left temporal-parietal lobes that resulted in a mixed aphasia in English, German, and French, and a short-lived right-sided weakness. As would be expected, he had difficulties in comprehension as well as in speaking. Critchley did not describe in full the details of the language impairments. Before the brain injury his work was characterized by fine, closely spaced, detailed illustrations consisting of minute strokes and cross-hatchings, and resulting in accurate representations. After the stroke, his artistic technique changed (see definition of artistic style in the introduction to this chapter) in the sense that there were fewer detailed strokes and figure identity was characterized by strong contour lines. This could be interpreted to mean that intact regions in the right hemisphere contributed to the global and wholistic configuration now that critical regions in the left hemisphere were damaged and could not contribute to the details and fine lines within the contour frame. The work of McFie and Zangwill (1960) would certainly support this conclusion. Still, as with the other artists described above, the ability to paint and illustrate was not abolished by the damage. What changed drastically was the manner of depiction.

Zlatio Boyadjiev (ZB)

The Bulgarian painter, Zlatio Boyadjiev (also referred to sometimes in the neuropsychological literature as ZB), suffered a left hemisphere stroke in 1951, when he was about 48 years old, which resulted in severe right-hand paralysis and mixed aphasia (Zaimov, Kitov, & Kolev, 1969). For many years afterwards the aphasia consisted of both the Broca-type and the Wernicke-type, and was accompanied by alexia and agraphia. In the few years after the stroke he drew a bit but not much is known about his artistic productions from those years. Starting around 1956 new works emerged and were exhibited in museums; he learned to use his left hand in order to paint (the right was paralyzed). Boyadjiev was very prolific between 1956 and 1972 (he died in 1973). He continued to paint, and his ability to depict realistic figures was largely unchanged. The new work was well executed, very aesthetic, and highly regarded. However, compared to the pre-injury artistic techniques, several interesting changes occurred. The colors became less exuberant and somewhat less varied, the number of figures in a given composition declined, there was now a blending of imaginary and real themes in a single composition, and there was less convergent perspective than prior to the stroke. Indeed, a number of paintings seemed to lack depth altogether, with figures appearing piled in a vertical plane, not unlike traditional Chinese paintings. This in itself is surprising given that only left hemisphere damage is suspected (no CT (computerized tomography) scan or MRI is known to have been taken). One would have expected absence of convergent linear perspective to be associated with a right hemisphere lesion. Also, a sort of a balanced left–right mirror symmetry emerged in his compositions that was not present previously. The new symmetry could reflect the fact that he now was using his left hand, the right hand, his dominant hand, was paralyzed. The mirror symmetry contributed to an "abstract" appearance of the whole picture, although the individual figures were often highly representational. The balanced mirror symmetry lends an impression of regularity and stability. The new paintings, highly skilled and aesthetic, appear somewhat "flat" compared to the convergent perspective and depth representation in his pre-stroke paintings. Nevertheless, his post-stroke works are exhibited in Bulgarian museums.

Parietal lobe cancer

A 72-year-old professional artist who suffered from a fast growing cancerous tumor, glioblastoma, in the left parietal lobe presents an interesting case (Marsh & Philwin, 1987). In the five months before surgical removal of the tumor, he suffered from mixed aphasia, inability to write his name on command, and similarly, inability to draw or copy on command. There were abnormal right arm reflexes, abnormal EEG (electroencephalogram) over the left hemisphere but particularly over the temporal lobe. After the tumor was removed, he appeared less aphasic than previously. Unfortunately, he died less than two months after surgery, and whether or not he painted then is not discussed in the published report. The authors compare two paintings, one made four years before tumor onset and one made around the time of the supposed appearance of the tumor. They observe that the second painting was composed with a shift toward the left so that there was greater emphasis of details in the left half than in the right half. It is not that there is a complete or even a partial neglect (ignoring or neglecting to pay attention to the half of space) of the right half of the canvas, a type of incompleteness of figures observed in patients with right parietal damage for the left half (see Chapter 8). It is an absence of details in the right half of the canvas as well as in the upper left corner that is interesting here. The authors emphasize that the whole canvas was filled with lines and paint. Defined human figures were painted only in the lower three-quarters of the canvas. Thus, this case illustrates a shift of attention to the portions of the visual field controlled by the non-damaged hemisphere. The damage in the left parietal lobe altered the composition as a whole while his drawing skills remained largely intact.

Polish art professor

The Polish artist RL was a professional artist and also a professor in the art department in the University of Lublin (Kaczmarek, 1991). The stroke occurred at age 51 in the left frontal lobe; he became aphasic and developed right arm paralysis. A second stroke a short while afterwards resulted in paralysis of his right leg. Neuropsychological testing revealed an inability to describe the theme of pictures (suggesting presence of simultanagnosia), digressions, poor memory for stories, confabulations, inability to derive the essence of read or spoken stories, limited vocabulary, difficulties in planning, and emotional lability. His artistic skills were preserved but the subject matter of his art changed. Specifically, whereas prior to the stroke he focused on figurative symbolic topics, afterwards he was unable to produce such themes. Subsequently, increased artistic productivity was accompanied by increase in language abilities (Kaczmarek, 2003). Unlike Zlatio Boyadjiev, however, he produced landscape paintings that showed good perspective and depth, and no distinct organizational strategy of left–right symmetry emerged in his paintings. His post-stroke art was highly aesthetic, he was able to sell it, his craft and talent clearly remained intact, and eventually, thanks to consistent art and cognitive therapy, he regained his ability to depict symbolic art again.

Jason Brown's artist

Are there selective effects of aphasia on art production? Jason Brown (1977) provides the following brief description of another professional artist:

> This 73-year-old woman was a professional artist, strongly right-handed without a family history of left-handedness. She suffered a stroke with right hemispheric lesion and left hemiparessis (i.e., a crossed aphasia) and presented characteristic features of phonemic (conduction) aphasia. Preliminary studies of her sketching, both spontaneously and as illustrations to short stories, demonstrated no apparent alteration in artistic ability.
>
> (Brown, 1977, p. 168)

Art production following right hemisphere damage

Film director

Federico Fellini was not only a highly acclaimed film director and screenplay writer, but also a professional cartoonist and painter. He made his last film in 1990, *The Voice of the Moon*. His highly regarded films, including *La Strada* in 1954, *The Nights of Cabiria* in 1957, *La Dolce Vita* in 1960, *8½* in 1963, *Juliet of the Spirits* in 1965, and *Satyricon* in 1969, received numerous awards, among them the illustrious Oscar award. At the age of 73 (August 3, 1993), he suffered a stroke in the right temporo-parietal junction, which resulted in neglect of the left half of space, and motor and sensory deficits in the left half of the body (Cantagallo & Della Salla, 1998). The neglect extended to difficulties in reading, clinically known as neglect dyslexia (ignoring the left half of words by not reading them out loud due to presence of hemi-neglect; see Chapter 8). Yet, there was no neglect agraphia, that is, he could write complete words. He was aware of the motor condition in his left hand and the neglect deficits. Despite this awareness, however, he was unable to compensate for the neglect deficits. There were no language impairments or a general cognitive decline. His sense of humor remained unchanged. He did not have prosopagnosia, a deficit in recognizing previously familiar faces that can occur following damage to the right parietal lobe (De Renzi, 1999; Landis, Cummings, Christen, Bogen, & Imhof, 1986), and he did not have a memory deficit. Despite the fact that he showed neglect of the left half of space, his drawing abilities, particularly the humor in his spontaneous cartoons, remained unchanged. The lines were firm and confident, their character was the same, the figures were just as recognizable as previously, and the humor depicted appropriate. Amazingly, while he ignored the left half of a straight line in the line-bisection test, the cartoons he drew on the right half of the page were complete and whole (if anything was missing on the left half, this could be attributed to the schematic nature of cartoons). One would have expected the drawings to have many omissions on their left half, but this was not the case with Fellini. When, however, he drew figures from memory, upon request, some left-sided lines were omitted but then spontaneously corrected after further inspection. Spontaneously executed cartoons did not show left-sided neglect. The deficits that were observed were present in the first two month after the stroke. Afterwards, no evidence of neglect in drawings was noted. The major lesson from Fellini's case is that his drawing skills were clearly not obliterated by the brain damage, that cartoon humor remained, that the lines and strokes were firm, and that no major changes in overall artistic style or techniques occurred. He died on October 31, 1993, not long after the stroke.

Sculptor Tom Greenshields

An established well-known British artist, the painter and sculptor, Tom Greenshields, suffered a stroke in his right hemisphere at age 75, in August 1989 (Halligan & Marshall, 1997). Subsequent to the stroke he had left visual hemi-neglect of space, mild weakness in the left arm and leg, and visual field blindness in the left lower quadrant. All of this implies damage in the right parietal lobe, as well as in the posterior region of the right frontal lobe, and possibly damage in the right occipital lobe; no localization information from brain imaging or neurological examination is provided in the published report (Halligan & Marshall, 1997). Although he was a right-handed person, he was forced to switch his manual activities to the left hand eight years prior to the stroke because an accident damaged his right hand. Working with his left hand did not prevent him from producing art for sale throughout the world. After 1989 we see an artist suffering from sensory-motor weakness in the left hand, the only hand he apparently can use for his art. In the few months following the stroke he concentrated mostly on the right half of both drawings and sculptures. Some spatial distortions and deformities were reportedly observed as well in some of the figures, but those were most apparent in the left half. The obvious deficits diminished slowly within a year; some were still seen afterwards particularly in drawings and paintings (presumably none of the those early impairments were seen for sculptures). Throughout the period between the time of the stroke and the artist's death five years later (in 1994), artistic skills, as judged from the character of the lines and their coherent relationships, remained intact and applied appropriately, including the production of non-canonical perspective views. His case, too, illustrates preservation of artistic skill despite right hemisphere damage and highlights the pervasive influence of talent and lifelong practice.

Color neglect artist

Left hemi-neglect (see Chapter 8 for discussion on hemi-neglect) can extend to colors and be more prominent for colors than for visual space itself. Such a rare case of an artist was described by Blanke, Ortigue, and Landis (2003b). A 71-year-old professional painter had a stroke in the right posterior parietal lobe that resulted in visual blindness in the left lower quadrant of the visual field and a mild left hemi-neglect. There was no sensory-motor loss on the left half of the body. Attention to detail was applied mostly to the right half of drawings while the left half was somewhat incomplete. The most interesting feature in the post-injury art, however, was an exaggerated neglect of color application in the left half of the painting. Thus, even while contour lines were produced in the left half, colors were more obviously absent in that half. All of this lasted for only six weeks after the stroke first occurred. Afterwards, the color neglect disappeared. No lasting changes in artistic techniques were noted. The important clue from this case to art production is that spatial layout and color are subserved by separate attentional mechanisms. (In this context, it is interesting to observe that several autistic artists, discussed in Chapter 4, did not use much color in their highly skilled graphic drawings, and when it was used, it was not imaginative and was applied within strict drawn contours.)

Swiss artist

A locally established Swiss artist, 54 years old, suffered from two right-sided strokes separated by approximately six days, resulting in an extensive lesion in the right parieto-temporo-occipital junction (Schnider, Regard, Benson, & Landis, 1993). The damage resulted in left-sided paralysis, left hemi-neglect, visual hallucinations, delusions, and mood changes. There were no impairments in recognizing familiar faces, environmental sounds, facial emotions, or colors; no impairment in verbal or non-verbal memory was observed. In order to under-stand some of his symptoms, it is important to note that about fifteen years before the stroke incidents, the patient suffered from visual hallucinations when under the influence of the hallucinogenic drug, LSD. In the ensuing year or so after the stroke, his art consisted mainly of charcoal and pencil drawings. A few days after the second stroke he centered his drawing mostly in the right half of the paper, but, at least as judging from the published drawings, all the individual figures that were depicted were completed on their left side. They appeared whole. The striking feature of this new work was the blending of text material and figural drawings. Such combinations in his art lasted for a brief period (four weeks) but during that period he also engaged in lengthy verbal dialogues that were not characteristic of his pre-stroke state. The amount of detail in his drawings following the stroke did not differ from the pre-stroke days.

However, interestingly, the neglect of space did not necessarily manifest in the left half of the paper but rather in the left half of a figure depicted in the right half of the paper. Thus, there was a "hole" of incompleteness due to the right hemisphere damage but this appeared in the right half of the com-position as a whole. Such a form of expression suggests that not all com-ponents of a single painted composition are controlled by a unitary cognitive process and embodied in a single idea applied to the canvas. The idea may consist of an image of the whole composition but the execution of the idea requires shifting attention to specific components (consisting of figures, whole forms, whole shapes).

In this artist's case, no obvious loss of talent, skill, or creativity was observed. Nor was there a major change in artistic style or topics of interest. He did not abandon his work in oil paintings. The principal change consisted of left-sided neglect, and that was not particularly gross. He did suffer from mood changes and irritability, both of which prevented him from further elaborations of individual drawings. "The character of lines and shades, the basic compositions, and his ability and desire to express himself through art, however, were preserved" (Schnider et al., 1993, p. 254).

French painter

Another case is that of an accomplished professional French painter who had a right hemisphere stroke at the age of 66 years (on April 15, 1973), which resulted in left-sided paralysis and left hemi-neglect (Vigouroux, Bonnefoi, & Khalil, 1990). He was well known both for his paintings and drawings (iden-tity was not revealed). After a period of depression (that occurred after the stroke) had dissipated he began to draw and paint again, and prolifically. There was, as would be expected, visual hemi-neglect in his work, particularly in the initial phases after the damage. The spatial organization of his com-positions was described as being excellent, the overall artistic style did not change, nor did the topics that interested him previously. Forms, character and firmness of lines, and proportionality were also largely unaffected.

Anton Raderscheidt and Otto Dix

In 1974 the German neurologist Richard Jung published neurological description of several artists who suffered from damage in the right hemisphere, and in whom left hemi-neglect was also present. The neglect ranged from mild to moderate. After reviewing, pondering, and discussing their cases, Jung (1974) observed that the damage did not bring a halt to artistic productivity, nor to alterations in previous subject matter. Skills remained unchanged in all of these artists. One painter was the renowned German expressionist, Anton Raderscheidt, who suffered a right parietal lobe stroke on October 1967, but went on painting until his death a few years later. The changes that took place in his work are hard to define but it is clear upon viewing that they were produced skillfully (Gardner, 1974). Another artist was Otto Dix, the renowned German expressionist. Figure 2.2 illustrates some of his (few) works produced after the stroke.

On the following page:

Figure 2.2 a, b, c, d Post-stroke drawings by Otto Dix (1891–1969), the well-known and highly regarded German artist. His pre-stroke work has been published and is available on the internet (http://www.artcyclopedia. com/artists/dix_otto.html). He suffered a unilateral right hemisphere stroke in November, 1967 (Jung, 1974) and only a limited number of his works after that is known. He was 75 years old at that time. Initially he was paralyzed in the left hand and suffered from some hemi-neglect in the left half of space. Both the paralysis and the neglect dissipated with time. In **2.2 a** we see the centering of the tree on the right half of the paper; the subsequent **2.2 b** drawing shows greater concentration of details in the right half of the tree sketch but no gross neglect of the left half. (Reprinted with permission from H. H. Wieck (1974). *Psychopathologie musischer Gestaltungen*. Stuttgart and New York: Schattauer, p. 69). **2.2 c** A year later, in 1968, we see his self-portrait with no traces of any left neglect. He continued to create art after the stroke. © 2004 Artists Rights Society (ARS), New York / VG Bild-Kunst, Bonn. His ability, skills, creativity, and ideas were all clearly preserved despite the brain damage. (Printed with permission from the Artists Rights Society.) He made drawings as well as several lithographs in color after the stroke. "The range [of colors] had been simplified and the colors are set down beside one another almost pure. A few days before his death, Dix said he intended henceforth to content himself with a less complex construction and a smaller number of colors, and to work less for exactitude of delineation and more for contrasts. New insights and, in view of the condition of his health, the desire to realize more quickly ideas that still pressed upon him both played a part in his ultimate change of style [technique]" (Loeffler, 1982, p. 134). **2.2 d** This is a portrait of the painter Josef Hegenbarth, painted by Dix in 1961, six years before his stroke. © 2004 Artists Rights Society (ARS), New York / VG Bild-Kunst, Bonn.

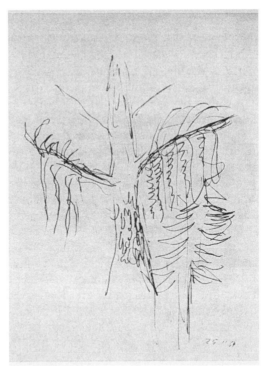

(a)

(b)

(c)

(d)

Lovis Corinth

Lovis Corinth (1858–1925), a renowned German artist, innovative, and skillful, was another artist described by Jung (1974). On December 1911 he suffered a stroke in his right hemisphere, which resulted in left hemi-neglect that was not long lived, and a left-sided weakness. Following the stroke, his drawing abilities remained excellent, the character of lines, proportionality of entire figures, details, receding planes, all indicated preserved skills. As early as February 1912, no distortions or abnormal exaggerations were seen in his self-portraits, even as he accurately attempted to depict his own facial expression; there was, however, evidence of a mild neglect of the left half of the canvas. There was also a system of very careful diagonal hatchings in the background that appeared to go from right to left (Butt, 1996). This system seems to have been new. In a landscape drawing that he prepared a few months later, in the summer of 1912, he used his careful, deliberate hatching system to impart an impression of light entering the scene from the right side, those straight lines of the hatchings representing light rays. His power of observation had not been altered by the right parietal stroke. For example, he depicted the asymmetry in his eyes that developed subsequent to the stroke, namely, a larger left than right eye. The spatial features of compositions went unaltered, in the sense that there was a logical proportionality and receding planes, although there appeared to be less deep convergent perspective than previously. What had changed seemed to be apparent in the oil and watercolor paintings, specifically, brush strokes appeared broader, color patches larger than before, and there was abundance and widespread use of white color touches. Together, his compositions appeared coherent and one wonders if a naïve observer could identify anything amiss.

Ambidextrous Polish artist

The case of an ambidextrous contemporary Polish artist has been reported by Pachalska (2003). In art production, the ambidexterity expressed itself in outlining the figures with the left hand and drawing in the details with the right hand. In daily life, she wrote predominantly with the right hand (but could write with the left hand as well) and mainly used the left for eating. The artist, Krystyna Habura, suffered a massive right hemisphere stroke at age 61. A CT scan showed involvement of the frontal, temporal, and parietal lobes. Afterwards she had mild motor aphasia and left hemiparessis. The aphasia consisted of slight anomia, slowing of speech output, and difficulties in initiating speech. At first, she complained of absence of imagery. In addition, neuropsychological tests revealed some impairment in spatial orientation, writing, and drawing. In the period right after the stroke the artist was unable to draw and paint. Later, after a period of multiple art therapy sessions for eight weeks she began to draw and paint again. As a result of these sessions the artist developed a new subject matter that consisted of combining drawing and writing on the same surface. These were called "painted letters." No evidence for scaling or spatial errors in compositions was reported, despite damage in the right hemisphere. However, whereas before the stroke she drew a close likeness of Einstein's face, after the stroke a similar attempt at drawing him did not produce a close likeness. She eventually became an active and prolific artist. In all, her drawing and painting skills remained unchanged and led to successful exhibition and sale of her post-stroke works. Pachalska summarizes the artist's case thus:

> The fact that she was ultimately able to return to an active artistic career is eloquent evidence against any argument that something essential to artistic creation was destroyed in her brain. This is not to say that the effects of the stroke on Habura's art were transient or reversible. The post-stroke, post-rehabilitation works are different. Technically she recovered most of what she lost, but not all: the line in the later works is somewhat less strong, sure, crisp, and the details are not always worked out with the same precision as before. Although she returned to some of the themes that had interested her before the stroke, her thematic range after rehabilitation included much greater interest in suffering and despair, while most of the social and political commentary characteristic of some earlier work disappeared.
>
> (Pachalska, 2003, p. 54)

Slow brain diseases

Parkinson's Disease

Horst Aschermann

Horst Aschermann, a known and established artist specializing in sculpture, decorative art, ceramics, and vases, was born in Thüringen, Germany, in 1932 (Lakke, 1999). Onset of Parkinson tremor was in 1965, particularly in the right hand. In 1970 he began taking L-Dopa. In 1975 his condition began to deteriorate because of increased hyperkinesia and dystonia (muscle contractions that result in abnormal painful postures), but no signs of dementia were observed. As of 1999, the right hand tremors continued to be severe, speech became unintelligible, and the dystonia had worsened. The disease hampered his ability to use a hammer and chisel. So he resorted to using clay-plaster, and this in innovative ways. Despite many years with the disease, he continued to create art work, sculptures and drawings that consistently received high praise. His productivity did not diminish even despite debilitating motor control. In the twenty years after the onset of symptoms, he produced twenty-seven works, which include two large bronze reliefs.

Parkinson's artists

The works of twenty-six professional artists with Parkinson's disease (eight women, eighteen men) were evaluated by Lakke (1999). Their works before and after the onset of symptoms were analyzed and the results described in the publication. None suffered from dementia, which often accompanies the disease. The artists either made a living from their art, or had been artists their whole lives. Some never received any formal art training while others did. They created paintings in oils, in watercolors, paintings on silk, drawings, sculptures, cartoons, graphic designs, stained glass sculpting, textile designs, and architectural plans. The artist who drew cartoons worked for *Playboy* magazine; he did not lose his wit after disease onset and no alteration in artistic style was observed. In the other artists, technical alterations were noted consisting of direction of hatchings, implementation of the tremor itself (putting it to use to create special effects), slightly tilted composition because of difficulty in maintaining vertical centrality, including slight tilting of the objects being depicted, and asymmetrical emphasis on one side of the canvas relative to the other side (but not as is seen in hemi-neglect cases). Some artists were not aware that they slightly tilted objects in their depictions. Importantly, Lakke observed that their art continued to mature and evolve, and they developed as artists even while the disease progressed.

Dementia

Commercial artist MH

An extensively studied case is that of MH, a commercial artist (Franklin, Sommers, & Howard, 1992). At age 77 years she was seen by a neurologist and found to have general cortical atrophy but more pronounced in the area of the left lateral sulcus (see Figure 1.4); this was presumed to have arisen from vascular causes (not progressive) including possibly a small stroke. Neuropsychologists administered a series of tests that revealed presence of anomia (word-finding difficulties) and serious deficits in language and pictorial comprehension. Otherwise, her speech was fluent. She had no impairments in copying drawings of simple figures or in real-life drawings of modeled objects (e.g., fork, comb, orange). To be sure, the latter drawings had touches of shadings that talented, experienced artists apply to their work. Her artistic talent was further demonstrated in copying Botticelli's *Portrait of an Unknown Man with a Medal*. The work on an excellent pencil reproduction of the head took several weeks. It was a very close likeness to the original. But when she was asked to draw objects from memory, after being given only the object's name (e.g., comb, glasses, chair, pencil), her drawings were poor; they were sketchy, representing outlines and lacking any of the nice artistic shadings that she applied when she drew the same or similar objects from models. Some were missing convergent perspective and representation of depth. This was particularly apparent in drawing a bus, book, suitcase, matchbox, pipe, and eyeglasses. Rendition of space was not missing in a spoon, apple, bucket, table, or chair. This is interesting if only because right parietal regions control productions of two-dimensional renditions of spatial depth; her cortical atrophy was bilateral (even if the most salient symptoms were linguistic, consistent with extensive atrophy in the localized language-related region in the left hemisphere). However, despite the brain damage she was still able to engage in commercial artwork.

The significant clue from this case study is that artistic output is not related to artificial psychological tests in the laboratory. The case can serve as an illustration of the notion that artistic expertise and talent have multi-representations in the brain, due to lifelong overpractice, which possibly are subserved by extensive neuronal networks, including subcortical regions. There may not be any neuropsychological tests that can ever tease out the components of art. All the interesting dissociations in performance by this artist do not explain the preservation of her artistic competence.

Corticobasal degeneration

Book illustrator and painter

A professional illustrator and portrait painter, age 68 years, developed several sudden neurological symptoms. He behaved inappropriately (associated with frontal lobe damage), was unable to find his way in familiar surroundings (associated with right parietal damage), could not relocate personal items (memory deterioration), developed difficulty in dressing himself (dressing apraxia, associated with right parietal damage), and had emotional outbursts. Personality changes were noted as well; he became apathetic, irritable, and was unaware of his condition (Kleiner-Fisman, Black, & Lang, 2003). In another three years, additional symptoms appeared: he began to show intellectual decline, there was left hemi-neglect of space, some visuo-spatial deficits, sensory loss in the left limbs, and abnormal reflexes on the left side. There were no obvious language deficits. An MRI of his brain revealed generalized atrophy throughout the brain but more pronounced in the right hemisphere, including the right brainstem. Another imaging technique, single-photon emission computed tomography (SPECT), revealed marked atrophy in the right hemisphere and the left frontal region. The medical diagnosis was corticobasal degeneration. His ability to paint had not changed essentially throughout this period but there were alterations. Specifically, faces were distorted, facial features were misrepresented, brush strokes became wide, paint was applied in greater quantity to certain parts than was necessary, color use changed, and there was a striking loss of detail. The colors now appeared brighter than prior to the illness. Also, the paintings now lacked fine details needed for real-life representations, and the appropriate size-ratio of body parts appeared distorted. He was aware of the changes in his paintings at this point but his attempts to correct what he perceived as imperfect were not successful. Reportedly, his dissatisfaction and frustration eventually led to giving up painting altogether.

Alzheimer's disease

Willem de Kooning

Willem de Kooning (1904–1997) belonged to the Abstract Expressionism art movement and is regarded as one of the important artists of twentieth-century art. He is believed to have suffered from dementia for the last twenty-five years or so of his life (Espinel, 1996). The issue of slow changes (alterations) in the brain as opposed to sudden changes are discussed in Chapter 4. The dementia and concomitant brain damage may have been due to several neurological causes including Alzheimer's disease, severe alcoholism, arteriosclerosis, hypothyroidism, poor nutrition, and effects of prescription drugs. By the mid-1970s, a time when the dementia was noticed, friends and associates reported that he suffered from progressively increased memory lapses and there was a noticeable physical deterioration as well. At that time he was in his early seventies, not an unreasonable age to see onset of dementia, including Alzheimer's. Some Alzheimer's disease cases show asymmetrical involvement of the cerebral hemispheres. In de Kooning's case, there is no information regarding this possibility. His productivity was beginning to drop, in the mid-1970s, presumably because motor control and cognitive capacities became compromised. But, then, after reportedly receiving help from his former wife and several of his friends, productivity increased so that between 1981 and 1986 he reportedly created 254 paintings, which were abstract (in keeping with his lifelong artistic style), displayed curvy lines, and with smoother boundaries than previously. (It should be stressed, however, that there is controversy among art historians regarding the nature of the help.) Of those 254, only 40 have been exhibited and they received mostly positive reviews.

During those five productive years, when he received help, he was presumed to already be suffering from Alzheimer's disease (brain tissue biopsy, to the best of my knowledge, was not undertaken). Any changes in artistic techniques (consisted of creating curvy, repetitive lines as opposed to straight lines and angles) observed between 1981 and 1986 in his paintings may already have begun in the early 1970s. There is debate concerning when exactly and why those curvy, sinuous wide lines made their appearance in his work. There was also a major change in the choice of colors in the 1980s compared to earlier years. Toward the end, fewer elements appeared and fewer colors were applied. Large areas of canvas were unpainted whereas his technique had been previously to fill every empty space. The paints were applied thinly now whereas previously they were thick. The changes in color may not be surprising given observations that several aspects of color perception, particularly in discriminating blues and greens is affected in Alzheimer's disease (Wijk, Berg, Sivik, & Steen, 1999a). Moreover, it should be pointed out that age alone would have affected his vision (see Chapter 3): with increased age there is reduced sensitivity to contrast (Jackson & Owsley, 2003). The curvy, widely spaced, and smoothly applied brush strokes could be seen by his aging visual system better than the tightly packed strokes of his younger and visually healthier days. Regardless, de Kooning was an established, creative, innovative, and highly regarded artist whose work from before the 1970s was widely exhibited throughout the world. In the last seven years of his life, a time when the disease was taking a very heavy toll, he did not produce very much art, whereas at the beginning of the disease he was able to produce.

How can the end-period technique changes, within his established abstract representation, be characterized in the context of his lifelong art endeavors? De Kooning was an abstract expressionist who painted discordant, disharmonious lines that together added up to a particular dynamic expressive message, one that is diametrically opposite to classic, figurative style. When his brain disease was taking its toll, de Kooning did not start producing figurative art. In fact, he continued producing abstract art. This shows that his lifelong interest in non-figurative art survived the ravages of the disease.

Portrait painter

William Utermohlen (born 1933), an established portrait painter living in Britain, was interested in drawing from an early age. He began to experience memory problems and deterioration in writing around the age of 57. Formal neuropsychological tests at age 61 revealed global cognitive impairment (e.g., in verbal memory, arithmetical calculations, visuo-spatial and visuo-perceptual tasks) and an MRI showed generalized cortical atrophy, with no asymmetry (Crutch, Isaacs, & Rosso, 2001). The pattern of impairments and damage together indicated the presence of Alzheimer's disease. Facial memory did not appear to be compromised. As the disease progressed from age 61 and on, several stylistic changes appeared. Paintings went from being realistic and balanced to being more and more abstract. Facial distortions were introduced. Perspective and depth were by and large lost while form and color were still used. However, judging from the few published examples, color was applied with broad brush strokes and different shades of color appeared unblended, giving an impression of patchiness. He did not go on to produce art similar to de Kooning's. Whatever was produced was consistent with his artistic essence. Around age 65 he resorted to drawing with pencil. Confirmation of Alzheimer's disease diagnosis was obtained at that age when another MRI and neuropsychological evaluations were administered.

Both of these cases illustrate the fact that artistic production is possible during the early and middle stages of the disease. The fact that alterations in technique emerge is indication of cognitive alteration stemming from progress of the disease, including the onset of motor impairments and visual deterioration (Rizzo, Anderson, Dawson, & Nawrot, 2000; Wijk et al., 1999a). The cognitive alterations consist of increasingly poor memory, visuo-spatial deficits, and verbal impairments (Koss, 1994). The visuo-spatial deficits are well documented (Henderson, Mack, & Williams, 1989). The end stages of the disease signal artistic decline and seem to preclude further production because, possibly, there is loss of motor control, motivation, severe cognitive decline, and, importantly, disinhibition presumably indexing frontal lobe deterioration.

Commercial artist

A third case is that of German artist Carolus Horn (Maurer & Prvulovic, 2004), who earned a living from illustrations and drawings for commercial advertising. During World War II he was imprisoned in a Russian prisoners of war camp; he drew scenes from that period and claimed that doing so helped him live through the whole experience. Around age 61 years he began to display signs of Alzheimer's disease. The early symptoms appeared in conjunction with a heart attack and a bypass surgery, and were interpreted at that time to be associated with the heart condition. Poor memory as well as language impairments and visuo-spatial difficulties emerged as the disease progressed. He continued to paint throughout this period with visible technique alterations and manner of expressing his art.

The most obvious markers of the disease in his art were mild visuo-spatial distortions of scenic spatial layouts in facial features distortions. As the disease progressed, however, the colors changed: they became stronger and brighter, and were applied throughout the canvas. In the pre-disease paintings there are few colors and they appear subdued. During the disease there seemed to have been a preference for colors in the middle and long wavelength range, yellow-red. In addition, small realistic graphic details present in the pre-disease days seemed now to be absent by and large. Instead, a painting technique, within the bounds of his figurative style, seemed to have emerged with further disease progression. The brush strokes and careful composition symmetry were retained, as was the case in the pre-disease days. But strong regular black lines now delineated contours and forms. This suggests alterations in his visual system, including the retina, in which there is further reduction in contrast sensitivity. The strong black lines helped him see what he was doing. On the whole, the new compositions depicted stylized human figures and objects, faces lacked individuality even as they were highly colorful. Ornaments were now added, left–right mirror symmetry emerged, and paintings became less and less realistic, although they did not become abstract. As with de Kooning, CH did not go on to develop a diametrically opposite manner of artistic style. And his works went on to be just as aesthetically pleasing as those produced during the healthy period.

Maurer and Prvulovic (2004) summarize the end stages in Horn thus:

> A second important change in CH's artwork within the severe stage of his disease could be attributed to a disturbed visual contrast sensitivity. This is the minimum amount of visual contrast a person needs to resolve light-dark boundaries in a stimulus. It is known that AD-patients [Alzheimer's disease] are more impaired in the lower than the higher spatial frequency range (Cronin-Golomb et al., 2000; Cronin-Golomb, Rizzo, Corkin, & Growdon, 1991). Since low frequency information is more important for face discrimination this may explain CH's impairment in object and face recognition, which led to the inability to visually recognize his wife for instance and as such had serious interpersonal consequences for himself, his wife and the caregivers. The implications of this inability can be seen in his painting. It is very likely, that CH downsized objects and persons in his later drawings in order to compensate increasing deficits of low-frequency contrast sensitivity.
>
> (Maurer & Prvulovic, 2004, pp. 243–244)

Near the end of his life, there was a further change in his technique but at this point his ability to paint saw a sharp turn for the worse; he drew only individual objects (as opposed to whole scenes), simple lines, geometrical forms, and a few scribbles. However, even those creations retained an "artistic flair."

Progressive aphasia in fronto-temporal dementia

Art teacher

The effects of dementia on art production by an established local artist and a high school art teacher have been investigated by Mell, Howard, and Miller (2003). At age 57 she was diagnosed with progressive aphasia syndrome, a type of language-related dementia. The authors refer to the artist's condition as fronto-temporal dementia (FTD). The aphasic symptoms evolved for ten years before she decided to retire from teaching. She also exhibited social disinhibition, consistent with frontal lobe atrophy. Her speech was non-fluent and effortful. Language comprehension was normal only for simple commands. She had no problems in copying figures. She failed on tasks that measured frontal lobe functions. An MRI revealed moderate atrophy in the frontal lobes bilaterally, with more pronounced atrophy in the left frontal lobe. There was also a mild atrophy in the left temporal lobe. Artistically, she was exceptionally prolific even though the disease was several years in the making. Along with the decline in language and social disinhibition symptoms, there were changes in her artistic expression. As her condition worsened, colors were applied to the canvas in large bright patches, drawings became less realistic and sketchy (but not abstract), and judging from the published examples, faces and objects blended into each other in an incoherent manner. However, we do not see compositions made of blocks of colors, but rather we see a desire to depict figurative representations. Dark contour lines framing forms were now introduced, and this suggests alterations in her vision, whereby sharp contrast was needed for seeing properly (see discussion of previous case, CH, regarding contrast sensitivity). If we consider art to be a form of expression, then as her language expression worsened, so did her artistic expression. Her art expression became vague but did not become abstract. The important observation, however, is that the art continued to be produced even as other aspects of her mind were obviously deteriorating.

Not all aphasic conditions lead to the same artistic results. Other cortical conditions need to be taken into account. The Alajouanine case described above continued painting reportedly with no changes in technique. The art of this FTD patient did reflect extensive technique alterations because the brain deterioration was extensive, and included sensory impairments in vision.

Dementia with Lewy Bodies

Mervyn Peake

The British artist, Mervyn Peake (1911–1968) is well known for his poetry, illustrations, novels, and plays (Sahlas, 2003). He was highly prolific and extremely well regarded. He studied in art school and had his first exhibition in 1931. He is famous for his illustrations of survivors of the Belsen-Bergen concentration camp, an infamous German killing camp where hundreds of thousands of innocent people were murdered during World War II. He is also very well known for his Gormenghast novels, which he began to write in the early 1940s. In the mid-1950s, around 1956, he began to display symptoms of Parkinsonism and progressive cognitive deficits. When he was about 45 years old, tremor was detected in both hands and then spread to his legs. He developed a stooped posture and facial expression characteristic of Parkinson's patients. Around the time when the Parkinsonism symptoms developed, he began to experience visual hallucinations. Yet, he was able to concentrate on drawing many illustrations in the course of just one hour, only to stop abruptly and return to sitting silently. He displayed difficulties in writing, attention, and cognition. Memory deficits were not apparent among those initial symptoms. Rather, fluctuations in cognitive and attentional activities and visuo-constructive problems were more salient. Such a constellation of symptoms, although representing a dementing process, is not seen in patients with Alzheimer's disease. The nature of his neurodegenerative disease was a matter of much debate at that time, and persisted to the present day, until the insightful publication by Sahlas (2003).

Sahlas (2003) proposes that the symptoms that afflicted Peake add up to a diagnosis of dementia with Lewy bodies, a neurodegenerative disorder now considered a variant of Alzheimer's disease. The symptoms include Parkinsonism, visual hallucinations, and visuo-perceptive impairments (perceptual, spatial, and constructional). Several brain sites are atrophied, including cortical and subcortical regions. The hallmark of the neuropathology is the presence inside some brain neurons of Lewy bodies, intracytoplasmic inclusions that mark the disease process, although how they originate is not known.

Peake's illustrations and poems reflected his distillation of experiences during the hallucinations and psychotic states, when he had paranoid delusions. However, on the whole, his writing style began to disintegrate as the dementia progressed. He ended up being treated with neuroleptics (to which he did not respond well at all) and anticonvulsant shock therapy. There was no doubt that there was deterioration in all of his art forms (although publications showing his art works from that period are not available for direct comparison with the pre-illness days). He died at the age of 57.

The early stage of the neuropsychology of art can provide patterns of post-damage artistic behavior more than it can provide a predictive model. Such models are difficult to arrive at when there is rarity of cases on whom to perform the observations, where the bottleneck rests in mostly non-numerical subjective observations that cannot be scrutinized through reproducibility, and cannot lead to adequate generalizability. The reproducibility of data issue notwithstanding, artists adjust to the damage in their own unique ways (see functional reorganization discussion in Chapter 4). By contrast, convergent evidence from multiple experimental approaches and varied neurological etiologies has helped shape and formulate neuropsychology theories since the nineteenth century. All scientific theories gain momentum this way. Nevertheless, important consistent artistic patterns emerged here and they are preservation of skills, aesthetic rendering, creativity, talent, and desire to produce art (see also Chapters 3, 4, 5, 6, 11, and 12).

Summary

The visual artists described here continued to be artistically expressive despite presence of severe neurological conditions, regardless of etiology. Importantly, laterality of damage did not seem to interfere with either creativity or productivity. The foregoing demonstrates that individual artistic style (defined in the introduction to the chapter), perfected and worked out by established artists prior to acquired brain damage, by and large survives the damage. It is generally assumed that preserved functions are supported by multiple neuronal circuits and that there is redundancy of functional representation. Currently, active research in anatomical reshaping consequent to brain damage is focused on language recovery. With regards to art, it appears that the essence of artistic being (the quality of an artist's work that remains constant) survives brain damage although the neural substrates of artistic preservation remain unexplored. Artists specialized in figurative and representational art do not suddenly start producing abstract art in the post-damage years. Such preservation illustrates resilience of highly practiced skills. Skill and talent preservation probably reflect the effects of damaged tissue in combination with healthy tissue. Both mechanisms interact with each other in production of the art.

Alterations in artistic approach or techniques are evident following left or right hemisphere damage. The precise nature of alterations when present is subject for debate and interpretation, given absence of clear definition of the components of art or their quantification. Furthermore, established artists appear to retain their motivation and expressive capabilities independently of language expression. Indeed, the evidence points to dissociation between linguistic expression and artistic expression but this does not necessarily stem from left–right hemispheric specialization. One mode of expression need not interfere with the other, need not exclude the other, and the two need not be mutually antagonistic. Although visual art requires normal visuo-spatial perception and cognition, the absence or degradation of such cognition does not seem to interfere with the production of aesthetic, creative, and skilled art works.

Further readings

Caplan, D. (1987) *Neurolinguistics and linguistic aphasiology: An introduction.* Cambridge: Cambridge University Press.

Chollet, F., & Weiller, C. (1994). Imaging recovery of function following brain injury. *Current Opinion in Neurobiology, 4*, 226–230.

De Leeuw, R. (Ed.). (1998). *The letters of Vincent Van Gogh.* New York: Penguin.

Gardner, H. (1974). *The shattered mind.* New York: Vintage.

Heilman, K. M., & Valenstein, E. (Eds.). (2003). *Clinical neuropsychology.* Oxford: Oxford University Press.

Hughes, R. (2003). *Goya.* New York: Alfred A. Knopf.

Kalbfleisch, M. L. (2004). Functional neural anatomy of talent. *Anatomical Record, 277B*, 21–36.

Kertesz, A., & Poole, E. (2004). The aphasia quotient: The taxonomic approach to measurement of aphasic disability. *Canadian Journal of Neurological Science, 31*, 175–184.

McCarthy, R. A., & Warrington, E. K. (1990). *Cognitive neuropsychology: A clinical introduction.* San Diego, CA: Academic Press.

Mohr, J. P. (1976) *Broca's area and Broca's aphasia, Vol. 1.* New York: Academic Press.

Pizzamiglio, L., Galati, G., & Committeri, G. (2001). The contribution of functional neuroimaging to recovery after brain damage: A review. *Cortex, 37*, 11–31.

Weiller, C. (1998). Imaging recovery from stroke. *Experimental Brain Research, 123*, 13–17.

Zeki, S. (1999). *Inner vision: An exploration of art and the brain.* London: Oxford University Press.

3   The eye and brain in artist and viewer

Alterations in Vision and Color Perception

Introduction

Traditionally in neuropsychology, sensory deficits are interpreted before reaching conclusions regarding cortical control of behavior. To infer the central influences on art, we need to explain and accommodate peripheral influences, those arising from sensory deficits. Alterations in visual acuity and color perception in either an artist or a viewer can arise from sensory visual impairments and interfere with how forms and colors are rendered. The outcome of such changes needs to be considered in conjunction with other neuropsychological influences on art. As healthy individuals age, they suffer a gradual decline in visual acuity. The most common change in normally aging adults, for example, is presbyopia, the loss of flexibility in the eye's crystalline lens, leading to the blurriness of closely viewed objects (Jackson & Owsley, 2003), and there is no logical reason to assume that aged artists are not affected as well (see diagram of the eye in Figure 3.1). Color impairments can begin at the level of the eye itself and may be caused by disease. Simple aging can also contribute to alteration in color processing by the central nervous system (Wijk, Berg, Sivik, & Steen, 1999b) even when there is no specific eye pathology. As will be made clear in this chapter, however, there are various eye conditions that modify form perception and color sensations without detriment to the creative, artistic, or expressive aspects of art.

Eye defects can also affect detecting changes in illumination, brightness spectrums due to surface refraction, of shadows emanating from the ambient field, or subtleties in shades of gray. Color assists in isolating meaningful shapes set against mixed backgrounds; although color deficient individuals lead normal lives, they can make use of monochromatic cues. Evolutionary explanations for human color vision lie in geographical, environmental and food resources available to our primate ancestors (Dominy & Lucas, 2004). Detecting edible fruits in leaves' green background is considered a major contributing adaptive force in primate trichromatic evolution. In the retina, specialized color sensitive receptors are initially exposed to light, and chemical reactions known as retinaldehydes (derived from vitamin A) set off electrical neural signals to the brain (see further explanation in subsequent

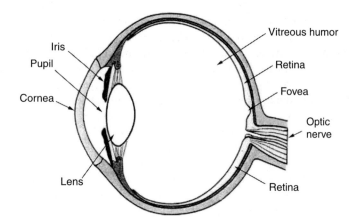

Figure 3.1 The cornea and lens are critical for seeing focused images. These two structures project outside images onto the retina in the back of the eye. The elasticity of the lens enables us to accommodate vision to close and distant objects. From infancy onward the lens undergoes progressive changes, which affect its transparency, and ultimately, color vision. One such change is increased yellowing of the lens. With aging, the yellowing prevents the retina from receiving short wavelengths, and, in addition, causes a glare effect in sunlight, due to decreased transparency. Also, with maturity the alteration in color vision is most noticeable in blue (the short wavelengths) and green (medium wavelengths). The fovea also undergoes changes (loss and degradation of photoreceptors) that compromise seeing details. Thus, we would expect alterations in how artists depict the visual world on canvas due to the status of the eye. Artists such as the Impressionists painted outdoors a great deal. Their fascination with light may have affected the health status of their eyes and may have contributed to their characteristic fuzzy paintings.

sections). Not all color sensitivities evolved simultaneously; receptors sensitive to blues are thought to be late-evolving, for example. Thus, the nature of their genetics (Deeb, 2004), vulnerability to disease, and functionality in human vision could partially explain the use of blue in art (see Ball, 2001).

In visual art, form and color are frequently combined in a single composition. Color is a vital component of seeing and navigating in the visual world and is thus an integral feature of visual art; it does not, however, define such art. After all, a large portion of visual art is not in color, and color-blind artists can still produce art, whether with color or not. In Venice, in the sixteenth century, for example, painters sometimes presented their initial ideas to patrons in monochromatic paintings (Gage, 1993). Those artists used a technique known as *grisaille*, a method of depicting forms in shades of gray. In the early 1950s, the American Expressionists in New York started to paint in black paint on white background; these artists included Jackson Pollock, Robert Motherwell, Adolph Gottlieb, and Willem de Kooning. The objects, shapes, and forms in the visual world all have colors associated with them, not because they themselves "possess" color, but because they induce the perception of color in the human brain via neuronal codes and the brain's computation of light's wavelengths (Ball, 1999). Symbolic use of color by early anatomically modern humans has been uncovered in conjunction with burial in an ancient cave (Hovers, Ilani, Bar-Yosef, & Vandermeersch, 2003). The neural code for interpreting light entering the eye begins its work the moment the light strikes the retina. The association between seen objects and their evoked colors is what gives the latter their significance or meaning. An artist's use of colors conveys that artist's particular intelligence, talent and skill as well as the health status of the eyes.

Color perception impairments due to non-sensory causes are also discussed in this chapter. The underlying brain regions controlling and processing color cognition have actively intrigued neurologists and neuropsychologists since the nineteenth century. Studies of neurological patients with focal brain damage have provided a number of clues into color-understanding deficits. Unilateral focal damage in posterior brain regions does not eliminate perception of or discrimination between colors (Cole, Heywood, Kentridge, Fairholm, & Cowey, 2003; Heywood & Kentridge, 2003). Various tests have been devised to isolate the underlying nature of color impairments. On the whole, neurological cases with acquired isolated color deficits are rare. Nevertheless, we have learned from neuropsychological test performance that there is dissociation between perceiving colors and knowing their meaning, between subjective color knowledge and wavelength discrimination, between memory and colored forms, between knowledge of the language of colors and other types of knowledge, and between other combinations of these functions (Davidoff, 1991). Both the brain's and the eye's roles in the processing of colors are discussed in this chapter with regard to the visual arts, as are the visual systems and vision impairments of established artists.

Localization of color processing: effects of brain damage

Color in the brain

Visual systems in each cerebral hemisphere can process colors when the response is not verbally yoked or the task does not have a heavy linguistic component. The projection of the visual tracts in each hemisphere are depicted diagrammatically in Figure 3.2. Geschwind and Fusillo (1966) described the case of a patient with damage in the left occipital lobe and the splenium (the posterior third of the corpus callosum) who could not name colors – a result one would expect from a left hemisphere lesion – but could nevertheless discriminate among various color patches. In Roger Sperry's psychobiology laboratory, Colwyn Trevarthen (1974) studied the complete commissurotomy patients (corpus callosum, anterior and hippocampal commissures were cut surgically down the midline) in the Bogen-Vogel series (also known as the Caltech series: Sperry, 1968, 1974), and found that they

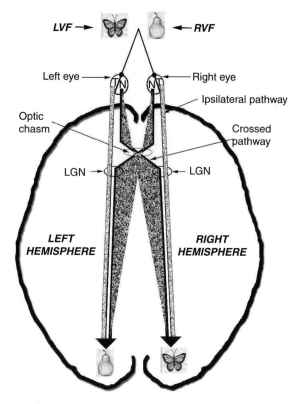

Figure 3.2 A schematic diagram showing top view of the two hemi-fields and visual
pathways. With both eyes focused on a single spot, visual information
appearing left of the spot is in the left visual half field (LVF) while information appearing right of the spot is in the right visual half field (RVF).
The detailed, focused images in either one of the two half fields are transmitted to the back of the brain, the occipital lobes, via the crossed
pathways (originating in the nasal half of each eye, labeled N). Non-
detailed, gross information is transmitted via ipsilateral pathways (originating in the temporal half of each eye, labeled T). Based on this anatomical
arrangement of the visual pathways, it has been possible to apply the hemi-
field technique to test the competence of the left and right hemispheres in
normal people. Before reaching the primary visual cortex in the occipital
lobes, the majority of the axons first project to the lateral geniculate body
(LGN) in the thalamus. The LGN represents the first synaptic contact that
retinal axons make after exiting the retina. Further neuronal processing
and computation are performed on visual input received by the retina. At
this junction, information from the two eyes does not blend appreciably.
Axons from each eye terminate in separate layers of the LGN. Not all of
the axons that cross at the chiasm end in the LGN. Some proceed to the
superior colliculus. The information transmitted via those fibers is not as
detailed as that transmitted via the retinal-LGN route. The geniculostriate
visual pathway, known also as the primary visual pathway, relays signals
from LGN neurons to the primary visual cortex, V1 (Area 17), in the
occipital lobes.

could recognize and identify – albeit non-verbally – colors shown in the left and right visual half fields (see Bogen & Vogel, 1962).

While the issue of color-sensitive regions in the brain has been debated, discussed, and described since the nineteenth century, the published detailed work of Zeki in the 1970s and 1980s on color-specialized regions of the visual area 4 (V4) in monkeys (through the technique of single-cell brain recording) confirmed with greater precision than previously what many neurologists had observed on human patients (Damasio & Geschwind, 1985). Neurological cases with acquired isolated color deficits were rare in the nineteenth century and are rare nowadays. Nevertheless, the earliest reports were often accurate in pinpointing localization to the lingual and fusiform gyrus regions at the junction of the occipital and temporal lobes (Mackay & Dunlop, 1899). In his book on color cognition, Jules Davidoff (1991) describes and reviews several such early papers, many published in German. The prominent English-speaking neurologists of the era were not ready to accept a brain center for color processing, arguing instead that in many of the published cases documenting retinal and acuity deficits, it was difficult to distinguish between primary visual damage – that is, either to the eye itself, or to the optic nerve or optic pathways – and actual central cerebral damage. Despite evidence to the contrary, this mode of thinking persisted for more than half a century. It wasn't until Meadows' (1974) review of color perception deficits following localized brain damage that the way was paved for reconsidering that a color-specialized area existed in posterior cortical regions. Meadows (1974) described the underlying brain localization in cerebral achromatopsia (impairment in distinguishing hues following brain damage) after reviewing fourteen published achromatopsia cases and reporting on three who underwent postmortem brain examination. His overall conclusion was that the color impairment in these cases must have been due to damage in the inferior junction of the occipital and temporal lobes, specifically in the region of the lingual and fusiform gyri (see Figure 3.3), with the suggestion that these regions are essential for color discrimination. We now associate these regions with the color-sensitive neurons in a monkey's V4 (Zeki, 1993) or a human's V8 (Cowey & Heywood, 1995; Tootell & Hadjikhani, 2001) visual areas.

Traditional tests of color perception in neurological and neuropsychological studies are described in a book by Birch (2001) as well as in a chapter on the neuropsychological aspects of color perception and cognition by De Renzi (1999). One of the first of these tests was Holmgren's Wool Test, devised in the nineteenth century. Many of the papers in the neurological literature devoted to color perception used this test. Subjects were asked to put together small woolen skeins belonging to specific categories of colors and shades. The examiner named one color at a time and the subject then attempted to pick up from the array (placed on a gray background) all those that matched the named color. In lieu of actually naming the target color, the examiner could also simply show a sample and have the subject pick up all the skeins in the array that closely matched or were identical to it. The test is

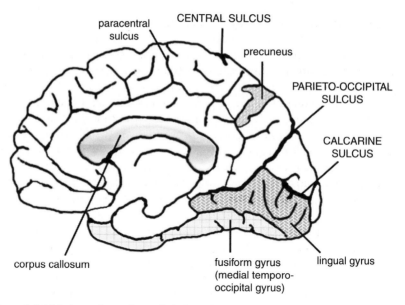

Figure 3.3 This is a schematic medial view of the cortex, showing the location of the lingual gyrus, fusiform gyrus, and the precuneus.

rarely used nowadays because it is now known that the very act of categorization into similarly colored skeins may involve more than just perception (De Renzi, 1999). At present, tests such as the Farnsworth-Munsell Hue Tests (28, 40, or 100 hues) are used because, with the hues equated for brightness, color perception deficits can be detected with greater accuracy (see Birch, 2001, for details).

Achromatopsia and hemiachromatopsia: hue discrimination impairments

Cerebral achromatopsia is a perceptual impairment in which visual acuity is not compromised. Generally, the condition arises following damage to the anterior basal portion of the occipital lobes, either unilaterally or bilaterally. Only one visual half field or both may be affected, as in hemiachromatopsia, and the critical defect is seen in the field's upper quadrant. There may be a color defect in the lower quadrant as well, but the upper quadrant bespeaks damage involving the fusiform and lingual gyri. Meadows (1974), in his summary of achromatopsia cases, reported no examples of inferior quadrant achromatopsia. Interestingly, bilateral damage in these regions does not lead to a doubly severe form of achromatopsia. Cases with hemiachromatopsia are particularly important for understanding the underlying brain mechanisms in color processing because such patients have a color deficit in only a portion of their visual world. Patients with full field achromatopsia report that the world is grayish, dull, and that colors are faded; they also have great difficulty matching hues. In daily life, they rely on smell, touch, and sound to distinguish among objects whose color is critical to their identification.

The essential feature in achromatopsia cases is that other aspects of their visual world are intact. Thus, visual acuity or spatial orientation, form and object recognition, reading, facial recognition, as well as many other cognitive abilities based on vision, are all preserved. Nor do such patients necessarily have difficulties in providing the names of colors from memory, or from knowing what color a particular ripened fruit or vegetable should have, or naming what the color of the sky is on a cloudless day. Instead, their problems lie in matching, distinguishing, sorting, or arranging colors, and they may also not be able to actively imagine an object's color in their mind (Levine, Warach, & Farah, 1985). Focal lesions accompanied by circumscribed behavioral deficits pertaining to colors further support the notion of functional specialization in the brain.

An important report on left hemiachromatopsia has been published by Albert and associates (Albert, Reches, & Silverberg, 1975). The case was a 59-year-old man who suffered from damage in the posterior region of the right hemisphere. His most salient color deficit was the inability to match colors in the left visual half field. At the same time, however, he was able to name colors of various objects from memory (for example, the color of a tomato), match colors in the right visual half field, and recognize all objects presented in his left and right visual half fields. Color discrimination and form discrimination are dissociable functions, and in this case, the subject was spared damage to his visual form-processing region.

Damasio and associates described a hemiachromatopsia neurological case in whom physiologically evoked visual brain responses were preserved for processing dichromatic black and white but not red and green (Damasio, Yamada, Damasio, & McKee, 1980). The color-discrimination impairment in this patient was in the left visual half field and the central damage was in the posterior region of the right hemisphere. Specifically, the anatomical localization of the damage was in the lingual and fusiform gyri while the calcarine fissure region was spared (see Figure 3.3). This was an important paper, as it emphasized anatomical localization with careful behavioral tests. An achromatopsia case reported by Heywood, Wilson, and Cowey (1987) is of particular interest because of the research team's elegant approach to getting at the underlying deficit; they demonstrated that despite the colorless world of such patients, it is nevertheless possible for them to match different shades of gray. Case CB was a 28-year-old man who, following a serious traffic accident, underwent neurosurgery to remove blood clots in the right fronto-temporal region, though there may have been damage to the left hemisphere as well. Brain imaging did not reveal damage to the occipital lobes. When tested on color matching, the man had great difficulty discriminating green, yellow, red and blue hues and less in matching different shades of gray. Compared to normal subjects, however, his matching of the shades of gray was somewhat slow and impaired. This case demonstrates a selective loss of the cortical neurons that process trichromatic colors but not of those that process dichromatic shades, and shows that there is a minute breakdown of neuroanatomical representation for different aspects of color processing. Generalizing from the above to colored art works, shadows depicted in shades of gray or black involve separate neuroanatomical regions.

In an effort to gain further insights into cerebral localization of color perception, neuroimaging techniques were used to study a case involving a 68-year-old woman exhibiting features of hemiachromatopsia following a left hemisphere stroke (Short & Graff-Radford, 2001). Her problem with colors was evident upon examination of the upper quadrant of the right visual half field. All colors she saw in that part of her visual world had a grayish tinge, while color perception in her left visual half field was intact. Her ability to discriminate shades of gray was not tested. An MRI revealed damage in the medial junction of the left occipital and temporal lobes, which includes the lingual and fusiform gyri; the calacrine cortex (in the occipital lobe) was spared. Although the left-sided damage in this patient extended deeper into the temporal lobe, including the hippocampus region, the color discrimination deficit was attributed mostly to damage in the lingual and fusiform gyri, in the region of the inferior junction of the occipital and temporal lobes.

Acquired central dyschromatopsia

The subjective color of the visual world has a neuroanatomical basis. Dyschromatopsia is a partial inability to discriminate colors despite good vision (Kennard, Lawden, Morland, & Ruddock, 1995). Meadows (1974) describes a case with acquired dyschromatopsia thus:

> Other disturbances occur occasionally; colours may appear altered, unpleasant, excessively bright or varying in intensity from time to time. A patient with bilateral posterior cerebral artery ischaemia studied by the author . . . whose acuity is admittedly somewhat impaired but nevertheless does not often interfere with recognition of everyday objects, complains that both colours and faces seem unpleasant and that colours appear excessively bright. On a sunny day their intensity dazzles him. The colour disturbance varies in severity but is always present to some degree. Occasionally he develops a type of visual perseveration for colour; for example, after looking at a red London bus his entire environment has appeared red for up to half an hour.
>
> (Meadows, 1974, p. 628)

A particularly circumscribed lesion in the anterior region of the occipital lobes may give rise to a type of dyschromatopsia in which the visual world appears continuously tinted by a color, say gold or red. At least two such cases have been described (Critchley, 1965; Rondot, Tzavaras, & Garcin,

1967). The 1995 case described by Kennard and associates (1995) had what appeared to be only partial destruction of the color-processing center. The patient was thus able to discriminate some colors under specific illumination conditions while failing to do so under other conditions.

The case of an art professor

The rare case of an art professor and a color expert, KG, who suffered a stroke in posterior regions of both hemispheres, was investigated with fMRI imaging (Beauchamp, Haxby, Rosen, & DeYoe, 2000). The damage was in the ventromedial occipital-temporal regions and included areas normally occupied by the lingual and fusiform gyri. It was not, however, severe enough to produce total achromatopsia. The spared color discrimination suggested that the patient suffered from dyschromatopsia. This was quite unexpected given the bilateral nature of the damage. The fMRI revealed that spared regions in the left color-cortex preserved at least some color processing, which accounted for the less than total achromatopsia. What is so interesting about this case, and illuminating for neuropsychology, is that the left color-cortex processed color information coming in from both visual half fields! Normally, information from the left visual half field is processed in the right hemisphere and vice versa. In the case of KG, input from the left half field may have either crossed over callosal fibers or come in via ipsilateral pathways. The authors suggest that these ipsilateral pathways, ordinarily weak transmitters of gross information from the external world, became functional following the damage. The other proposed explanation is that in an expert with a sharp sense of color (in addition to being an art scholar, KG had previously worked in paint manufacturing), the color specializing cortex was sculpted functionally and anatomically differently from that of ordinary individuals. In the case of KG, it may have been the left cortex that saw the greatest reorganization, perhaps even prior to the damage. However, since the damage in the right side was more extensive than in the left, we cannot be sure that a similar pre-damage reorganization did not take place there as well.

An artist with color agnosia

Color agnosia is the loss of knowledge and meaning of colors. Gordon Holmes (1945), the well-known neurologist, provided the following illuminating description of an artist with posterior brain damage with color agnosia:

> Another man was a competent artist, but since his stroke he has been unable to use colours and states they had lost their natural significance for him. He is not colour blind, for he can name most colours and can select them when given their names, but when tested with Holmgren's wools it was found he was unable to sort out colours, for example, to select the various shades of red or green. He is, however, unable to

associate colours with familiar objects. When he was asked the colour of the sky, of grass, or of a rose, his replies, if correct, were based on verbal associations, not on the association of the colour with the object; colours are for him no longer properties of objects. This colour agnosia also results from disease of the lateral surface of the left occipital lobe in the neighborhood of the visual cortex.

(Holmes, 1945, p. 359)

With color agnosia, either the semantic store for the meaning of colors is damaged or else the access routes to this store are compromised, particularly those projecting from the visual modality. The bulk of evidence points to posterior cortical areas in the junction of the occipital and temporal lobes for attaining color meaning. Color agnosia is the dissociation between the concept of a color and its object; the meaning of a color is lost possibly due to a disconnection between the regions representing the object and its color representation. Cases of color agnosia are even more rare than those of achromatopsia, but their very existence illustrates the relationship between color and meaning, between colors and objects. While hues can be discriminated and named in such cases, the association between the color and visual objects is lost. Language deficits alone cannot explain this particular agnosic disorder. The left junction of the occipital and temporal region including the anterior fusiform area is more often implicated than the same region in the right side, not only in individual case studies but in large group studies as well (Basso, Faglioni, & Spinnler, 1976; De Renzi, 1999; De Renzi & Spinnler, 1967; De Renzi, Faglioni, Scotti, & Spinnler, 1972; Goldenberg & Artner, 1991; Hecaen, 1969; Hecaen & Albert, 1978; Holmes, 1945; Lewandowsky, 1908; Meadows, 1974).

Distinguishing between mere perceptual problems and cognitive linguistic versus non-linguistic impairments is not trivial. For years neurologists used tests that failed to isolate the nature of the color disorder. The person credited with devising appropriate and valid tests to tease out the association between an object and its color, and thereby show knowledge of the color's meaning, was Lewandowsky (1908; see also Davidoff, 1996; De Renzi & Spinnler, 1967). He had a patient who had suffered a left posterior stroke, probably involving the occipital lobe, and who subsequently could not provide the names of colors or point to patches of color named by the examiner. Similarly, he could not recall the names of objects whose color the examiner provided. It became necessary to devise a test in which words or other overt linguistic components were excluded. Lewandowsky (1908) thus came up with an elegant test consisting of black-and-white line drawings of familiar objects, requiring the patient to fill each one up with the appropriate color(s) chosen from an array of colored pencils. His patient failed to fill the line drawings correctly, indicating that the color problem was due to several factors related to perception, language, and cognition. Years later, De Renzi and his associates, as well as many other investigators, began using

Lewandowsky's effective line drawing coloring test (De Renzi & Spinnler, 1967), now considered the definitive method for determining the presence of color agnosia. Color agnosics may paint a banana blue, the sky brown, the Earth purple, strawberries yellow, and so on. In some of the larger studies of color agnosics, there seems to be a greater prevalence of left hemisphere damage (De Renzi & Spinnler 1967; De Renzi et al., 1972).

Health status of the eyes in visual artists

Brain damage in established artists informs answers to only some of the questions regarding the components of art. The eye informs the brain in the first place; seeing clear, focused images of the external world depends on the integrity and health of the eyes (see Figure 3.1). In artists, a breakdown in the process of utilizing light normally for vision can compromise and alter the final artistic product. We see shapes, forms, color, contours, and patterns in the external world because they reflect light that enters the eye and stimulates special receptors in the retina, which, in turn, give rise to sensations of color. The retina itself is brain tissue and the photoreceptors are actually specialized neurons. Normally, light enters through the pupil – the opening in the iris – which constricts or expands depending on the amount of light that hits it. Then the cornea and the lens focus the light rays on the retinal receptors. The region of the retina responsible for seeing fine details is the fovea, a small area with an especially high density of photoreceptors. When we fixate our gaze to write, paint, sculpt, read, or embroider, for example, we are using foveal vision. We see images of the external world with clarity despite the fact that light goes through several layers of cells and liquid before hitting the receptors that send neural signals to the brain, and despite the fact that the image on the retina is inverted (see Figure 3.4). Exploring these normal mechanisms of vision and how the brain processes neural signals arriving from the eyes is critical for gaining insights into the neuropsychology of art. This section discusses the breakdown in normal functioning of the eye and the visual system in artists.

Color deficiency and color-blindness

The fact that choice of color is not essential to what constitutes art can be seen in the works of accomplished color-deficient artists, of whom few are known, although given the prevalence of color-blindness among males, we would expect more artists to have some forms of this condition. Several currently practicing highly successful American cartoon and comic artists, including Mort Drucker, John Byrne, and Mike Kaluta, have some form of color-blindness (Cooke, 2001). Pickford described the case of American artist, Donald Purdy, who had color deficiency particularly for greens (Pickford, 1964). Charles Meryon of France was a color-blind artist who painted with colors, illustrated, engraved, etched, and created beautiful and highly

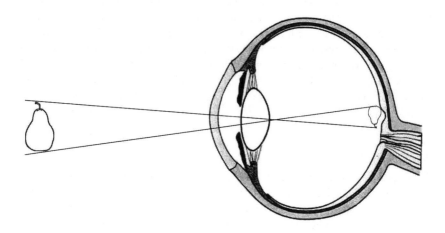

Figure 3.4 When light enters the eye and reaches the retina, the projected image is inverted. Only when neural signals from the retina reach the brain, the image is computed neuronally to an upright position. Furthermore, the image on the retina, in each eye, is two-dimensional but the brain applies computations that incorporate the inputs from both eyes to yield an image in three dimensions.

regarded drawings. He eventually gave up using colors, resorting instead to detailed black-and-white works (Collins, 1999; Marmor & Lanthony, 2001; Ravin, Anderson, & Lanthony, 1995).

Specific artists are discussed later in the chapter. The rate of color-blindness in the male population is currently around 8 percent and there is no reason to believe that professional artists would be spared, particularly given its hereditary component. Color deficiency when present in artists illustrates that color is but one component in art expression and emphasizes instead the critical roles of talent, spatial abilities, expertise, skill, and sensitivity to shading and light in rendering the complete product. This and the extensive range of achromatic art is indication that form and shape play a stronger role in conveying the artist's message.

Defective color vision affects limited features in the artist's creation but does not detract from its composition or aesthetic effect on the observer. The disorder is commonly found in males, transmitted through the X chromosome of the unaffected mother. The condition arises in the retina when the cones responsible for reacting to certain wavelengths of light are either entirely missing or grossly defective. In general, the most prevalent type of color-blindness is the red–green defect in which the afflicted person is particularly unable to differentiate between red and green hues. A less common defect is blue–yellow blindness (tritanopia), the inability to distinguish between these two colors. In both types the ability to distinguish objects on the basis of saturation and brightness remains intact. In other words, a light red may not be identified as red by a red–green color-blind person, but it can be distinguished from a dark red. In an even rarer condition, there is complete color-blindness to all hues, with the afflicted person seeing the world in monochrome (grayscale vision). Partial color-blindness exists in people who have only a few defective cones specialized to process one type of wavelength, their color sensation deficits varying from mild to severe. The English artists Constable and Turner, who used a great deal of yellow, are suspected of fitting into this category, but this is far from certain (Lanthony, 2001).

Specialized neural cells in the retina

A simple definition of light is that it is energy consisting of particles (photons) that oscillate in specific frequencies (wavelengths). The rate of photon oscillations also informs shapes, forms, or contours. Fast frequencies describe short light wavelengths while slow frequencies describe long ones. For example, blue is represented in short wavelengths, red in long wavelengths. Our subjective perception of color is determined by the brain through its neural computations of the input that comes in through the eyes. Two photoreceptors in the eyes containing photopigments are cones and rods. The cones are functional in daytime and are sensitive to color (see subsequent sections in this chapter), while the rods are functional in extremely low illumination and are sensitive to movement (they can react to levels of illumination – light versus dark – but not color). There are approximately 120 million rods and 6 million cones in each eye (Kaufman, 1974). The cones are located in the macula region of the retina, particularly in the fovea, whereas the rods are found in peripheral retinal regions outside the macula. Given the predominance of foveal vision in humans, these regions "need" to be sensitive to motion and movement in the visual field for adaptive protection. That way, while we focus on details with our fovea, specialized motion-sensitive rods detect a movement that can signal danger.

Both the cones and the rods first send neural signals to the horizontal and bipolar cells, which, in turn, signal the next level in the chain, the ganglion cells. These cells consist largely of the large magnocellular (M) and small parvocellular (P) cells. The M cells receive input primarily from the rods, the P cells from the cones. The P cells are concentrated in the fovea while the M are found in regions outside the macula. Only the P cells react to color; the M cells react to movement and faint light. The important thing to realize about the ganglion cells is that they "capture" the external world in what is known as their receptive fields, the size of which is determined by the extent of the cells' dendritic arborization (Livingstone, 2002). In the fovea, where the P cells are concentrated, the receptive field of individual ganglion cells is minute whereas peripheral to the macula, where the M cells are concentrated, receptive fields are large. This implies that focused vision requires the action of many ganglion cells. Moreover, the ganglionic operations also suggest that computational processes begin at the level of the retina, even before reaching the brain (Livingstone, 2002).

Visual pathways and the two visual half fields

The ganglion cells give rise to the axons that together form the bundle of fibers known as the optic nerve through which further visual neuronal signals are transmitted to the brain (Goldstein, 2001). Figure 3.1 provides a diagram of the primary visual pathways. Light information falling on the nasal parts of the eyes is transmitted via two separate optic nerves which converge at the optic chiasm and then cross over to the opposite side. That is, the optic nerve from the left eye continues on to the right hemisphere and vice versa. Fibers from the temporal halves of each retina do not cross over at the chiasm but rather continue on the same (ipsilateral) side. The detailed, focused visual information of the external world is transmitted via these variously routed fibers. In all, the great majority of fibers leaving the eye (approximately two-thirds) cross over to the opposite side while about one-third do not. Moreover, it appears that despite the fact that there are approximately 120 million rods and 6 million cones in each eye, there are only about 1 million fibers leaving the retina through each optic nerve. This further confirms the suggestion that visual information from the eye is already converted into small, efficient neural units that are then relayed to the brain.

Before reaching the primary visual cortex in the occipital lobes, the majority of the axons first project to the lateral geniculate body (LGN) in the thalamus. The LGN represents the first synaptic contact that retinal axons make after exiting the retina. Further neuronal processing and computation are performed in the LGN on visual input received via the retina. At this junction, information from the two eyes does not blend appreciably, with axons from each eye terminating in separate layers of the LGN. Additionally, not all the axons that cross at the chiasm end in the LGN; some proceed to the superior colliculus. The information transmitted via those fibers is not as detailed as the information transmitted via the retinal-LGN route. The geniculostriate visual pathway relays signals from LGN neurons to the primary visual cortex (also known as V1 (Area 17)) in the occipital lobes, and is known as the primary visual pathway (for a review, see Leff, 2004).

After initially synapsing on the neurons in the V1 region of the visual cortex, two separate visual pathways, sometimes called "streams," are formed consisting of further neuronal signals that travel forward carrying neural codes toward the front of the brain (Ungerleider & Mishkin, 1982). These are commonly called the dorsal (superior) and ventral (inferior) visual streams. The dorsal stream is the "where" system while the ventral stream is the "what" system. The "where," a spatially oriented information system, feeds into the association areas of the parietal lobes to inform us where objects are located in space (and consists of further subtle subdivisions (Rizzolatti & Matelli, 2003)). In contrast, the "what" system reaches the inferotemporal cortex, in the inferior portion of the temporal lobe, where information is coded about object identity. These two streams work parallel to one another, and it is possible, through behavioral tests on neurologically impaired patients, to demonstrate that when one stream is damaged, the other may remain intact.

Brightness in paintings

Color contrast facilitates luminance contrast in judgments of visual form. Normally, shading provides visual clues to object shape and identity, and to the perception of motion. Color vision also contributes to such recognition and perception by differentiating luminance gradations arising from shading and shadows from those that arise due to surface reflectance (Kingdom, 2003).

A critical determinant in how colors are perceived is their brightness. In addition to the amount of light that is reflected from a given surface, the angle from which the observer views the object plays an important role in its perceived brightness. Looking at a painting, we receive one type of signal from its colors and another signal from the brightness of those colors. The color blue, for example, seems less bright to us than yellow. Indeed, the degree of brightness in a painting contributes to its aesthetic value and general compositional appeal. The role that shades of brightness play in paintings is to convey depth, shape, texture and movement, as well as mood. In paintings, artists make use of subtleties in luminance to create contrasts between background and foreground, while with line drawing, they create borders that are easily processed by the visual system. Consider Picasso's line drawing of a woman's nude back. Just a few crisp lines on white paper and we, the observers, interpret it as the back of a nude woman; the drawing contains no hatching, smoothing or blending into subtle gray scales. In the real world there are no crisp lines, no sharp demarcations, yet we immediately understand Picasso's representation.

In human visual perception of art, light and dark are another dimension of the aesthetic experience. This is amply demonstrated in theatrical stage performances and particularly in films, where directors and cinematographers have tremendous artistic flexibility. Specifically, sitting in a darkened room watching a black-and-white movie brings out light-versus-dark accents in a way that is unlike viewing black-and-white still photography, where the ambient environment is flooded with light.

Color and light in the art of film

Lighting in motion pictures is a critical aspect of the filmmaker's art – central to what makes a movie what it is. Imagine how dull it would be to sit in a darkened movie theater watching a film shot with non-varying light. Used in the right way, light accentuates faces, emphasizes and de-emphasizes critical moments, induces doubt or clarifies ambiguous situations, molds and shapes the actor's figure, creates impressions of depth, speeds up slow-moving objects or slows down fast ones, creates smoke where there is none, enhances colors, and performs innumerable other critical functions that give rise to meaning. Cinematographers manipulate light in order to convey non-verbal messages that are an essential support to the central meaning and theme of the film. Particularly interesting cinematic lighting effects are seen in black-and-white films.

The famous cinematographer, Sven Nykvist, known for his work with director Ingmar Bergman, has described his approach to lighting (Nykvist, 2003) as follows:

> The most important task of the cinematographer is to create an atmosphere. The foundation of the film is always the script, and the director is the person with the vision of how that script should be realized. Actors give the story life, and it is the cinematographer who has the task of carrying out the intentions of the script and catching the moods and feelings that the director wants to convey. I mostly perform these tasks by using very little light and little color. There is a saying that a good script tells you what is being done and what is being said and not what someone thinks or feels, and there is some truth in that. Images, not words, capture feelings in faces and in atmospheres, and I have realized that there is nothing that can ruin the atmosphere as easily as too much light. My striving for simplicity derives from my striving for the logical light, the true light. I cannot deny that my job has become easier with the new and more light-sensitive film stocks, but the conclusion is always the same. A naturalistic light can only be created with fewer lights, sometimes none at all. At times I have used only kerosene lamps or candles. It may be that my spare lighting stems from the sparse light we have in Sweden compared to more southern countries and especially California. Ingmar Bergman and I studied this beautiful light extensively and learned that simplicity is the key for natural cinematic light.
>
> (Nykvist, 2003, p. 10)

The interpretation of space stems from visual experience where faraway objects are fuzzier than those in close-up. Similarly, our experience with shadows enables us to interpret pictorial representations that use bright versus dark colors to emphasize light and shadowing. The manipulation of light together with a knack for selecting the most effective vantage points informs the art of the world's most talented cinematographers. How they use light to photograph faces and objects, and to capture the relationship between the two, is what makes their films remarkable. The widely known and highly regarded American film director John Ford provides his insight (Sharpe, 2001):

> I can take a thoroughly mediocre bit of acting, and build points of

shadow around a ray of strong light centered on the principals, and finish with something plausible – anyway that's my one boast. If you'll watch in any of my pictures you'll see the trick I use for special effect: while the stars are running through their lines a diffused glow settles over the background assemblage, which at the same time begins to murmur and then to talk intelligibly. And the louder the voices, the stronger the glow, until the main actors are merely part of a group and the general realism is achieved. It always works. Good technique is to let a spot follow a bit player with an important line or two of dialogue across a shadowed set until his part of the scene is finished too.

(Sharpe, 2001, p. 19)

Light–shade defines shapes while simultaneously increasing the impression of depth in the viewer's mind. This is one of the pictorial cues that give rise to depth perception. Film is after all a two-dimensional art form, albeit one that, through movement, can create an additional real-life illusion that still pictures cannot.

What compromises colors in the eye of artist and viewer?

The cornea and crystalline lens of the eye allow us to see clear, focused outside images by projecting them onto the retina. The elasticity of the crystalline lens enables us to accommodate our vision to close and distant objects. Thus, the health of the cornea, lens and their supporting muscles is what determines how focused that image will be.

Let us suppose the artist suffers from an eye condition that compromises vision such as a persistent eye infection, hereditary retinal disease, a lens abnormality, color-blindness, color deficiency, macular degeneration, atrophy, or even normal age-related alterations (Nathan, 2002; Trevor-Roper, 1970). Moreover, consider the variability in the concentration of cone photoreceptors in the retina, or in sensitivity to short versus long wavelengths of light. The visibility of shapes and forms, the clarity of light and colors – all can be compromised by poor vision due to impaired or damaged eyes. We would expect such variables to shape artistic style without affecting talent or skill.

In her book on Cézanne, Mary Lewis (2000) quotes the French master: "Now being old, nearly seventy years, the sensations of colour, which give light, are for me the reasons for the abstractions that do not allow me to cover my canvas entirely" (Lewis, 2000, p. 307). And again, commenting on his vision in 1905, a year before his death:

I believe I have in fact made some more progress ... It is, however, very painful to have to state that the improvement produced in the comprehension of nature from the point of view of the picture and the development of the means of expression is accompanied by old age and a weakening of the body.

(Lewis, 2000, p. 322)

To his son he likewise noted: "I regret my advanced age, because of my colour sensation" (p. 322). Cézanne was reportedly also myopic, but did not regularly wear glasses; he felt that wearing them did not benefit his work (Nathan, 2002). In other words, he liked the world that he saw through poor vision.

The cone photoreceptors can be compromised genetically or through disease. The cones are concentrated in the macula, the region immediately surrounding the fovea. Some diseases, such as macular degeneration, lead to partial sight and loss in the perception of some colors. Consider the following: as measured in wavelengths, red is long, blue is short, while green and yellow are of medium length. Immediately around the fovea there is a paucity of cones reacting to short wavelengths (blue) and a relative abundance of cones reacting to long ones (such as red and brown). Blue, therefore, is not a color we see with foveal vision (Kaufman, 1974), and may be the last hue compromised in macular degeneration. On the other hand, red may be the first to go if the fovea is compromised. Normally, with regard to light wavelength sensitivity, there is great individual variability in the topographical distribution of cones. For this reason it has been difficult to construct a generic map of cone-pigment distribution. It is entirely possible that gifted visual artists have uniquely organized cones, not only within the macula, but around it. Moreover, the pigments in cones may have particular neurochemical reactivity, unique in some visual artists. Indeed, there has always been a question in psychology and philosophy about sensations not being the same across individuals.

From the time we are born, the eye's crystalline lens undergoes progressive changes which affect its transparency, and ultimately, our color vision (Trevor-Roper, 1970). With maturity, this is most noticeable in perception of blue (short wavelength) and green (medium wavelength). One such change is increased yellowing of the lens, but whether this is due to a pigment already present at birth or increased exposure to sunlight is not yet clear. With aging, the yellowing prevents the retina from receiving short wavelengths, and, in addition, causes a glare effect in sunlight due to the tendency of light to reflect off the lens (again because of decreased transparency of the lens) (Gaillard, Zheng, Merriam, & Dillon, 2000). The fovea also undergoes changes (loss and degradation of photoreceptors) with aging that compromise the seeing of details. Thus, variables in the eye would expectedly alter how the visual world is depicted on canvas. Artists such as the Impressionists painted outdoors a great deal; their cognitive fascination with light may have affected the health of their eyes because of extensive exposure to sunlight.

Both the natural yellow pigment in the lens and the yellow pigment in the macula itself have an effect on light that ends up stimulating the photoreceptors. With increasing age, the amount of filtering and refraction due to this yellowness would logically lead to changes in the perception of colors, and presumably the choice and use of colors. However, again, there is tremendous variability in this natural yellow pigment and the degree of refraction that occurs.

Cataracts and consequences to clarity and colors

Cataracts typically develop in some people with advancing age. A cataract is a film that forms over the lens of the eye, causing blurred vision. This film also makes the lens thicker and less elastic (compromising accommodation to distance viewing, for example). Some people are known to be more susceptible to cataracts than others (e.g., diabetics, alcoholics, smokers). Prolonged exposure to bright sunlight, hereditary circumstances, and diabetes increase the chances of developing cataracts at a younger age than usual (Trudo & Stark, 1998). Vision becomes severely limited since the cataract prevents normal entry of light to the retina, which, in turn, leads to blurred, foggy and fuzzy vision. The artists Claude Monet and Mary Cassatt suffered from serious cataract conditions in both eyes (discussed below).

Cataracts and myopia have a selective effect on color vision, and ultimately on what colors artists choose in their paintings. In both conditions, short wavelengths such as blue and violet are absorbed by the lens and consequently do not project well on the retina. On the other hand, long wavelength colors such as red do penetrate the thickened lens (Trevor-Roper, 1970). After cataract removal, for instance, artists can suddenly see blues and may overcompensate by applying them everywhere in their paintings. Because reds are easier to see, some artists, as they develop cataracts or become increasingly myopic, seem to prefer red tones. For example, as Renoir aged, reds became preponderant in several of his late paintings. This observation has fed speculation that his vision had become impaired (Trevor-Roper, 1970).

Dopamine and colors

Dopamine, a major inhibitory neurotransmitter in the brain, is found abundantly in the retina, where concentrations increase markedly during light adaptation. Its presence in the retina is not unique to humans, but occurs in all mammals and many other vertebrates. Dopamine somehow regulates cone sensitivity to colors (Shuwairi, Cronin-Golomb, McCarley, & O'Donnell, 2002). In cocaine addicts, for example, dopamine levels typically increase during cocaine use but levels either drop off or become irregular during withdrawal. Blue cone insensitivity during the withdrawal phase suggests that dopamine regulates specific color-sensitive cones (Roy, Roy, Williams, Weinberger, & Smelson, 1997). Thus, when levels of dopamine in Parkinson's, schizophrenia, depression, or normal aging decline or fluctuate, color vision is altered (Djamgoz, Hankins, Hirano, & Archer, 1997; Jackson &

Owsley, 2003). In normal states, mood changes due to the action of dopamine in specific regions of the brain may cause alterations that could have an effect on the cones' sensitivity to blue. If this should occur in artists, the results could explain their choice of pigments.

Specific established artists with compromised vision

Let us consider the works of several artists who have suffered from poor vision due to various eye defects (Dan, 2003). They are Pissarro, Monet, Cézanne, Degas, Kandinsky, Leonardo, and Rembrandt.

Camille Pissarro

One of the founders of Impressionism was Camille Pissarro (1830–1903). He was born on the Caribbean island of St. Thomas, grew up and began drawing there, and eventually moved to Paris where his friends included other notable Impressionists. He painted prolifically and consistently. In 1888, a reoccurring infection developed in his right eye (Ravin, 1997b). The style of the paintings he produced during the subsequent years may have been shaped by the nuisance infection as well as by his sensitivity to cold weather and the eye patch he needed to wear over his right eye (Ravin, 1997b). The colors and shapes in his work are not as crisp as they were prior to his eye infection. Reportedly, during the post-infection period, he often preferred painting indoors and favored views he could see from his window (Eiermann, 2000). Nevertheless, the paintings he produced in his last fifteen years remain true to his exceptional artistic talent.

Claude Monet

Claude Monet (1840–1926) is one of the most famous Impressionists, considered by some to be the "father" of the school. Indeed, its name came from Monet's painting, *Impression, Soleil Levant*, displayed in a Paris exhibition in 1874. He and Pissarro were friends who worked together and participated in joint group exhibitions. In 1912 Monet was diagnosed with cataracts in both eyes, although in 1908 he was already complaining of poor eyesight (Ravin, 1997a), indicating that the cataracts might have begun developing at that time. Surgery to remove cataracts and restore vision is now routine and usually successful; in Monet's time, however, the surgery was not a sure thing, a fact of which the artist was certainly aware. In 1913, a leading ophthalmologist diagnosed exceedingly poor vision in his right eye and prescribed powerful corrective lenses for distance (as well as for close-up vision in his left eye). Monet had cataract surgery on his left eye in 1923, but it was not entirely successful (Ravin, 1997a). Throughout this whole period of poor vision and cataracts, he continued to paint, though his choice of colors changed and his forms became less focused. Fuzzy images characterize many of his paintings, yet we the viewers derive pleasure from looking at them. His talent was unaffected, and the powerful aesthetic appeal of his famous water lily series, begun in 1914 and painted through 1920, continues to this day. What guided his creative expression were his talent, extensive skills, and the concepts stored in his long-term memory, and what contributed to the appearance of the final product was the fuzziness of his poor vision.

Paul Cézanne

Paul Cézanne (1839–1906) was another prominent member of the Impressionist school. The French painter reportedly suffered from myopia (nearsightedness) and diabetes (Mills, 1936). Diabetes eventually compromises vision by constricting small blood vessels in the eye as well as altering the water balance within the crystalline lens (Trudo & Stark, 1998). His outdoor painted scenes do not emphasize color and the lines do not delineate clear-cut forms. Compared to these scenes, his indoor still-life close-ups do emphasize color (yet still with somewhat ill-defined forms). This is in keeping with the notion that near vision facilitates attention to detail. However, even here it has been suggested that some subtle distortions in his work may be attributed to poor focal vision with a resultant emphasis on peripheral vision (Mills, 1936). Consider *The Card Players*, painted in 1882. Earlier, observing Cézanne's artistic style, a leading critic of the time, Thadee Natanson, confirmed that the style reflected an interest in anything but the precise depiction of objects, emphasizing instead the juxtaposition of those objects or color patches that together make up the painting's composition (Thomson, 2002). Cézanne's eyes do not detract from his extraordinary artistic talent and aesthetic sense. We may posit, however, that his innovative style was influenced by the impaired health of his vision.

Edgar Degas

Edgar Degas (1834–1917), famous for his paintings of ballerinas, suffered from poor vision believed linked to several causes, including a familial hereditary condition. His vision problems seem to have begun around age 36 (Ravin & Kenyon, 1997), particularly in his right eye. Because he suffered from sensitivity to strong light, he avoided painting outdoors which likely explains his emphasis on indoor scenes. In this regard he was different from other Impressionists who, in their art, preferred to express their fascination with light and its effects on trees and water. Degas's sensitivity to light together with his problems distinguishing colors has suggested to some that he may have suffered from a form of retinal degeneration affecting central vision (Ravin & Kenyon, 1997). Eventually, he lost central vision bilaterally, and applied his attention to what he saw around the focal point (Mills, 1936). His later works, shaped by the further deterioration of his eyesight, emphasized certain colors and blurred forms; his experimentation with sculpture and pastel drawings reflects the ill health of his vision at that time (Ravin & Kenyon, 1997) (it is apparently easier to use pastels than oil paints when vision is compromised). Again, his productivity, originality, creativity, and talent remained intact.

Wassily Kandinsky

Wassily Kandinsky (1866–1944) began painting seriously only around age 30. He studied art in Munich, Germany. There is a great deal more emphasis on color in his paintings than on representational shapes. This may be due to his myopia (interfering with the accurate perception of forms and shapes). Indeed, he is credited with starting the "modern" school of abstract art in which geometrical forms supplant naturally occurring ones, and in which color patches and non-verbal shapes are heavily emphasized. With no clearly recognizable forms, colors became the unifying themes of his paintings (Critchley, 1987), a style perhaps reflective of his extremely poor vision.

As stated earlier, normal aging can influence color choice even in the absence of identifiable eye disease (Jackson & Owsley, 2003; Wijk et al., 1999b). Aging compromises visual acuity, stereopsis, brightness contrast, and adaptation to darkness, to mention but a few visual functions (Pitts, 1982).

Leonardo and Rembrandt

Leonardo da Vinci (1452–1519) and Rembrandt (1606–1669) both continued to paint beyond age 60, but their later works seem somewhat "darker" than those from younger days (Trevor-Roper, 1970). They are believed to have had normal vision throughout their lives. Normally, with advanced age, presbyopia and other changes discussed above compromise color vision – for instance, a normal degradation of the retinal macula (Weale, 1997). Similarly, with this degradation, particularly in the fovea, there would be a loss of detail vision, which might explain why many details present in the paintings of a young artist are not there when he or she grows old. Color preferences also change with age, at least in non-artists (Wijk et al., 1999b). In any case, the paintings produced by maturing artists can be interpreted and understood against the backdrop of age-related changes in their eyes (Weale, 1997).

Additional well-known visual artists affected by poor vision were Pierre-Auguste Renoir, Georgia O'Keeffe, and Edvard Munch (Dan, 2003). Others such as Vincent van Gogh displayed interesting visual effects in his paintings believed to be due to neurochemical imbalances.

Vincent van Gogh's colors

Vincent van Gogh (1853–1890) is famous not only for his paintings but also for being hospitalized in an insane asylum, for cutting part of his ear off, and for committing suicide at a relatively young age (Blumer, 2002; Devinsky, 2003). There has always been debate about the motivation behind his unusual artistic style, those wavy lines, all the yellows (particularly after 1886), and how it all relates to his supposed insanity. He did indeed suffer from visual and auditory hallucinations sometimes, and spent time in an insane asylum, but all of this cannot explain his phenomenal, extraordinarily beautiful, time-less, and influential paintings. In the end, it cannot even be said about him that he was schizophrenic. As an active member of the artistic community of his times, he was influenced by works of other artists and this can explain in part the basis for some of his artistic decisions. For example, he was influenced by Japanese paintings and woodblocks (see Munsterberg, 1982). He was not the only practicing artist at that time to be influenced by works from the Far East. But he did suffer the side-effects of bad habits, as judged from his letters, reports by his friends, and some surviving medical records (Arnold, 1992). First, he was addicted to absinthe, an alcoholic drink con-taining toxic compounds, one of which is now known to be alpha thujone. When drunk in excess, it can lead to neurological disorders, psychosis, hal-lucinations, and epileptic seizures. This was true not only for van Gogh but also for many of the other people drinking it at that time. Toulouse-Lautrec, the French artist, was also addicted to absinthe and suffered its consequences in a mental asylum for a brief period in 1899. Under experimental conditions, toxic doses of thujone were found to induce epileptic convulsions. The drink is now outlawed but not before it took a heavy toll on French society in the nineteenth century and fifteen years into the twentieth century. It was finally banned there in 1915 (Arnold, 1989). Alpha thujone is now known to block the chloride channel on the gamma aminobutyric acid type A (GABAA) receptor and thereby promote its convulsant effects (Harris, 2002; Hold, Siri-soma, Ikeda, Narahashi, & Casida, 2000). Second, van Gogh suffered from pica, a mental disorder characterized by the urge to eat non-food items such as paint, sand, pencils, and many other substances. He was known to ingest his paints, which were mixed with turpentine, to drink kerosene, with which he used to fill his lamps for light, and to drink camphor in order to alleviate his insomnia. Third, he took bromide to alleviate some of his neurological symptoms. Fourth, he took digitalis to alleviate his epilepsy, and drank san-tonin to alleviate gastrointestinal discomfort. The latter two compounds, if taken in excess, are known to cause xanthopsia, that is, yellow vision. The world appears as if pigmented with yellow. It turns out that van Gogh took everything excessively, except nutritive food, and it is highly likely that his "yellow paintings" reflect chemical changes in the retinal photoreceptors. The chemicals must have suppressed the action of some of photoreceptors while enhancing the action of other receptors. The exact mechanisms are not understood. The effects on the brain were reversible since the hallucinations, psychotic states, and xanthopsia were not permanent. Finally, van Gogh did not eat well and thus suffered from nutritional deficits. One reason for this, besides the drinking and excessive smoking, is the possibility that he suffered from a gastrointestinal disorder known as acute intermittent porphyria, which prevented him from retaining real food, digesting properly, and developing a strong appetite. All of these explanations do not explain everything or nearly everything about his art or his choice of colors (the blue irises, the white iris, blue skies, blue walls, green leaves, dark colors in his early period, the one prior to 1986, and so on) but they provide a workable background against which to understand features of his art.

Van Gogh's famous ear-cutting incident could have been exasperated by emotional upheavals associated with his brother's impending marriage (and the loss of his exclusive attention to van Gogh) as well as an uncomfortable relationship with his friend and colleague, the artist Gauguin (De Leeuw, 1998). Van Gogh committed suicide a year and half after he cut off his ear. He is known to have worked on producing art tirelessly and consistently. Even when he spent time in the insane asylum, he went on painting beautiful works. If he had been a seriously mentally ill person, he would not have been able to sustain focused attention on his art and to work so consistently and deliberately, to say nothing of his continued originality and creativity. There were no alterations in his depictions of depth, faces were not deformed, objects were not misshapen, proportionality and scaling were retained, forms were recognizable, paints were controlled with the same careful brush strokes, and balanced compositions were produced. Despite all his mental anguish he produced at least 638 paintings between 1886 and the time of his death in 1890. They are admired by critics and non-critics alike, sought after, exhibited, and still retain their enormous aesthetic appeal.

Preservation of artistic abilities is illustrated further in the interaction between neurological disease and sensory impairments in another famous professional artist. The case of Goya, described next, is one such example.

Francisco Goya's illness

Francisco Goya (1746–1828) was a highly innovative artist who was drawn to artistically chronicling social and historic events and was extremely interested in depicting the cultural and societal values of his day (Hughes, 2003). His talent was recognized early on in his life through his sketches of people. Around age 14 he became an apprentice to an established painter, after which he studied and worked in Rome, returning to Madrid to pursue his art. Around 1784 he became a court painter to King Charles IV and Queen Luisa. Goya suffered from several physical ailments (Critchley, 1987; Ravin & Ravin, 1999), which, in 1792, had him complaining suddenly of poor balance, dizziness, deafness, and worsening vision. A year later Goya reportedly was completely deaf and his visual acuity somewhat compromised. He began experiencing bad dreams – "sounds in his head" – and suffering periods of depression. At this time he was about 37 years old. Numerous medical explanations have been offered in hindsight, with the most reasonable being that he suffered from a rare viral infection, possibly Vogt-Koyanagi syndrome, associated with inflammation of the eyes and ears and leading to total deafness (Vargas, 1995). This type of illness occurs abruptly, and corresponds with some of the reports on Goya circulating at that time.

And yet, from age 62 to 73, he produced more than 700 paintings as well as numerous etchings, sketches, and drawings. He had enormous energy, sometimes completing a portrait within several hours. No spatial distortions are noted in these works, the character of his lines remained excellent, and he continued to innovate. His colors, however, became somewhat darker, and his subject matter took on a nightmarish quality. In one of his letters he says he is blind and cannot read or write (and yet he was able to go on painting). Interestingly, however, in the last years before his death, his paintings reportedly became more colorful. The remarkable aspect of Goya's art is that it continued to grow and develop, even though he himself was experiencing poor vision and mental anguish stemming from a physical condition.

Summary

Neuropsychology distinguishes between sensory and central impairments and takes both into account in obtaining the global picture. Visual artists are affected by eye health, the quality of their vision, and the functioning of the brain's color processing regions. What gets displayed on canvas is a reflection not only of artistic skills, but also of eye-related influences as well. It is possible that the Impressionists' style of art evolved in part because their vision had been compromised by disease (e.g., the cataract-clouded perspective of Monet) and excessive exposure to sunlight. Similarly, neurological diseases could affect the colors artists choose, and even normal age-related changes to vision can influence an artist's work (examples of the latter include both Leonardo and Rembrandt, who may have suffered alterations to their color vision with the passing of the years). Thus, in considering the neuropsychology of the visual arts, it is useful to explore sensory visual processing as well.

Degrees of illumination, light and dark manipulations, are another dimension of the aesthetic experience amply demonstrated in theatrical stage performances and particularly in films, where directors and cinematographers apply tremendous artistic flexibility to emphasize story elements. Watching a non-color movie in a darkened theater brings out light-versus-dark accents unlike viewing black-and-white still photography, where the ambient environment is flooded with light. Colors are but one special dimension of art that invokes aesthetic sensation; achromatic manifestations bring forth a strong aesthetic reaction as well. Through the use of shadows to depict gradation in light, artists give volume to objects and scenes. One way two-dimensional figures gain a three-dimensional look is when light is shown to reflect off them and paint is applied to depict shadows cast by them. These are some of the techniques artists employ to represent features of reality without resorting to colors.

Further readings

Cole, B. L. (2004). The handicap of abnormal colour vision. *Clinical and Experimental Optometry*, *87*, 258–275.

Dan, N. G. (2003). Visual dysfunction in artists. *Journal of Clinical Neuroscience*, *10*, 166–170.

Davidoff, J. (1991). *Cognition through color*. Cambridge, MA: MIT Press.

Livingstone, M. (2002). *Vision and art: The biology of seeing*. New York: Harry N. Abrams.

Nathan, J. (2002). The painter and handicapped vision. *Clinical and Experimental Optometry*, *85*, 309–314.

Perkowitz, A. (1999). *Empire of light: A history of discovery in science and art*. Washington, DC: Joseph Henry Press.

Zajonc, A. (1995). *Catching the light: The entwined history of light and mind*. Oxford: Oxford University Press.

4 Special visual artists

The effects of autism and slow brain atrophy on art production and creativity

Introduction

The artwork of special artists with brain damage can potentially reveal quite a bit about the neuropsychological nature of talent. Extraordinary isolated talent in otherwise cognitively and socially handicapped autistic individuals has been a source of puzzlement to neuropsychologists and scholars for a long time (Mottron et al., 2003; Sacks, 1995; Selfe, 1977; Treffert & Wallace, 2002). The well-described autism cases of Nadia, EC, and Stephen Wiltshire produce graphic line drawings in black and white showing realistic objects, small and large, from models, pictures, and memory on a level that very few non-autistic individuals can achieve. However, there is little or no abstraction in their productions. The drawings are proportionately correct, details are faithfully rendered, and they depict three-dimensional space. Not only are they executed at a level that few in the general population could ever achieve, but also they can mentally rotate a given object in their mind's eye and then render that image on paper. This is truly remarkable, especially considering that artistic savants comprise a very tiny fraction of the autistic population. However, despite the fact that they display such graphic skills from a very young age, these skills do not substantially improve, develop, or change in significant ways, as they grow older, even following attempts to provide them with art lessons. Because there is no serious artistic growth and there is absence of other artistic qualities, their concurrent flawless performance in neuropsychological tests designed to measure visuo-perceptual, visuo-spatial, and visuo-constructive abilities questions the generalizability of such tests to art production.

The following sections in this chapter explore two groups of atypical artists, the autistic savants and dementia patients who became artistic after onset of their disease. The age at which the remarkable artistic skills emerge in both groups lies in opposite ends. Review of their accomplishments and deficits unravels components in the relationship between art, talent, and brain. In this context, it is important to now discuss the effects of slow brain changes on behavior in general and artistic behavior in particular, and the role of functional reorganization in art production with brain damage.

Untypical artists

Savant Visual Artists

The first such case to be described fully was of Nadia, a young autistic girl who from a very early age (3½ years) appeared to make remarkable sketches of horses from different perspectives (Selfe, 1977). Normal adults, let alone children, cannot produce such drawings. She was autistic; she did not respond to verbal requests, nor was she aware of danger; she appeared to be emotionally uninterested and socially uninteractive. As a baby there was already a lack of responsivity. She was diagnosed as autistic with mental retardation. At age 5 years or so she underwent medical examination that revealed normal skull X-ray, but an electroenchephalogram (EEG) pattern indicating mild wave abnormality in the right hemisphere. The examination also revealed abnormal photic response, which is typically associated with epilepsy, although she herself did not suffer from epilepsy. Her productions were black and white line drawings; there was little if any color in them. Creations expanded to include a variety of objects and continued to express remarkable skill as she grew older, but reportedly only through age 6. That is, her drawing abilities progressed between $3\frac{1}{2}$ and 6 years of age, and afterwards they remained the same. Moreover, Nadia did not display particular creativity or originality, even as she displayed remarkable imagery skills such as mental rotations of two-dimensional representations (Cooper & Shepard, 1984; Shepard & Hurwitz, 1984; Shepard & Sheenan, 1971). In the normal brain, such skills are associated mainly with right hemisphere specialization. Even when she took intensive art lessons at her school, her skills did not improve or expand. Eventually, when in her teens, she gave up drawing and a marked deterioration in her productions was observed, which, at this point resembled work by untalented children. Her language skills were poor from the start. Only when she was 12 years old did she begin to use two-word phrases, for example. Language comprehension remained equally very limited. It was only somewhat better in Ukrainian, the language spoken by her parents at home. She could not read or write, and her language abilities remained very limited (Mottron et al., 2003; Selfe, 1995).

By comparison, the case of another intellectually compromised individual, EC, reveals that remarkable drawing skills, including those that display the use of mental rotations, can be clearly achieved when language is fully present (Mottron et al., 2003). This is the case of a 36-year-old adult diagnosed with high-functioning autism but whose language was in the low average range. He began to draw skillfully around age 7 or 8, skipping, as Nadia did, the normal stage of scribbling that ordinary children go through. He, too, rendered realistic objects in black and white line drawings. There has been very little use of colors or shading in his productions, but perhaps more so than in Nadia's. Unlike Nadia, who stopped drawings in her mid-teens, he continued to display his graphic skills for many years (and probably still does into his forties).

Thus, the presence of language competence and remarkable drawing skills are not mutually antagonistic.

All of EC's line drawings are precise, outlines of objects or landscapes. The lines are firm, careful and precise:

> he draws on A4 paper using a lead pencil or ball-point pen, occasionally using the edge of a sheet as a ruler for his alignments, but otherwise able to draw perfect lines, circles, ellipses or ellipsoids. He never uses an eraser, even when using a lead pencil. He never needs to sketch, since he never makes a mistake: the first line is always the final one. During a copying task, E. C. turns the sheet at his convenience to draw straight lines in the sagittal plane. Consequently, the orientation of the sheet may be completely independent from the model. He is able to reproduce his previous works without a model. The backgrounds of his drawings are sometimes the same: a whole display may be used repeatedly with a striking metric similarity in several drawings. The drawings stop at the edge of the sheet regardless of the outline of the configuration in the real world. Therefore, it is not rare to have a half-complete object or person with an essential part missing.
>
> (Mottron & Belleville, 1995, p. 641)

In other words, the authors are saying that EC does not scale his images to fit the page. Although the scaling is not random, they are also saying, in so many words, that he is not creative in the sense that he uses the same backgrounds for his drawings.

The experimental laboratory studies with EC revealed important clues about linear perspective and vanishing point (Mottron & Belleville, 1995). Both EC and Nadia made use of linear perspective in their drawings but there were errors in depicting realistic depth with the principles of the vanishing point. Mottron and his associates indicate that EC was able to detect discrepancy in perspective views with an accuracy level better than normal subjects, yet when he had to construct scenes with vanishing points he was not very good at doing so. Thus, they propose, rightly, that this ability is a deliberate conscious effort, an intellectual feat, something that EC and Nadia lacked. The spatial depth that EC did portray must have relied on other cognitive abilities than those used by artists who construct scenes with accurate vanishing points. A plausible explanation is that he drew outside his mental sketchpad, the pad he held in his mind's eye, which was supported with a very well functioning working memory. He visualized and rotated images in his mind and then "copied" the image onto paper. The same explanation could apply to Nadia. Invariably, autistic savants have exceptional visual memory. But such mental visualizing, apparently, does not facilitate accurate depiction of scenes of vanishing points. The latter requires a conscious, cognitive, and intelligent effort. The mental three-dimensional visualization may be useful for single objects, for mentally rotating them and viewing them from various perspectives, but not as directly useful for vanishing point depictions. That is not to say that artists who are very good in depicting vanishing points are not good in three-dimensional visualization. The two abilities may well coexist in a normal artist. The brain abnormality in these exceptional autistic artists affects the ability to correctly make use of vanishing point, and the lesson learned here is that high cognitive intelligence is required for such execution.

Oliver Sacks, who extensively observed and studied several autistic visual artists, noted that despite their remarkable graphic skills, the incredibly precise visual realism they are able to represent on paper, they do not develop artistically or improve substantially in time (Sacks, 1995). They do have excellent memory, most likely better than normal. They must also have very good eye–hand coordination dedicated to drawing movements. However, they might not be very good in dart throwing. Furthermore, as I see it, the Nadia and EC cases demonstrate dissociation between identified neuropsychological visual measures and precise graphic renditions of reality. Performing well on laboratory tests that tap components of visual perception certainly does not predict excellent graphic skills. The same tests may also not explain production of beautiful, innovative, original, captivating, timeless art. Nadia and EC did not make discoveries through repeated practice and exploration. Of the two, EC had a higher intelligence, and, it is he who learned to use different artistic techniques (from cartoons) and thus modified his artistic repertoire to an extent, albeit limited. Timeless art shows the use of deliberate intelligence, development, change, experimentation, distillation of ideas, abstraction, thoughts, and growth. Such deliberate skills cannot easily be teased apart by current neuropsychological tests.

Sacks describes in detail the remarkable work of another autistic savant, Stephen Wiltshire, whose graphic talent was first noticed around the age of 5 years (Sacks, 1995). He was interested in depicting cars, but at about age 7 years he started to show consistent drawing interest and fascination in buildings, whether from real models, pictures, or from memory. His drawings appear to have more purposeful shadings than either Nadia's or EC's, but there is very little use of colors, and when there is color, it is simplistic. He too made black and white sketches. They are all remarkably realistic and skillful, appearing as if drawn by an adult artist even though he was only a child when he drew them. "Stephen's art at seven was clearly prodigious, but at nineteen, though he may have developed a bit socially and personally, his talent itself had not developed too greatly" (Sacks, 1995, p. 225).

> Stephen's development has been singular, qualitatively different, from the start. He constructs the universe in a different way – and his mode of cognition, his identity, his artistic gifts, go together. We do not know, finally, how Stephen thinks, how he constructs the world, how he is able to draw and sing. But we do know that though he may be lacking in the symbolic, the abstract, he has a sort of genius for concrete or mimetic representations, whether drawing a cathedral, a canyon, a flower, or

enacting a scene, a drama, a song – a sort of genius for catching the formal features, the structural logic, the style, the "thisness" (though not necessarily the "meaning"), of whatever he portrays.

(Sacks, 1995, p. 241)

The use of color, when it is used, is not imaginative, striking, or unique in these exceptional autistic savants. This is in sharp contrast with the remarkable accuracy with which pictures or models are drawn. Even the case of Richard Wawro, the Scottish autistic savant who uses colors extensively, is not remarkable in how colors are incorporated into the final composition (Treffert & Wallace, 2002). He does not use models for his works, focusing mainly on available pictures and his memory. Although he says, and others around him have confirmed this, that he is fascinated by light and its effects on objects, there is no indication that he has explored light in innovative ways.

Separate neuronal pathways process colors and forms, and their integration in a single composition is a reflection of *binding*, a psychological concept that explains the integration of several distinct functions (Kalat, 2002; Shafritz, Gore, & Marois, 2002). The integration is what gives rise to a unitary percept. A natural question in the context of the autistic savants is whether or not high order binding for form and color is impaired. The tentative answer is that such binding may be missing in such artists.

There is no question that the autistic artists discussed in this chapter have drawing talent and remarkable skills. If they had not been born with neurological brain dysfunction, the kind that gave rise to the autism in the first place, they might have grown into highly accomplished artists. What is missing from their art is the abstraction, development, ideas, and symbolism, all of which could be due to absence of normal binding. Another clue to art and brain may come from what is so striking in their productions, namely the very realistic visual renditions, the photocopy-like attribute, which includes highly spatial and mnemonic features. An explanation for this is offered here in terms of lack of interference from other neuronal networks, which normally exist in non-autistic individuals but that are missing or have not developed in the autistic artists. In other words, their skills are realized only because limited neuronal networks are operational. That vision processing cortical regions are intact is obvious, and these have excellent connections to the frontal motor cortex, especially the hand area representation, enabling direct execution of what is seen. The posterior parietal and temporal lobes must be highly functional bilaterally and connected to the motor cortex as well, given their excellent mental rotation capabilities (done in the mind's eye).

Other critical neuronal networks may be functionally disconnected from this system, a possibility suggested by the findings in an fMRI study of language in high-functioning autistic individuals (Just, Cherkassky, Keller, & Minshew, 2004). White matter fibers may be compromised as well. The semantic system, not necessarily the one subserving linguistic meaning alone, but rather a system that stores experiences and their meanings could be disconnected. This would be a highly interactive system, connecting concepts derived from several sources and modalities – cognition, emotions, social relationships, context, language, general intelligence – and providing a rich source of knowledge, explicit and implicit, for application in art production. But, of course, none of this explains the neuroanatomical nature of talent per se.

Comparison to musical savants

Musical autistic savants exemplify the dissociation between composing and performing. While the great majority of visual autistic savants can and do create drawings and paintings not seen in depictions by others, this is not so with musical savants; they perform more than they create, and what is performed they have heard previously. They possess remarkable memory for musical and other sounds, and have demonstrated above normal ability to mimic in singing or on an instrument (typically piano) musical pieces they had just heard (Miller, 1989; Peretz, 2002; Sloboda, Hermelin, & O'Connor, 1985; Young & Nettelbeck, 1995). The first publicized case was that of Tom Wiggins ("Blind Tom", 1849–1908). He was born a slave on an American plantation and became an accomplished concert pianist (Southall, 1979). Unlike visual autistic savants, who do not have sensory deficits, Treffert (1989) notes presence in musical savants of a triad of symptoms consisting of blindness, mental retardation, and exceptional musical performance skills. The well-known musical savants, Thomas Wiggins, Leslie Lemke, Derek Paravincini, Rex Lewis-Clack, and others, exhibit this cluster of symptoms. These savants improvise previously heard tunes, melodies, and songs but their ability to compose and invent new pieces is debated (Hermelin, O'Connor, & Lee, 1987; Hermelin, O'Connor, Lee, & Treffert, 1989; Sacks, 1995). In all cases, mimicking developed very early in childhood (as young as 2 years in some) but the mimicking is not restricted to musical sounds alone; entire conversations, environmental and animal sounds, can all be recalled and repeated flawlessly. Although musical skills appeared spontaneously, without instruction, all the accomplished musical savants eventually received musical instruction, have been associated with professional musicians as they grew older, and participated in concert performances. There are no detailed descriptions of the sequential progress achieved through training nor of the role that the instructors had in so-called compositions. In contrast to all of this, visual autistic savants hardly benefit from instruction and they create their works spontaneously. Future investigation of the brains of these exceptional musicians may contribute to our understanding of their exceptional musical abilities, which are remarkable given the brain anomalies and the blindness (Heaton & Wallace, 2004; Peretz, 2002).

Fronto-temporal dementia

Bruce L. Miller and associates have published several important cases of patients who developed artistic skills in the course of FTD, a brain disease that affects the temporal lobes more than the frontal lobes (but the reverse can also occur), and in whom there was hemispheric asymmetry in cortical atrophy (Miller, Ponton, Benson, Cummings, & Mena, 1996; Miller et al., 1998; Miller, Boone, Cummings, Read, & Mishkin, 2000). Their productions as a group vary widely (paintings, photographs, and sculptures). On the whole, the works are realistic representations with little abstraction. The emergence of artistic work is explained in the publications in terms of possible selective deterioration of inhibitory influences normally operational through the connections between the temporal lobes and the frontal lobes. Specifically, it is proposed that the disease process gradually produces disconnection between the anterior temporal lobes and orbitofrontal regions but not with dorsolateral and medial frontal regions. Presumably, the latter regions remain intact, permitting initiative and planning of the art. The orbitofrontal region is implicated in the disconnection because the patients display social disinhibition. Preservation of parietal and occipital regions in both hemispheres probably facilitated visual input and constructive abilities. Disconnection from other regions, notably subcortical, is likely to have occurred as well. Importantly, however, it was suggested that the selective disconnection involving the frontal regions *has* led to enhanced interest in the visual world and somehow this has led to the desire to produce art works, all in ways not quite understood. At a certain point of their degenerative condition, typically near the end of their lives, they became unable to produce art at all.

The most impressive of all their cases was a successful businessman who suffered from progressive dementia since age 56 but who previously did not receive art lessons (although it is not known if he created art spontaneously on his own, prior to the dementia). Yet, when his illness developed and progressed he nevertheless painted detailed, realistic, and careful works, even while he was undergoing the effects of the dementia; he suffered from social disinhibition, remoteness, emotional blunting, verbal anomia, and memory deficits. His work was exhibited locally and he received awards. At age 67 years his productions started to show deterioration and at 68 years he produced bizarre figures. He had bilateral atrophy of the temporal lobes, but less activity in the right temporal lobe than in the left, as determined by PET (positron-emission tomography). The MRI showed worse atrophy in the left temporal lobe. Brain activity in the posterior right parietal and occipital lobes was high. His creative output for a period of ten years is impressive in light of the degenerative brain process.

How do we interpret the foregoing? The capacity to create, conceptualize, and rely on abstract cognitions must have existed premorbidly. There are no published data on the percent of normal retirees in the general population who begin to engage in artistic activity after retirement for the first time. If we knew the percentage we would be in a better position to evaluate the significance of art emergence in dementia. These FTD cases were a successful businessman, an advertising entrepreneur, and an inventor before onset of the disease process. If dementia leads to production of art works then why is it that all people with dementia do not have these abilities? The capacity to paint, draw, sculpt, and so on, could have been there in the first place, premorbidly, even if unexpressed artistically. How does their art compare with art of undemented, normally aged adults who begin to paint upon retirement? The explanation proposed here is that the initial professional skill, although not in the field of art, has shared components with artistic skills, and the shared skills are somehow resistant to brain damage, possibly because of repeated use, over-practice, and redundant representation in the brain.

The view proposed here is that the dementia process somehow facilitated skills, abilities, and certain talents that existed before. And what existed before does not have to be artistic. The damage caused by the dementia could lead to generalization transference from one skill to another, the skill of communicating, and the skill of abstract cognition, say. One example is that of another dementia patient, not part of this group: he was unable to communicate with words in the last six months before his death, but he was nevertheless able to communicate with his caretakers through simple drawings (Thomas Anterion, Honore-Masson, Dirson, & Laurent, 2002). They were artful yet not elaborate as those produced by the patients described above (see elaboration of this case at the beginning of Chapter 8). Whereas before disease onset the businessman excelled in talking and convincing people to buy products, or to make money, this business skill – whatever it is – now translated into painting. The underlying cognitive process in skill transference has not yet been clarified, let alone the neuroanatomical and neurophysiological underpinnings in such transference.

Preservation of skills despite extensive brain damage due to Alzheimer's disease was also reported for a musician with twelve years of formal training and forty years as a music editor (Crystal, Grober, & Masur, 1989). He was a pianist who practiced playing the piano on a daily basis and regularly involved his family in music listening to various compositions. After the disease set in, he was no longer able to recall composers' names or titles of their compositions, something that he was very skilled in doing in the pre-morbid stage, while he was able to play the same composers' compositions on the piano. This case illustrates the dissolution of specialized, highly localized functions such as language (naming, in this case) and diffuse representation of certain non-verbal skills.

Slow brain alterations

The effects of slow brain changes on art: serial lesion effects

Recovery of function depends on the rate with which the brain damage occurred, even when the damaged area is large (see Kapur, 1996). The "momentum of lesions" is a concept long understood by clinical neurologists. Stanley Finger (1978) reviews this important topic. For the past 200 years neurologists and neuroscientists have known that slow progression of brain trauma has less detrimental effects on cognition than sudden trauma. This was observed as long ago as 1824 by neurologists who conducted experiments on the effects of brain excisions on animals. The British neurologist John Hughlings Jackson advised in 1879 that neurological symptoms be understood in terms of speed of damage spread. The notion of "momentum of lesions" originated with his observations. He noted, further, that symptoms end up being more permanent with the fast than with the slow variety. Constantin von Monakow observed in 1897 that coma does not necessarily accompany intracerebral hemorrhage when the bleeding is slow. Later, in 1914, he observed that slow-growing tumors in Broca's area might not necessarily result in aphasia. Brain excisions of a specific region that are done in multiple surgeries can obliterate detrimental behavioral symptoms altogether. This is known as the serial-lesion effect. Damage due to slow-growing tumors is not considered equivalent to damage caused by a stroke. Brain tumors can be slow growing, taking years to develop, or they can develop quickly, as in glioblastoma. Thus, in neuropsychological studies that investigate the effects of unilateral focal lesions on specific cognitive functions, it is vital to exclude patients whose lesions are caused by slow-growing tumors; patients with sudden stroke onset are typically better suited for such studies.

Neuronal readjustments to injury are optimized when the damage occurs in small steps. The exact mechanisms of the reorganization and reshaping are not established but it is believed that functions previously controlled by dedicated regions slowly "encroach" on nearby regions as their regions become compromised, incorporating their neuronal components into existing undamaged circuitries. They do not necessarily "cross over" to the other hemisphere. By gradually blending into nearby regions, modified neuronal circuits take over support of lost or partially lost functions. The result of such sharing is that behavioral deficits become less distinctive and hard to tease out in neuropsychological examination. However, neuronal rearrangement is not equally possible throughout brain, or even the cortex. The precise nature of neuronal plasticity remains to be determined.

In the twentieth century, specific experiments were carried out on laboratory animals to determine the difference between single versus serial cortical ablations. The basic finding was that animals with single surgery were more impaired than animals with successive removals of the same region. This is despite the fact that with repeated surgeries there were multiple brain entries resulting in adhesions, scars, and healing complications. A critical finding in this field was when an inadvertent experimental procedure provided some clues. Steward and Ades published this work in 1951 (see discussion in Finger, 1978). Monkeys who underwent two surgeries with an inter-operative separation period of seven days were less impaired on a retention task of an auditory discrimination task than those who underwent surgical removal of the same area in a single operation. Those results inspired further systematic investigations of the effects of multiple- versus single-stage surgeries in other laboratories.

Functional reorganization

The behavioral compensation that takes place in slow-progressing brain diseases masks profound deficits caused by loss of actual tissue and further complicates attempts to determine localized regional functional control. There is no reason to assume that such a process does not evolve in slow dementing diseases such as fronto-temporal dementia, Pick's disease or Alzheimer's disease, cortico-basal degeneration, and the degenerating disease of the composer Ravel (discussed in Chapter 5). As the brain is being compromised piecemeal fashion, sub-region by sub-region, neuronal mechanisms undergo adjustment. The adjustment allows normal functioning of some skills and abilities to carry on as before, and, at the same time, in some cases gives rise to new expressions. This could explain what happened to the 57-year-old art teacher and artist described by Mell and associates (2003), for example, and other artistic cases with slow progressive brain diseases.

Some neuronal reorganization can occur even in adulthood, everything else being equal (Jenkins & Merzenich, 1987; Kapur, 1996; Ovsiew, 1997). The possible ways in which the reorganization can occur are as follows. First, tissue surrounding a small area of damaged tissue may provide the platform for new axonal sprouting that continues to make connections to intact target regions (Duffau et al., 2003); second, previously minor pathways, perhaps "evolutionarily old", become dominantly active; Third, presence of damaged tissue itself provides impetus for synaptic readjustment of neighboring intact tissue. There is hard-wiring in the central nervous system but this is not a fixed template that applies equally to all human skills and cognitions (Kapur, 1996; Knecht, 2004; Mohr, 2004). To be sure, the central nervous system comes with several windows of plastic opportunities in development known as critical periods; they allow adjustment and modification depending on age of occurrence and type of external environment and interactions with it. The window closes for many skills around the age of puberty. And even in the course of development from birth to puberty, several such mini-windows of opportunity open and close for various skills. The upper limits on neuronal plasticity in adulthood have not been identified yet. A discussion of this biological issue is beyond the scope of this book (historical background to the medical thinking behind neurological functional recovery is in Mohr,

2004). Although the upper limits on neuronal readjustment and functional reorganization are not certain, promising clues are slowly being gathered through neuroimaging investigations (Chollet & Weiller, 1994; Weiller, 1998). This is particularly so with regards to language recovery following left hemisphere damage, in childhood as well as in adulthood (Heiss, Thiel, Kessler, & Herholz, 2003; Knecht, 2004; Knecht et al., 2002; Liegeois et al., 2004), and following stroke in adults (Dombovy, 2004; Heiss, 2003).

The foregoing illustrates some of the considerations that should contribute to inferring preservation of function following unilateral or diffuse brain damage, including art expression. Numerous neural factors are at play and can account for the artwork of aging individuals not previously known to be artists. There is currently no ready or simple explanation for art production in FTD as long as the underlying mechanisms involved are uncertain. Clearly there is some form of functional reshaping and compensatory neural take-over. Inborn art-relevant talent (and power of abstraction) may have been present all along in the artists with FTD. Cognitive abstraction can be viewed as a type of invariant human ability that survives extensive neuroanatomical damage. Comparing autistic savants and dementia patients, talent may be "enhanced" as in dementia patients or "spared", as in autistic savants. The notion of *underconnectivity* due to white matter abnormality in autism has been proposed, based on an fMRI study (Just et al., 2004). In sum, in both conditions, there is some sort of tissue isolation due to deteriorating or undeveloped neural systems and elimination of interference from normally inhibiting pathways.

Summary

Autistic savants produce graphic drawings that are by and large realistic representations with little or no abstraction. They seem to possess innate drawing skills and graphic talent despite extensive neuronal brain malfunctioning. They represent but a small fraction of autistic individuals and their productions can be matched by a select few of the general population. Little benefit, if at all, is gained by them from art training. The artistic productions created by some neurological patients who have not produced art until the start of a dementing process, fronto-temporal dementia, could suggest that selective atrophy in neuronal connectivity in such cases leads to emergence of new expressions. Arguments are presented to question this assumption in light of evidence from serial lesion effects. In all, since both types of artists – autistic, whose skills develop very early, and dementia patients whose skills may appear and disappear coinciding with late onset incremental brain atrophy – are severely handicapped by an otherwise poorly functioning brain, a fundamental question about art is raised; specifically, the underlying brain mechanisms for talent.

Further readings

Fitzgerald, M. (2003). *Autism and creativity: Is there a link between autism in men and exceptional ability?* London: Brunner-Routledge.

Frith, U., & Hill, E. (Eds.). (2003). *Autism: Mind and brain*. Oxford: Oxford University Press.

Heaton, P., & Wallace, G. L. (2004). Annotation: The savant syndrome. *Journal of Child Psychology and Psychiatry, 45*, 899–911.

Hou, C., Miller, B. L., Cummings, J. L., Goldberg, M., Mychack, P., Bottino, V., & Benson, D. F. (2000). Autistic savants. *Neuropsychiatry, Neuropsychology, and Behavioral, Neurology, 13*, 29–38.

Jenkins, W. M., & Merzenich, M. M. (1987). Reorganization of neocortical representations after brain injury: A neurophysiological model of the bases of recovery from stroke. *Progress in Brain Research, 71*, 249–266.

Just, M. A., Cherkassky, V. L., Keller, T. A., & Minshew, N. J. (2004). Cortical activation and synchronization during sentence comprehension in high-functioning autism: Evidence of underconnectivity. *Brain, 127*, 1811–1821.

Mohr, J. P. (2004). Historical observations on functional reorganization. *Cerebrovascular Disease, 18*, 258–259.

Muhle, R., Trentacoste, S. V., & Rapin, I. (2004). The genetics of autism. *Pediatrics, 113*, 472–486.

Sacks, O. (1995). *An anthropologist on Mars*. New York: Alfred A. Knopf.

Sacks, O. (2004). Autistic geniuses? We're too ready to pathologize. *Nature, 429*, 241.

Selfe, L. (1995). Nadia reconsidered. In C. Golomb (Ed.), *The development of gifted child artists: Selected case studies* (pp. 197–236). Hillsdale, NJ: Lawrence Erlbaum Associates, Inc.

Simonton, D. K. (1999). Talent and its development: An emergenic and epigenetic model. *Psychological Review, 106*, 435–457.

Simonton, D. K. (2000). Creativity: Cognitive, developmental, personal, and social aspects. *American Psychologist, 55*, 151–158.

Snyder, A. (2004). Autistic genius? *Nature, 428*, 470–471.

Snyder, A. W., Mulcahy, E., Taylor, J. L., Mitchell, D. J., Sachdev, P., & Gandevia, S. C. (2003). Savant-like skills exposed in normal people by suppressing the left fronto-temporal lobe. *Journal of Integrational Neuroscience, 2*, 149–158.

Treffert, D. A. (1989). *Extraordinary people: Understanding "idiot savants"*. New York: Harper & Row.

5 Musical art and brain damage I
Established composers

Introduction

In the neuropsychology of music, a distinction is often made between musical expression and musical reception. Expression consists of composing on one end of the musical production spectrum, while singing and instrument playing are on the other end of this spectrum. Reception is listening to music. The neuroanatomical underpinning of music composing is elusive largely because there are so few cases of established composers with well-defined brain lesions from whom functional localization could be inferred. By comparison, the brain's control in singing and instrument playing is somewhat better explored (see Chapter 6). What has emerged gradually, despite some inconsistencies in findings, is that sub-components of music are asymmetrically controlled by the brain's hemispheres and that the total musical expression relies on the specialization of both hemispheres (Baeck, 2002b). Currently, there does not appear to be a specialized brain "center" dedicated to music but rather the bulk of the evidence points to the interaction of multiple, distributed neural networks (Peretz, 2002; Peretz & Coltheart, 2003).

The perception of music is another feature that shows inconsistency in experimental studies largely because musical processing is complicated by effects of musical training (covered in Chapter 6). Nevertheless, some behavioral patterns have emerged thanks largely to an accumulating body of data from brain-damaged patients, normal subjects, and neuroimaging techniques. The overall hemispheric pattern with regards to the sub-components of music is that while the left hemisphere specializes in the perception of timing and rhythm, the right hemisphere specializes in pitch and timbre perception. The temporal lobe in each hemisphere comprises the predominant brain regions associated with music perception. But no specific brain lobe, or region, is yet known to be associated with the composition of music. This chapter explores the available neurological and neuropsychological evidence on composers.

In the majority of musical artists, talent is expressed at a very early age. The neuroanatomical understanding of this talent is elusive; it plays a critical role in musical productivity and seems to be resistant to brain damage of various etiologies. There are probably strong genetic components but how these talent-related "musical genes" manifest themselves has not been determined, nor have any such genes been identified thus far. Bach, for example, had many children, some became composers and some did not. And not much is known about his grandchildren and their contribution to music. And what of Mozart's children and grandchildren, for example? Not much is known there. Judging from the well-known and accomplished composers, extraordinary musical talent seems to have a short "shelf life" within families. This is a puzzle that may eventually be untangled by research into genetics and patterns of inheritance of musical talent (or any artistic talent). Neuronal computation associated with persistence, attention, and memory may not always interact well with neuronal circuits that control artistic creations. There may be a maladaptive neuronal coupling that prevents the required artistic expression. As with the visual artists, clues about talent and creativity in music have come from observing the rare cases of established artists with acquired brain damage. It would appear that regardless of the nature of the damage, or its extent and localization in the brain, composition of new works can carry on. Moreover, the "musical artistic essence" is spared in that musicians adhere to the same expressive artistic style as before the damage. The fact that in some cases art is created for a long while into the illness illustrates that musical talent, creativity, and productivity engage multiple brain regions.

Localized brain injury in published cases of composers seems to involve mostly the left hemisphere. In the few cases with slow degenerative disease, we can assume bilateral hemispheric involvement, albeit with some asymmetry affecting the left more than the right. Absence of localized damage in the right hemisphere somewhat complicates reaching parsimonious conclusions.

Composers and slow brain disease

Maurice Ravel

The composer, Maurice Ravel, was born in Ciboure, France, in 1875 and died in 1937 (Otte, De Bondt, Van De Wiele, Audenaert, & Dierckx, 2003). His father was a pianist but made a living as an engineer. Maurice had piano lessons at an early age. He was enrolled at the Paris Conservatoire at age 14 but after a few years quit (only to return a few years later to study with the composer Gabriel Fauré). His medical history reveals signs of neurological problems: he suffered from general weakness, insomnia, and poor appetite. In 1916, when he was 41 years old, his health was substantially reduced and he had to undergo surgery for the relief of dysentery. Earlier, the military did not want to enlist him because he suffered from a hernia and general weakness. Then, when he was 53 years old, his handwriting changed dramatically and an amnesic lapse occurred during a concert when he was playing his very own composition. The next year, he continued to suffer from insomnia and reported that he had difficulties in starting new projects. Later, when he was 61 years old, he asked to be relieved of his duties as a judge in a musical competition, explaining that he might fall asleep in the middle of the competition. In 1932, at age 57 years, he had been involved in a car accident. Also, around that time, when on a tour in Spain, he lost his luggage and other personal belongings. In the summer of 1933, his health continued to deteriorate and neurological symptoms became exacerbated. He showed signs of incoordination while swimming (he was known to have been a very good swimmer) and his writing legibility became worse. The doctors who took care of him discussed aphasia and memory deficits. By 1934 his handwriting had become barely legible (the agraphia involved poor penmanship); he continued to be apathetic and flat affect was discernible on his face (Alonso & Pascuzzi, 1999). At this point he already had difficulties in reading (alexia), speaking and comprehending (aphasia), and writing (agraphia); he had difficulties playing the piano (poor interdependent bimanual movements), he could not copy very well (dyscopia); writing to dictation was laborious, whether this was words or musical notes, and his musical writing was no better than his letter writing. However, he continued to recognize notes and melodies when he heard them, including his own, noticed when errors were made in the melodies, and noticed when a piano was out of tune. But he could not read musical notes by sight, or name notes that he heard (Alajouanine, 1948). In all, it would seem that the disease affected his left hemisphere more than the right hemisphere.

The well-known French neurologist, Theophile Alajouanine, visited Ravel between 1933 and 1936 and wrote this in a 1948 *Brain* article:

> Though all artistic realization is forbidden to our musician, he can still listen to music, attend a concert, and express criticism on it or describe the musical pleasure he felt. His artistic sensibility does not seem to be in the least altered, nor his judgment, as his admiration for the romantic composer Weber shows, which he told me several times. He can also judge contemporary musical works.
>
> (Alajouanine, 1948, p. 234)

About ten days before he died, a craniotomy was performed. The surgeons lifted the right frontal skull bone and discovered a brain that was not atrophied at least in that region (the right frontal lobe). They also did not see a tumor or meningioma, or presence of intracranial pressure. He died after a short period of unresponsiveness on December 28, 1937. No postmortem was performed (Alonso & Pascuzzi, 1999).

Localization and further discussion of Ravel

The initial symptoms progressed into expressive problems with language but not so much in language comprehension; eventually there were changes in personality, and apathy and flat affect developed. This latter implies damage in the frontal lobes. All in all, the constellation of symptoms suggests that the fontal lobe and anterior regions of the temporal lobe were affected the most. But the flat affect also suggests the involvement of the dopamine system, particularly the pathway of the substantia nigra, nucleus accumbens, and the basal ganglia. Dopamine exerts inhibitory action on GABA neurons. Losing dopamine through disease leads to loss of motor control. In Parkinson's disease, for example, the great majority of dopamine producing neurons are lost well before symptoms first appear. In this disease, there is also a flat affect in the face, since the control of muscles everywhere is severely compromised. Ravel did not have the typical symptoms of Parkinsonism (tremor, rigidity). Nevertheless, could there have been a progressive loss of dopamine neurons in the substantia nigra, the neurons that project to the motor regions of the cortex through the basal ganglia, and have projections in the frontal lobes? And the general weakness observed by military doctors much earlier could have been the beginning of the dopamine abnormality, or else showed the abnormal activity of the dopamine receptors in the frontal lobes. Furthermore, the bimanual incoordination was an inability to execute interdependent bimanual movements, the kind expected in an etch-a-sketch toy (the two hands are required to create a single line with a built-in pen). In playing the piano with both hands, the action of the hands must result in a single event, the piece. The two hands must act together to produce the composition, and this is accomplished interdependently; one hand cannot go off on its own, so to speak, without affecting the single outcome. Thus, it may be useful to consider the following finding: patients with commissurotomy, partial or complete, have great difficulties in executing such interdependent movements (but not with parallel bimanual movements) (Preilowski, 1972; Zaidel & Sperry, 1977). It is possible, then, that commissural fibers were compromised in Ravel's brain, preventing his two hemispheres from working together to coordinate this type of bilateral movement. Of course, these are speculations; not having the results of a postmortem examination, all we can do now is wonder and discuss the symptoms and what they might tell us about the underlying neuroanatomy. When Ravel died he was 62 years old. According to medical opinion, it is highly likely that the disease started when he was in his early fifties (Alonso & Pascuzzi, 1999).

There are differing opinions on the exact diagnosis, but there is consensus that by and large Ravel's condition was due to a slow brain atrophy-type process caused by a neurodegenerative disease that affected both sides of the brain. Pick's disease, fronto-temporal dementia, in which there is progressive aphasia, accompanied by corticobasal degeneration, in which movements are compromised (Amaducci, Grassi, & Boller, 2002), as well as traumatic brain injury caused by the car accident in 1932, all have been proposed. The latter is conjectured to have hastened symptoms consistent with Pick's disease (Otte et al., 2003). It has also been suggested that Ravel's symptoms can be explained as a chronic endocrine disease, congenital in nature, from which he suffered (Otte et al., 2003). His own father had a slow progressive dementing disease (its nature is not known). There is a genetic component in these diseases, particularly with a young age onset, so it is not unreasonable to assume that Ravel's brain disease was a type of slow developing dementia as well. The disease could not have been Alzheimer's disease because the hallmark of Ravel's symptoms was not a severe memory deficit, nor did he have a severe walking disability (also common at one stage of Alzheimer's disease). His symptoms do suggest a functionally asymmetrical progression affecting mostly the left hemisphere, although both hemispheres were subject to the degenerative process.

However, he composed until five years before his death, that is, until 1932. The symptoms first made their appearance about 1927, but that does not mean that degenerative conditions were not already present before that time. After 1927, the deterioration continued steadily in a downhill course. His famous composition, *Bolero*, was performed for the first time around 1931–1932, and is highly regarded. He must have written it after the first symptoms appeared. In 1931 he completed his Concerto in G, a musical piece that he started to write around 1929, or perhaps even earlier; there is some debate, particularly about the time when he began its composition. It is considered to have been completed in 1931 and first performed in January of 1932. One of his last pieces, the Concerto for the Left Hand (which he wrote for the famous philosopher Ludwig Wittgenstein's brother, Paul Wittgenstein, a concert pianist who lost his right arm in World War I) is believed to have been written between 1929 and 1930. The first performance was in 1931 and was not Ravel's last composition. The last compositions that he ever wrote were three songs for the musical *Don Quichotte à Dulcinee*, and that was in 1932 (Amaducci et al., 2002; Baeck, 2002a).

How did Ravel's disease express itself in his art? Experts differ on these effects, particularly on the *Bolero*, Concerto in G, and the Concerto for the Left Hand (Baeck, 2002a; Marins, 2002), seeing these works as a reflection of superior mastery, skill, and creativity. However, the roots of these works are embedded in his earlier work, in his earlier experimentation, and interests. As Baeck says,

> All through his career, Ravel produced contrasting works. Even in the same work, e.g., the Sonata for violin and piano, there are striking stylistic differences between the Allegretto, the "jazzy" Blues and the Perpetuum mobile. Actually, the stylistic peculiarities in the Concerto for the Left Hand are related to Wittgenstein's commission. In the nature of things, the G-major concerto has a stronger presence of the piano because Ravel wrote it normally for both hands, whereas in the Concerto for the Left Hand he had to create the illusion of writing for both hands.
> (Baeck, 2002a, p. 322)

In Ravel's work as in other established artists, there is remarkable preservation of productive artistic skills even as highly localized functions, such as language, become severely compromised.

Hugo Wolf

Another case of gradual damage in the brain and its possible effects on composing is that of Hugo Wolf (Trethowan, 1977; Walker, 1968). Wolf was born in 1860 in Windischgraz, Austria, and died in 1903. In the period spanning 1888 to 1891 alone he wrote over 200 songs. He did not compose between 1892 and 1894, but in the period spanning 1895 and 1897 he wrote an opera, *Der Corregidor*, started another opera, *Manuel Venegas*, which remained incomplete at the time of his death, plus about thirty songs. Wolf published his first songs when he was 28 years old. His musical compositions are highly regarded; the music is said to be a unique form of combining words, their meaning, and musical melody. He was admitted to a mental institution around September 1897. Previously he had physical signs of neurosyphilis and his behavior during rehearsals of *Der Corregidor* in 1896 was indicative of severe mental deterioration, particularly with regard to judgment. Subsequently, he reportedly suffered a psychotic episode while attending a festive party. Throughout his life he was known to experience bouts of depression, but the events in the two years before his death indicated presence of psychosis. Six months before he was institutionalized, he wrote his Michelangelo songs. The last of these three, "Fühlt meine Seele," was viewed as complex yet exquisite and having strong emotional tones. At the same time, others who were familiar with his works also felt that the Michelangelo songs were not first rate. Remarkably, while he was institutionalized he continued to revise his previous pieces; those revisions included work on "Penthesilea," "Italian Serenade," "Third Italian Serenade," the song "Morgenhymnus," and orchestral versions for two songs from the *Spanish Song Book* (Walker, 1968). In any case, the fact remains that he was able to compose despite brain damage from neurosyphilis and psychotic disturbances. One explanation is that the slow progression of the disease allowed neural adjustment and functional reorganization (Jenkins, Merzenich, & Recanzone, 1990) in this highly practiced musician in whom there were highly rehearsed musical skills, and overlearning (see Chapter 4, section on serial lesion effects).

French composer M. M.

M. M. was an established, award-winning composer of chamber music, piano concerti, and concerti for other instruments, particularly sacred music; he also performed on the piano in concerts (Tzortzis, Goldblum, Dang, Forette, & Boller, 2000). His piano training began at age 4. Around age 65 he underwent a quadruple coronary bypass surgery after which he began to complain of anomic difficulties as well as memory impairments. Deterioration in language became progressively worse in the next few years. A CT scan taken eight years after onset of these disturbances revealed bilateral atrophy in the peri-Sylvian areas suggesting a degenerative disease. The atrophy was greater in the left relative to the right side, and this explains the gradual and pronounced language deterioration, which took a downhill course. At the same time, he went on composing and earning his livelihood from it. The composed music continued to be sacred music. His concert piano activity, however, ceased around that time. Nevertheless, privately, in his home, he did continue to play the piano and even improvise on imaginary themes. Remarkably, despite the severe word-finding difficulties and other language deterioration, and what must have been gradual brain deterioration, he was able to name musical instruments correctly upon hearing their sounds.

This striking dissociation between verbal language of ordinary life and language of music is explained thus by the authors:

> Besides motor skills, cognitive aspects of musical function might also benefit from such an expanded cortical representation with overlearning. We propose that intensive practice and early acquisition of music may have provided M.M. with protection against loss of musical skills in the event of brain damage.
>
> (Tzortzis et al., 2000, p. 239)

Composers and localized damage due to stroke

Vissarion G. Shebalin

The case of a prolific Russian composer and professor of music, V. G. Shebalin (1902–1963), is highly revealing (Gardner, 1974; Luria, Tsvetkova, & Futer, 1965). He had damage in the left hemisphere, in the temporal lobe, from two strokes; the first in 1953 and the second in 1959. He suffered from hypertension for many years prior to the first stroke. The first stroke was not as devastating as the second one, and there were no obvious behavioral symptoms. He was 57 years old when he had the second stroke. It was then that he developed Wernicke-type aphasia: that is, he had severe comprehension difficulties, made speech errors (paraphasias), could not repeat sequences, and had difficulties in both reading and writing. There was no substantial change in his speaking despite receiving therapy. Even with the aphasia, he was able to interact with his students and evaluate their compositions. He continued to compose and work on pieces he had started before the stroke. He lived until he was 61 years old. Postmortem examination revealed a large area of damage spanning the left temporal and inferior parietal lobes plus a hemorrhaging cyst in the temporo-parietal area.

The critical feature of his case is that he went on composing and teaching. He composed his last symphony, the Fifth Symphony in C flat, after the second stroke. The stroke had occurred in 1959 and the symphony was reportedly completed in 1962. (It is not clear when he had started writing it; he may have begun before the second stroke.) The composition was highly regarded and received laudatory reviews, including from his friend and colleague, the composer Dimitri Shostakovitch. In the last three years of his life, Luria and associates (1965) report that Shebalin wrote numerous compositions which reflected his pre-morbid style. In other words he did not develop a new musical format. In this post-stroke period he wrote a sonata in four parts for violin and piano, a sonatina in three parts, two string quartets in three parts, numerous choruses, a suite for orchestra, music for numerous songs, orchestral music for an opera, a concertino for viola, and additional musical works.

However, it needs to be emphasized that he had two strokes in the same side, separated by about six years. The second was far more devastating, yet he was able to interact with his students, provide feedback on their work, and go on to compose his own music. He may not have been so successful with composing if it had not been for the first stroke; in the period that elapsed between strokes, the brain's reaction could have contributed to a modification of neural circuitry. Functional reorganization is likely to have occurred in the intervening years.

Jean Langlais

Jean Langlais was born in 1907 in La Fontenelle in Brittany, France, and died in 1991 (Labounsky, 2000). He was a composer and a highly renowned concert organist who was blind from age 2. Langlais performed in public throughout the world, taught organ playing, and both recorded and composed numerous musical pieces. He read words and musical notes in Braille. He suffered a stroke at age 77 years (July 1, 1984) in the left temporal and inferior parietal lobes (Signoret, van Eeckhout, Poncet, & Castaigne, 1987). Immediately afterwards he was paralyzed in the right side and had Wernicke's-type aphasia. The paralysis soon dissipated but not the aphasia. A month after the stroke he was unable to read or write, was reluctant to play the organ again because he had problems remembering previously familiar pieces, and his aphasia persisted. However, things started to improve: on October 24, about three months after the stroke, he was able to play the organ in a recording for French television. He started to teach soon afterwards, in November. His speech improved thanks to his family's help and hard work by his speech therapist, Philippe van Eeckhout. The course of his recovery in some cognitive domains was remarkable:

> His speech began to return, but mostly, mysteriously, in English, and therefore, as part of the beginning speech therapy, he was no longer permitted to use the language he had labored so hard to attain [French]. Much to everyone's chagrin, he reached a plateau after about nine months; from that time on improvements were only marginal. He was able, however, to carry on simple conversations. With the help of Marie-Louise [his wife] and his speech therapist, he learned to pronounce a few proper names but required practice before saying them. He used to keep a little list of names that he used frequently in his pocket. Numbers were

also impossible for him, except by counting aloud from one to add their components. He was unable to write or read Braille text or type at a typewriter.

(Labounsky, 2000, p. 316)

Nevertheless, he was able to compose, to read and write musical notes in Braille, and amazingly, to use the same Braille notations in writing the musical notes that he could not use when writing words. He also continued to engage in recording sessions of his organ playing.

The issue of memory problems surfaced: once, on March 2, 1986, when Langlais played an organ recital in the church of Notre-Dame, some memory lapses occurred during the performance. He continued playing to the end nevertheless and critics lavished high praise on his performance. He recorded for the last time in November of that year. That last recording also received highly positive evaluations from critics. In all, after the stroke he composed at least twenty-two new musical pieces. Of those, one was written for four cellos. His student and biographer said this:

> These last works are not substantially different in style from those written prior to his stroke, although their quality is very uneven (his need to express himself perhaps compromised his analytical objectivity). Throughout this period, the pull toward chant and a very simple style becomes even stronger, exceeding even that of Vingt-quatre pieces. Yet each new piece is fresh.

(Labounsky, 2000, p. 318)

After Christmas of 1990 Langlais no longer composed. Additional strokes compromised his health and mental condition, and he died five months later, on May 8, 1991.

Benjamin Britten

The British composer Benjamin Britten (1913–1976) was born in Lowestoft, England, and died at the age of 63 years (Carpenter, 1992). For many years he suffered from cardiac problems that interfered with his ability to conduct orchestras or play tennis. Finally, on May 7, 1973 surgery was performed in the National Heart Hospital, London, in order to replace a faulty heart valve. During the surgery his heart was discovered to have been enlarged; unfortunately, while on the operating table, some calcium particles from the machinery may have entered the bloodstream only to lodge in his brain, in the left hemisphere. He is thus believed to have suffered a small stroke, which resulted in weakness in the right side of his body. He could not find his mouth with his right hand, for example. The cardiac condition remained a problem till his death three years later, and the right side weakness impaired his ability to play the piano. He also had difficulties writing. But despite all of this he went on to compose new music as well as revise old compositions. He revised his String Quartet in D major, which was originally written in 1931, and he revised his operetta, *Paul Bunyan*, originally written over thirty years earlier. Some of the new musical pieces are "Canticle V," "Suite on English Folk Tunes: 'A Time There Was'," "Sacred and Profane," "Birthday Hansel" (commissioned by Queen Elizabeth II for the seventy-five birthday of the Queen Mother), and "Phaedra." He continued to write arrangements for string orchestra and folksongs, and he wrote a musical piece for solo cello in honor of Mstislav Rostropovich. All of these new works were extremely well received by the critics. If he had any features of amusia, these are not known. The extent of the damage in the brain is also not known. The fact is that he did not experience aphasia; this alone suggests that the stroke affected only a small brain region, probably only in the precentral gyrus (the motor cortex), involving only the arm and leg representation, while not extending to affect lateral regions of the left frontal gyrus where Broca's area is located.

American composer B. L.

This is a neurological case of a famous composer and conductor who suffered a stroke in his early seventies localized in the left occipito-temporal area (Judd, Gardner, & Geschwind, 1983). The event occurred while he was conducting. Following the stroke he had aphasia characterized by disturbances in comprehension as well as by agraphia and alexia. The agraphia and aphasia symptoms were short lived while the alexia remained. At one year after the stroke he started to compose; he had difficulties writing the notes at first and needed assistance. Gradually he began to write the notes himself. Within a few months afterwards, he was able to correctly write himself:

> He complained that he often failed to place his notes properly, for instance, a note intended for a space would wind up on the adjacent line. We therefore made him wide-lined staff paper, which helped significantly . . . At twenty months poststroke he wrote a 7 min piece for chorus and orchestra in five weeks with no assistance. Only a dozen errors or so were found in his score, demonstrating that his musical writing at this point was quite functional. His performance on musical dictation tasks was surprisingly poor, considering how well he wrote down melodies that he composed. At fifteen months poststroke he wrote only one of 5 short (3 to 5 note) melodies correctly, despite his requests for up to 4 presentations of each. The rhythms were generally correct, but he made errors of pitch. Given a 4 bar, 16 note melody, he requested 11 presentations and got it correct except for three minor omissions. He wrote down 4-chords to dictations flawlessly, but required 3 presentations of each. He made several errors in writing rhythms to dictations on long items, especially when the barring was not obvious.
>
> (Judd et al., 1983, pp. 449–450)

B. L. had worse memory for singing a song he had just heard versus singing a song he had just composed in his head. He may also have suffered from mild anterograde musical memory. Regarding his composition abilities,

> B. L.'s composing skills appeared undiminished. He worked more slowly, could not rely on reading his texts, and relied on the keyboard more than before his stroke because of shortcomings in writing and memory. For these reasons he attempted less ambitious works. Nevertheless, his post-stroke compositions have been well received. Independent critics consider them to be as good as his prestroke compositions, but musically somewhat more conservative.
>
> (Judd et al., 1983, p. 450)

George Gershwin

The relationship between the art of music composition and disease, even when no direct and clear localization for brain lesions is known, can help shed additional light on the nature of musical expression by professional musicians. Diseases that target body parts also cause some alteration in the physiology and neuronal circuitry of the brain. For example, bodily pain has some effects on cognition through modulation of emotions, particularly by raising psychological stress. Hormonal levels, blood pressure, toxic production by bacteria or virus, high body temperature, severely impaired digestion, are but some of the variables that may disrupt normal brain functioning. Consequently, non-brain disease can potentially influence the creation of musical composition. The following sections describe relevant medical conditions of several famous composers. In some cases the brain damage is known, while in others it is inferred from the medical condition itself.

The well-known American composer George Gershwin was born in New York on September 26, 1898 and died on July 11, 1937. Gershwin developed a large brain tumor, a glioblastoma, in the right temporal lobe, but unfortunately the true nature of the symptoms were ignored for a substantial period of critical time; he died at the age of 38 in Los Angeles, right after the operation to remove the tumor, on July 11, 1937. The big debate concerns the time at which the tumor began to grow, his age at that time, and what effect the tumor had on his work. This is the course of events: just at the end of 1936 he complained to the musician Mitch Miller that he smelled the odor of burning garbage when in fact nothing burning was present. Such olfactory hallucinations are the hallmark of temporal lobe problems (patients with temporal lobe epilepsy sometimes report an olfactory aura just prior to a seizure). But medical opinion pinpoints the serious manifestations of the tumor to a later date, namely to February 1937 (Silverstein, 1999). He continued to compose successfully the music for *Shall We Dance* and for *A Damsel in Distress*. It is not clear when he started to compose the music for these two musicals, but he certainly completed the compositions after the first symptoms appeared. However, he began but did not complete the musical score for *The Goldwyn Follies*. On February 11, 1937, Gershwin was conducting the rehearsal performance for *Porgy and Bess* in Los Angeles. Suddenly, he nearly fell off the platform but after steadying himself, continued conducting to the end. This happened in the afternoon. In the evening of that day he played his own piano Concerto in F with the Los Angles Symphony Orchestra. While playing, at one point he missed a few bars due to a brief amnesic episode. The audience was not aware and since the conductor realized what had happened, he managed to cover for him somehow. This lasted only a few seconds and Gershwin went on playing. Later he reported that when the lapse had occurred he smelled burning rubber. He underwent a medical examination but nothing amiss was discovered. Later on, in April 1937, while sitting in a barbershop he had more olfactory hallucinations as well as cognitive disturbances (Silverstein, 1999).

At the beginning of June 1937, a whole series of symptoms began that signaled a serious neurological problem but his doctors misdiagnosed them, believing he had psychiatric disturbances arising from a very stressful life in Hollywood, including a failed infatuation affair with Paulette Goddard, Charlie Chaplin's wife. During that June he felt dizzy, was irritable, and reported to be confused every morning. He suffered from headaches and showed lack of coordination on several occasions. Then, he was hospitalized at Cedars of Lebanon Hospital in Los Angeles and this was toward the end of June, 1937. They discovered presence of photophobia and impaired smell sense in the right nostril.

> He was discharged with a final note of "most likely hysteria." After discharge, Gershwin received daily psychoanalytic treatment and had a male nurse in constant attendance. He tried working but had difficulty in even playing the piano. He had two episodes of automatisms, which today would be recognized as complex partial seizures. The olfactory hallucinations became almost continuous, and the incoordination and lethargy both increased . . . On the afternoon of July 9, 1937, George Gershwin became drowsy and fell into a semicomatose state. He was readmitted to the same hospital, where he was now found to have bilateral papilledema with recent hemorrhages. He did respond to pinprick on the face, and a suggestive right facial palsy was present . . . Dr. Howard C. Naffziger arrived at the hospital at 9:30 in the evening of July 10, and felt that Gershwin's condition required immediate surgery. He consulted by telephone with Dr. Dandy, who remained in the Newark Airport and then proceeded with the surgery. A ventriculogram revealed a large right temporal tumor. . . . The operative procedures took some 5 hours, but George Gershwin did not regain consciousness. His temperature rose to 106.5 degrees F, and he was pronounced dead on July 11, 1937 at 10:35 am.

> (Silverstein, 1999, p. 5)

There has been some debate regarding the age of onset of symptoms, some believing they had started long before 1937. Accurately pinpointing them could go a long way to understand the role of his brain lesion on his composing abilities. The most convincing argument assumes that the tumor made its appearance in the early part of 1937. Glioblastomas are a type of cancerous tumors known to grow extremely fast, so it is reasonable to suppose that this is the correct time period. Gershwin probably would have been diagnosed earlier today, and he might have survived. The removal of the tumor would have undoubtedly included removal of the right temporal lobe. The subsequent full effects on composing and playing cannot be predicted because so little is known about the effects of severe right temporal lobe damage on these skills. However, as mentioned above, he did compose music after the serious symptoms began in February 1937.

Effects of syphilis on brains of composers

In the eighteenth and nineteenth centuries quite a number of musicians suffered from syphilis, a disease that affects the central nervous system. This devastating sexually transmitted disease took a very heavy toll, frequently leading to death, until the discovery of penicillin in the twentieth century provided a cure. The Italian composer Gaetano Donizetti (1797–1848), for example, is believed to have suffered from neurosyphilis, and some speculate that his ability to portray psychosis in his works (for example, *Lucia di Lammermoor* and *Anna Bolena*) stems from his own personal experiences with the effects of the disease (Peschel & Peschel, 1992)

   In men, the disease is characterized by the appearance of a chancre on the penis, but this heals within a few weeks to leave only a small scar (Roos, 1999). Then, a rash appears all over the body that causes embarrassment and leads to public isolation until it disappears. The rash is also accompanied by general bodily pain. There is also a stage in some cases when ulcerations develop on the skin, deforming the body parts they attack (penis, nose, lips, larynx). The last stage, known as tertiary syphilis, is a time when further damage occurs particularly to the heart and the brain. There is a stage in which no symptoms are obvious externally; this is the latent period. Historically, what caused syphilis was discovered in 1905, and in 1906 August von Wasserman developed the procedure for a test that could reveal the presence of the disease. Before penicillin there was really no effective cure and sufferers had to undergo painful treatment procedures; compounds consisting of mercury were applied directly to the skin, spread all over the body, and blankets were placed as wrappings. Then, sweating was induced in saunas. This procedure was applied from twenty to thirty days. Dietary restrictions were part of the treatment as well. Prior to Wasserman's test, medical doctors made their diagnosis on the basis of a scar on the penis (from the chancre), the rash, or hair loss. Medical historians claim that on the whole the course of transmission of this disease was not obvious to the people in the eighteenth and nineteenth centuries (Hetenyi, 1986; Roos, 1999).

Robert Schumann

Schumann was born in Zwickau, Germany in June 1810 and died in July 1856 when he was only 46 years old. From a very early age his musical talents were recognized. At age 7 he began his formal piano lessons, and sometime between the ages of 7 and 8 wrote his first musical composition, which consisted of piano music for dances. His piano lessons continued until he was 15 years old. He also received education in literature and the classics. In 1828 he started law school in Leipzig, and it was there that he met his future wife, Clara, who became a very well-known pianist. In Leipzig he lost interest in law studies, indulged in drinking and smoking, and is believed to have had several sexual relationships. When he transferred to a law school in Heidelberg, he continued to indulge in similar extra-curricular activities. In the winter he had alcoholic binges that resulted in auditory disturbances. He talked about suicide and plunged into depression, but then became euphoric as he emerged from the depression. In 1830 he returned to Leipzig but this time to take up piano lessons with Friedrich Wieck, Clara's father. Schumann lived in their house while receiving the lessons. At one point, Robert Schumann suffered an injury in his right hand, particularly affecting his ring finger (the cause of which is not clear to this day). He describes this in a diary entry dated January 26, 1830, by referring to a numb finger. In 1831 he wrote in his diary that a sore was developing on his penis (he had a steady sexual relationship at that time). While his piano virtuosity suffered as a result of the injury, he wrote three literary works, which were published. In 1834, he began a music literary journal, the *New Journal for Music* (*Neue Zeitschrift für Musik*). Between 1830 and 1840 he continued to write and compose, and finally in 1840 married Clara. In 1840 he was particularly productive but in January of 1844 he plunged into a long-lasting depressive episode. In 1845 he slowly recovered, but by 1852 there was a recurrence. He continued to compose nevertheless between 1845 and 1852. However, his mental health deteriorated substantially in February of 1854; he suffered from auditory musical hallucinations along with some visual hallucinations. He tried to kill himself by jumping into the River Rhine, in Düsseldorf, on February 27 of that year. On March 4 he was admitted to a psychiatric hospital at Endenich, near Bonn. While there he received numerous medications and treatments for his mental disorder. Still, the letters that he wrote to Clara from the hospital appear coherent. His mental state deteriorated greatly starting in August 1855 and leading to lack of interest in communicating, or in eating, and resulting in what is believed to be severe malnutrition. The proposed modern diagnosis is that he suffered from a bipolar disorder coupled with a neurological disorder possibly due to the effects of neurosyphilis on his brain (tertiary syphilis) (Lederman, 1999).

A postmortem examination by Dr. Richarz revealed a brain that weighed approximately 1338 grams, which is within normal limits for males. It also revealed the following:

> The pituitary gland was surrounded by a considerable amount of a "yellowish, gelatinous substance, which in places had the consistency of fibrocartilage." It has been suggested that this was a syphilitic gumma. According to Richarz, there was also a substantial amount of cerebral atrophy. An extensive area of ecchymoses [areas of hemorrhage, which originate with coagulation disorder or may reflect effects of hemorrhagic stroke] extended from the frontal lobe to the occipital lobe, greater in the left hemisphere than in the right. A number of peculiarities in Schumann's cranial bones have been described in the autopsy that historians have attributed to "ossifying periostitis" caused by syphilis.
>
> (Roos, 1999, p. 40)

It is interesting that the brain weighed as much as it did given the observation of cerebral atrophy. Even more interesting, however, is the left hemisphere atrophy considering his prolific writing; one wonders when the atrophy had begun, how quickly it progressed, and how the degree of progression correlated with specific productivity rates. Also of interest is whether this was uniformly present throughout the left hemisphere or there were regional patches with atrophy. Left hemisphere atrophy could explain his depression, particularly the last bout.

The relationship between Schumann's artistic work and his mental condition is of great interest:

> Several remarkably productive years, mostly notably 1832, 1840, and literally 1849 through 1853 can roughly be correlated with periods of high energy and emotional elation. Conversely, periods of very low compositional output seem to correlate reasonably well with episodes of depression or melancholy.
>
> (Lederman, 1999, p. 20)

(Slater and Meyer (1959) derived this information from a compilation of data on his works.) Even during 1853, when he was behaving strangely, including during conducting sessions, he managed to compose his Opus 118, "3 Clavier-Sonaten für die Jugend," the Violin Concerto in D, and his last work, Opus 134, the Introduction and Allegro for Piano and Orchestra.

Bedrich Smetana

Smetana, the famous Czech composer, was born in 1824 to a musical family. At age 6 years he already gave public piano performances. His first child, Friederika, was also exceptionally talented musically. When he was 50 years old, in April of 1874, the first symptoms of syphilis appeared in the form of skin ulcers and rash. Not long afterwards, he suffered dizziness plus a whole host of problems with his hearing: instead of the actual sounds from the A, E, and C flat chords, he heard high whistling sounds. It was discovered that there was a hearing loss in the right ear in the summer of that year and in the left ear in October. He also complained about auditory hallucinations (the nature of which is not clear). Around that time he was instructed to live in near auditory and visual isolation, asking friends to whisper when visiting him (Roos, 1999).

He continued to create despite the symptoms of dizziness and deafness. He composed *Hubicka*, his first opera during that period of isolation. In all, he wrote eight operas after he became deaf. However, it took him three years to write his last opera, *The Devil's Wall*. It was performed in 1882 and was not well received. His medical condition was, in addition, deteriorating substantially at that time. It was in 1881 that difficulties in speaking, memory, and concentration began to be apparent. In a letter that he wrote in December, 1882, he described having suffered two recent expressive aphasic episodes. In 1884 he began having visual and auditory hallucinations, unsteady gait, rage episodes, and the inability to recognize familiar people, including his children and friends (prosopagnosia). He also had swallowing difficulties, paralysis in the left facial half, and drooping of the right mouth corner. On April 23, 1884, he was checked into a psychiatric hospital in Prague. According to hospital records, he suffered from malnutrition and his hallucinations went unabated. He died on May 12, 1884, at the age of 60 years. A postmortem examination was consistent with a diagnosis of neurosyphilis, that is, it revealed "thickened meninges due to chronic inflammation, dilatation of the lateral ventricles and atrophy of the cerebral cortex and nervi acustici" (Roos, 1999, p. 37). Again, the question of interest is when exactly the atrophy set in; it is highly likely that it set in when he was trying to compose his last opera, and may have even been complete by then.

Franz Schubert

Schubert was born in Vienna, Austria, in 1797 and died in 1828, when he was only 31 years old (O'Shea, 1997; Schoental, 1990). From an early age he was exceptionally musically gifted. By the time Schubert was 18 years old, he had already composed "144 songs, including Erlkonig, two symphonies, two masses, two sonatas, five theatrical works, a string quartet and a number of choral works" (Roos, 1999, p. 38). Because of failed love affairs, it is believed that he allowed himself to be seduced into having sex with a prostitute in 1822, when he was 25 years old. He may have contracted syphilis as a result of that liaison. In the spring of 1823 he was very ill with the symptoms of the disease. He did not want to see friends, began losing hair, and started wearing a wig to cover up this fact. He began to complain about having headaches, probably due to inflammation of the meninges, one of the effects of the disease. Similarly, he reported the development of bodily pains. He was subjected to the common treatment at that time, mercury applications. In the year of his death, 1828, he managed to give a public performance in March, and to write the *Winterreise* song cycle and a couple of piano trios (Roos, 1999).

By the time Schubert died, delirium had set in; he was working at that time on his last symphony, but since he did not complete it, it is called, "The Unfinished" (Schoental, 1990). During the period of his illness, 1823–1828, he continued to compose new pieces including the "Wanderer" Fantasy for piano, the *Schöne Müllerin* song cycle, *Die Verschworenen*, the opera *Fierabras*, the A minor and D minor ("Death and the Maiden") string quartets, the octet for wind and strings, the C major symphony ("Great"), the piano sonata in A minor, many songs, and the string quartet in G major. Unfortunately, the results of a postmortem examination are not known, if it was performed at all.

Ludwig van Beethoven

Beethoven was born in Bonn, Germany, in 1770 and died in 1827 (Keynes, 2002; Kubba & Young, 1996). He was born into a musical family, his grandfather having been a professional musician and his father a singer, a violinist, and a pianist. He received his early music lessons from his father. By the time he was 7 years old he played in a public performance, and by the time he was 12 years old he had already published his first musical composition. At the age of 17 he worked to support his father and brothers by playing the viola (his mother had just died of tuberculosis, and his father's drinking had led to voice alterations and loss of work). When he was 21 years old, around 1791, he moved to Vienna where he studied with Joseph Haydn and Antonio Salieri. He composed and played while there. In 1801 we have the first documentation of a hearing loss. Then, in 1802, in a letter he wrote to his brothers, Beethoven says that the loss began in 1796 (five years after he left his family and moved to Vienna). In 1801 his hearing loss was selective to high tones emanating from people's voices and musical instruments. The loss in hearing began in his left ear. At that time, he writes that he was treated with mercury (the treatment commonly used for syphilis). Then, starting in 1807 he developed chronic headaches, and by 1814 developed difficulties in playing the piano, presumably because of his hearing loss. He is known to have visited prostitutes, a prescription for treatment of syphilis had been discovered in his papers, and his biographer and admirer, Alexander Wheelock Thayer, is said to have been so shocked by Beethoven's behavior that he was unable to complete the biography. He never married, but is known to have proposed to several women, who all turned him down. Together, then, there seems to be a strong possibility that his famous hearing loss was due to syphilis rather than to otosclerosis, or independent malfunctioning of the auditory nerves. The important thing to realize is that all his nine symphonies were composed between 1800 and 1827, well after his deafness had begun (Roos, 1999).

Sensory deprivation did not interfere with his creative compositions nor did it disrupt whatever process in his brain gave rise to aesthetic reactions in listeners. What is not obvious are the footprints of the deafness in his extraordinary music. How would his music have turned out if he had not been deaf, is a natural question to ask. It is important to mention that some believe that a musical change took place around 1817 (Cooper, 1985; Solomon, 2003), but the musical nature of this change is beyond the scope of this book. (In addition to Beethoven and Smetana, Fauré also suffered severe hearing loss and deafness when he composed many of his highly admired pieces, including the Second Piano Quintet, his opera *Pénélope*, and his last piece, the String Quartet.)

Beethoven's health deteriorated in December 1826. Doctors in Vienna noticed his swollen feet, liver abnormalities, and a jaundiced skin. In the early part of 1827 he was bedridden for four months. He died on March 26, 1827 after lapsing into a coma. The postmortem report was lost until 1970, when it was discovered in the Vienna Museum of Anatomical Pathology. The report said that the eustacian tube and the facial nerves were exceptionally thick, and the left acoustic nerve was thinner than the right nerve. In the brain, the region around the fourth ventricle (which is located below the cerebral hemispheres) was dense and vascular (Hui & Wong, 2000). These observations are extremely hard to interpret against the background of his musical talents. Nothing else is known from that examination to give us additional clues about his brain. The medical records kept by his physician were destroyed in a fire; it has been suggested that they were purposefully destroyed so that the facts of his illness will not be known.

Neurological consequences in established composers

Can postmortem and morphological assessment yield subtle clues regarding musical skills? In a review of published postmortem studies of brains of musicians and composers by Bentivoglio (2003), the impression that emerges is that there is no uniformity in exceptional neuroanatomical localization. For example, in the brain of Canadian-Japanese concert pianist and composer, Chiyo Asaka-Tuge (1908–1969), the left Heschl gyrus was determined to be exceptionally larger than the homologous gyrus in the right. Normally, Heschl's gyrus is larger in the left than the right but presumably in this musician, the degree of asymmetry was particularly large. In Smetana and Schumann no asymmetries were reported. In the brains of highly skilled musicians (conductors, cellists, singers) the middle and posterior portions of the first temporal gyrus were particularly developed bilaterally as was the supramarginal gyrus (see Figure 1.4). In singer Julius Stockhausen (1826–1906), the left second frontal convolution was particularly highly developed. The lack of uniformity in the postmortem findings, few as they are, reflect the broad spectrum of musicality, and supports other findings that music is not a single entity with a single major anatomical localization.

Summary

The composers with degenerative disease or localized damage involved mostly the left hemisphere. Scarcity of published cases of composers with localized right hemisphere damage prevents balanced conclusions regarding the contribution of each hemisphere's cognition to musical composition. The composers described here were able to compose despite neurological complications. Extensive training, skill overlearning, together with exceptional musical talent as well as inherited predisposition, are all factors that contribute to preserved abilities of composers following brain damage. Their craft incorporates a wide range of abilities. Functional representation of well-rehearsed musical skills (often from early childhood) and neuronal plasticity contribute to these spared skills. This is particularly true in slow, progressive neurodegenerative brain disease where functional reorganization in a brain reacting to loss of neurons and connections is highly likely. The course of the diseases in composers Maurice Ravel, Hugo Wolf, and M. M. was discussed in this chapter in the context of their productivity. Composers with unilateral stroke are rare. Composers Vissarion G. Shebalin, Jean Langlais, Benjamin Britten, and B. L. were discussed. On the whole, there is no consistent relationship between the ability to compose in these cases and laterality of damage. Similarly, the medical conditions that afflicted composers and professional musicians throughout the centuries have not halted their productivity, or creativity. Neurological conditions suffered by George Gershwin did not affect his works in obvious ways. Neurosyphilis was a devastating sexually transmitted disease before the discovery of penicillin. The disease took a heavy toll on composers Robert Schumann, Bedrich Smetana, and Franz Schubert. In addition, sensory deficits causing deafness in Smetana and Beethoven could have influenced the nature of their work but not their skills, craft, and talent. Perhaps the output would have been greater than it was if composers with neurological conditions had been healthy, but the fact is they went on composing despite some extreme neurological hardships. In all, the elusiveness of neuroanatomical underpinning of the artistic musical composition is attributed to multiple representation of musical skills and the plasticity of the brain in reaction to neural damage.

Further readings

Atenmuller, E. O. (2001). How many music centers are in the brain? *Annals of the New York Academy of Sciences*, *930*, 273–280.

Baeck, E. (2002). The neural networks of music. *European Journal of Neurology*, 9, 449–456.

Benzon, W. L. (2001). *Beethoven's anvil: Music in mind and culture*. New York: Basic Books.

Brown, S. (2001). The "musilanguage" model of music evolution. In N. L. Wallin, B. Merker, & S. Brown (Eds.), *The origins of music*. Cambridge, MA: MIT Press

Cooper, M. (1985). *Beethoven: The last decade, 1817–1827*. Oxford: Oxford University Press.

Critchley, M., & Henson, R. A. (Eds.). (1977). *Music and the brain: Studies in the neurology of music*. London: William Heinemann Medical Books.

Flor, H. (2003). Remapping somatosensory cortex after injury. *Advances in Neurology, 93*, 195–204.

Landers, M. (2004). Treatment-induced neuroplasticity following focal injury to the motor cortex. *International Journal of Rehabilitation Research, 27*, 1–5.

Marien, M. R., Colpaert, F. C., & Rosenquist, A. C. (2004). Noradrenergic mechanisms in neurodegenerative diseases: A theory. *Brain Research Reviews, 45*, 38–78.

Midorikawa, A., & Kawamura, M. (2000). A case of musical agraphia. *NeuroReport, 11*, 3053–3057.

Peretz, I. (1990). Processing of local and global musical information by unilateral brain-damaged patients. *Brain, 113*, 1185–1205.

Sloboda, J. A. (1985). *The musical mind: The cognitive psychology of music*. Oxford: Clarendon Press.

Solomon, M. (2003). *Late Beethoven: Music, thought, imagination*. Berkeley, CA: University of California Press.

Tuge, H. (1975). *An atlas of the brain of a pianist (1908–1969)*. Tokyo: Koseisha Koseikaku.

6 Musical art and brain damage II

Performing and listening to music

Introduction

Performing musical artists, whether opera or jazz singers, pianists, violinists, or organists, all display their craft, talent, skill, experience, and musical cognition. Both expression and reception are thus displayed. The accumulated body of experimental data suggests that total musical expression relies on the specialization of both hemispheres (Baeck, 2002b; Wieser, 2003). Currently, the general hemispheric pattern is that while the left hemisphere specializes in the perception of timing and rhythm, the right hemisphere specializes in pitch and timbre perception. Within each hemisphere, the temporal lobes are predominantly involved with musical perception and the frontal lobes in musical output and expression. The latter feature of music is associated with language and is an important issue for discussion in the context of music. Music consists of a variety of sub-components and fragments, not all of which are understood or defined, while the sub-components of language appear closely related to each other and to form a unified entity, one that requires single cortical control. Moreover, the sub-components of language are better understood than those of music. However, the bulk of the discussion in this chapter concerns disruption to musical abilities following brain damage or neurological intervention.

Art of music and language

In neurology and neuropsychology the attempt to distinguish between music and language stemmed from observations that patients with language deficits can sometimes show spared musical abilities (Basso, 1993). It is not uncommon, for example, to find a few intact musical abilities in a patient experiencing even global aphasia. Occasionally patients with Broca's aphasia can sing, and indeed sing the words that they are normally unable to utter. Similarly, patients with aphasia may also suffer from amusia. Indeed, more often than one would expect, aphasia and amusia arise from damage to the left hemisphere (Polk & Kertesz, 1993).

The famous case of Dejerine known as Monsieur C., whom Dejerine diagnosed as having alexia without agraphia, was, as it turns out, a trained musician (Hanley & Kay, 2003). He sustained damage in the left hemisphere, in the parietal and occipital lobes, and in the posterior region of the corpus callosum. This patient had as much difficulty reading musical notes as he had in reading words. Yet, he was able to sing both previously familiar and new tunes as well as play the piano and write musical notes. Discussion of musical training is in a subsequent section of this chapter. The symptoms illustrate commonalities in expressive aspects of language and music (not only in trained musicians). Unlike language, however, music has components that are specialized in the left hemisphere with other components specialized in the right hemisphere.

The principal shared commonality of music and language is temporality; that is, the units occur in sequential order and the order gives the sound its meaning (provide it and listen to it). This is unlike the perception of a painting, drawing, or a statue, where the whole stimulus is initially perceived at one time. With speech and music, the brain must not only understand the whole from the sequences, but also support ongoing memory for the order of occurrence. The caveat is that with speech, time intervals are wide compared to music's intervals. The speed with which the units of music congeal into a melody, even into a phrase, is faster than the unification of speech sounds into a meaningful whole. There is neuroimaging support for activation of Broca's area in both hemispheres during music listening (see Levitin & Menon, 2003). And the rhythmic speed of music increases when produced by a musical instrument and even more so when several instruments play together.

With melodies, it is difficult for most of us to know when sub-components, phrases, say, started exactly and when ended. This is not so with speech; we know the beginning and the end clearly. Ultimately, the influence of music on the listener reflects opposing neural computation from what is applied in language listening. Moreover, the anatomical underpinning for parts of language are by far better understood than for the sub-components of music.

The source of music production and language sounds provides a critical clue to the underlying neural support: the major instrument of language is speech. It was designed to be produced solely by a part of the human body, the mouth and larynx. Emitted speech is constrained by the limitations imposed by the very anatomical structures. With music, on the other hand, this does not have to be so: music can be produced by limbs alone, the mouth–lungs apparatus alone (vocal cords, larynx), or by both. The mode of production may have sculpted the nature of music, both neurologically and phenomenologically. Further, the connections to subcortical areas with musically related cortical regions may be more wide and diffuse than for language. This is regardless of whether at the dawn of human brain evolution music started off as a form of semantic communication or not. The fact that music production does not have to rely on the oral cavity alone suggests that it could expand broadly through recruitment of additional cortical areas and neuronal networks.

Amusia and the art of music

Agnosia for music is known as amusia (the loss of receptive knowledge of previously known components of music because of acquired brain damage). The amusia condition can include total auditory agnosia in which musical sounds are not recognized as being musical. As we said earlier, brain damage fractionates knowledge into units that can be observed, analyzed, measured, and understood. But with music, not all the components have been identified; consequently it has been difficult not only to ascertain precisely which musical features have been lost in the patient but also to understand the neuroanatomical underpinning of the various manifestations of amusic disorders. When diagnosis of amusia is made, it is assigned by neurologists who, commonly, are not trained musicians nor do they have at their disposal tests that can isolate parts of impaired musical knowledge. Nevertheless, a great deal has been learned through the good judgment and insights of neurologists and neuropsychologists dealing with such cases.

When there is gradation in the agnosia, two major subtypes are identified. First, tone deafness is the inability to discriminate tones on a musical scale, that is, to say whether the tone was in the low end of the scale or the high end (or somewhere in the middle). The patient reports that all tones sound the same. Second, melody deafness (amelodia) is the inability to recall a melody, either to name it or to hum it, even after clues are given, or even to sing it in the mind's ear. There are interesting functional dissociations in this condition: patients can still identify the instrument playing the melody as well as recognize wrong notes, and yet not be able to recognize the melody itself. Also, in some cases, previously familiar melodies sound as mere noise, particularly unpleasant noise (the sound of a screeching car, or of a hammer on a steel sheet). Also, it is possible for a patient to recognize melodies but not recognize wrong notes introduced while playing it (Basso, 1999).

On the whole, tone deafness is seen most often following damage in the left hemisphere while melody deafness is often found following damage in the right hemisphere, and the localization within each hemisphere can vary (Basso, 1999). However, exceptions have been reported as well, and in any case tone or melody deafness alone do not define all there is to music. Attempts to relegate music perception to the right hemisphere alone are fraught with problems given inconsistency in data and heterogeneity of subjects, and of testing methodology. Rather, a recent appealing suggestion based on a study of non-musically trained neurological patients with unilateral focal damage is that there is a great deal more interhemispheric integration in music perception whereby the total experience receives selective contributions from each hemisphere (Schuppert, Munte, Wieringa, & Altenmuller, 2000).

Tone deafness can also occur congenitally. Such cases have rarely been reported in the literature. One important study, however, explores this condition in a group of eleven adults reportedly experiencing tone deafness (Ayotte, Peretz, & Hyde, 2002). They were administered a battery of six tests that measured various components of music, including pitch, rhythm, melody, temporal judgment, contour, and melody memory. The overall finding was that the worst deficit was in pitch processing, and there were impairments in memory and recognition of music, singing, and keeping time through tapping. The researchers noted that all of these impairments were restricted to music; the subjects were able to recognize speech prosody, familiar environmental sounds, human voices, and interestingly, ten subjects could recognize and identify familiar songs from hearing the opening lyrics. Indeed, all subjects were exposed to music from an early age and some even took music lessons. Previously, Geschwind and Fusillo (1966) reported the case of a congenitally amusic patient who could not sing, discriminate between two pitches, or keep time, yet was fluent in four foreign languages. No specific brain damage is known to be associated with these cases.

A detailed and highly illuminating study of a single case of congenital amusia (tone deafness), Monica, was published by Peretz et al. (2002). Monica was unable to recognize or discriminate melodies, sing, or dance, despite having been given music lessons as a young child. Sensitive music and sound tests uncovered that what may lie at the bottom of her musical disability is a gross deficiency in perceiving changes in pitch, particularly for descending pitches. This was true regardless of whether the tones played to her were pure tones or piano tones, and whether the tone duration was, say, 700 or 350 milliseconds. Somewhat slightly better performance was observed when Monica perceived pure-tone changes (but only if the change was rising, not when falling). Her case reflects a clear-cut dissociation between language sounds and music sounds: she does not appear to have impairments in discerning speech intonations (e.g., she was able to monitor pitch changes in sentences ending in a question mark). Moreover, no brain anomaly has been found that can explain her congenital musical difficulties. Importantly, what all of this shows is that one of the critical features of musical understanding is decipherment of pitch, and that the rest of the dedicated neuronal music pathways in the brain are heavily dependent on normal pitch processing.

Music localization in the brain

When neurologists initially attempted to localize music in the brain, they noticed the prevalence of amusia in left hemisphere damaged patients. They did not fail to observe, however, that some right hemisphere damaged patients suffered from musical disorders as well. At the time when Solomon Henschen carried out investigations in the 1920s, the right hemisphere was regarded as being incapable of supporting anything worthwhile (by way of human cognition), except sometimes after the left hemisphere was damaged. So it is not surprising that the few right brain damaged patients with amusia were not seen as providing important clues about functional brain localization. He concluded, however, that both hemispheres probably play a role in music perception and production. His work was seminal since it spurred comments, criticisms, and debates (see Basso, 1993). Indeed, some views on music and hemispheric specialization point to both hemispheres rather than to only one (Baeck, 2002b).

The next important research period in the neuropsychology of music and the brain came in the early 1960s with the publications of Brenda Milner (1962) and Doreen Kimura (1964), which were based on work in the Montreal Neurological Institute on patients undergoing anterior temporal lobectomy for the relief of epilepsy. Milner administered the Seashore Musical Abilities Test to these patients and a group of control subjects and found asymmetries in their deficits: the right-sided group performed particularly poorly compared to the left-sided group and the control group in discrimination between two brief musical melodies and in timbre recognition; all groups were indistinguishable in rhythm discrimination. The Seashore test provides measures for several components of music, including rhythm, timbre, tonal memory, pitch, loudness, and duration. The strongest result that Milner obtained then was for the poor performance on timbre by the right-sided group. As it turned out, timbre discrimination shows right hemisphere activation in several functional neuroimaging studies carried out more than forty years afterwards (described further along this chapter). Being able to discriminate which instrument is playing may be not unlike telling which person is speaking. With regard to rhythm, however, the bulk of the evidence from functional neuroimaging studies since the early 1990s points to left hemisphere specialization (Wieser, 2003). This is consistent with the long-understood left hemisphere specialization in memory for temporal order (Efron, 1963).

Melodies and the role of musical training

Kimura (1964) investigated memory for melodies through the use of the dichotic listening paradigm; two simultaneous but different sounds are heard at the same time, except that one is administered to the left ear and the other to the right ear. This technique relies on the fact that under competing auditory conditions, the contralateral auditory pathways dominate. In Kimura's study, normal subjects heard one melody in one ear and simultaneously a different melody in the other ear; the question of interest was which melody will later be recognized from among a series of four melodies heard binaurally. The melodies heard in the left ear were recognized better than those heard in the right ear (Kimura, 1964). This study launched the argument that the right hemisphere specializes in musical perception, since not soon afterwards several other studies confirmed Kimura's findings. Previously, Kimura administered a dichotic listening task to normal subjects requiring that they say out loud the name of the number that they heard; one ear received one number while simultaneously the other ear received a completely different number; the numbers heard in the right ear were named significantly more accurately than numbers heard in the left ear (Kimura, 1963a, 1963b). These results were interpreted to show the specialization of the left hemisphere in language. On the whole, Kimura's two studies suggested that while one hemisphere was indeed specialized in language, as was already well known at that time, the other hemisphere, the right, specialized in music. Subsequent tests of musical perception revealed, however, that musical training plays a crucial role in hemispheric involvement.

The idea that training is important in obtaining information about the neuroanatomical underpinning of music from brain-damaged patients was first suggested in 1930 by Feuchtwanger (explained by Basso, 1993). In 1974 Bever and Chiarello demonstrated in a seminal study the influence of musical training in an experiment in which one group of subjects consisted of trained musicians (who had extensive training in a music school for at least five years prior to the testing) and another group of non-musicians (Bever & Chiarello, 1974). The task was to listen to melodies recorded on a tape (heard on a non-dichotic tape), detect a specific sequence of two notes and later say whether or not a given melody was already presented during the two-note sequence detection stage. There were many such trials. The results indicated a clear-cut difference between the two groups: trained musicians were better able to recognize the melody heard in the right ear while non-musicians recognized the melody better when heard in the left ear. This outcome suggested the opposite involvement of the two hemispheres in musical processing, with the left hemisphere being maximally involved in trained musicians and the right hemisphere being maximally involved in the non-musicians (Bever & Chiarello, 1974). These findings were subsequently replicated in other studies and the issue of training remains important in empirical studies of music. One study, for example, has demonstrated that trained pianists process musical notations differently from non-musicians and as a result of training and practice in their craft, the pianists have a spatial understanding of the world that is different from non-musicians (Stewart, Walsh, & Frith, 2004). The current view is that music perception is influenced by extent of musical training.

Unilateral brain damage in trained musicians

Playing a musical instrument by professional musicians following unilateral brain damage has not yielded a clear-cut picture of hemispheric control. As Basso (1999) summarizes, left hemisphere damage resulting in language comprehension impairments (Wernicke's type aphasia) had the following effects: a piano teacher went on to play the piano; a concert pianist in a chamber orchestra continued to play professionally; an organist continued to play the organ. On the other hand, similar hemispheric damage impaired piano playing in a piano teacher, in a conductor and orchestra director, and in a music student playing the guitar (but, interestingly, not singing). Right hemisphere damage resulted in the inability to play by an amateur accordion player and in the inability to play the organ in an amateur organist (also in Basso, 1999).

The loss of pleasure in listening to music is more often reported after right hemisphere damage than after left damage. But it should be stressed that there are more left hemisphere cases with amusia than with right damage. Consequently, because the sample numbers are unequal, the issue of pleasure from music in patients with unilateral damage is unclear. There is pleasure and there is pleasure, of course. When musicians listen to music their pleasure is "colored" by their knowledge of sub-components of music and their interplay in the whole musical structure. Experienced music listeners, those who have taken lessons or trained in listening selectively to music, derive listening pleasure of a particular sort. In non-musicians and untrained listeners, the absence of direct cognitive knowledge gives rise to a different sort of pleasure (Blood & Zatorre, 2001). Nevertheless, neuroimaging studies show that the right orbitofrontal cortex is active in most people listening to music that they enjoy (Tramo, 2001).

Cases of trained musicians with right hemisphere damage are exceptionally rare. However, a neurological report of such a case was published by Sparr (2002). The most striking deficit was this musician's amelodia. When first seen at the hospital, he could not recognize melodies that he previously knew, regardless of whether they were presented from recordings, played live on a piano, or sung; nor was he able to recognize tunes with lyrics containing words. By contrast, he could hum a tune from memory and he could correctly clap his hands to the rhythm of the melodies that he could not identify. Thus, he showed dissociation between rhythm and melody identification. At the same time, when given sheet music, he was able to discern the melody represented by the notes, categorize the style, and go on to explain which lines represented the melody; he could also explain the timing of musical instruments in a Stravinsky score. He had no problems in producing the pitch of single notes. He had problems reproducing sequences of four notes or longer, but not of three tone sequences. He did not suffer from atonality. At the same time, he was unable to identify instruments from their sounds, and could not match voices of famous people to their names, even when they were singing. The inability to associate sounds with their source is not unlike the timbre deficits seen in non-musicians following damage to the right hemisphere. Follow-up tests one month later revealed a 20 percent improvement in melody identification and this rate went up to 70 percent three years later. Still, even at that time, there was a lag between melody presentation and its identification. The neurologist reporting this case notes that throughout the patient remained unaware of his deficits and denied having these perceptual difficulties with music. The denial suggests anosognosia (denial of illness), a condition associated with right parietal damage. It is possible, then, that despite the fact that neuroimaging revealed only right temporal lobe dysfunction, that there was functional damage in the parietal lobe as well. In all, his amelodia was not accompanied by disorders in pitch, rhythm, or harmony. The critical contribution of this case is that it shows important dissociations in musical perception and understanding in a professional musician who despite localized brain damage goes on to use intact regions in both sides of his brain to process features of music.

The neuropsychology of singing

In non-musicians, singing may be controlled by the right more than by the left hemisphere. This has been observed in some patients who despite having aphasia caused by damage in the left hemisphere were able to sing previously familiar songs. This idea is further supported by observations of left hemispherectomy patients (left hemisphere is surgically removed) in whom surgery was after age 8 years. In these patients language production was minimal but singing was possible nevertheless. One of these hemispherectomy patients, RS, was noted by several investigators to sing with no disruption to pitch, tone, rhythm, or any other identified feature of music ("she sang like an angel" was one evaluative remark) (Gott, 1973; E. Zaidel, 1978). But it is not known if she was able to learn new songs after the hemispherectomy. This is an important distinction: do we need two intact cerebral hemispheres to learn music? Currently, we do not have an answer to this question.

The control of singing by the brain was investigated in experimental conditions in eight neurological patients by Gordon and Bogen (1974). The patients were evaluated for surgery to control generalized epileptic seizures that were resistant to medication; they were administered unilateral anesthetizing drug (sodium amytal), known also as the Wada test, to the left and right hemispheres separately, and were then asked to sing familiar melodies while the unilateral anesthesia was in effect. When the left hemisphere was anesthetized and the right was awake (and able to control the singing), patients could not immediately sing nor utter any words. The singing began as soon as the patient was able to utter a single word. Once that occurred, melody singing proceeded with clear pitch and rhythm. When the right hemisphere was anesthetized, and the left was in control of the singing, the patients were able to speak (because control of language was in the left hemisphere) but their singing was impaired in seven out of eight cases. When patients succeeded in singing, there was rhythm, although it was a bit slow, pitch was poorly executed, and the singing was characterized as being monotonic. (The poor control over tonality confirms the observations from tonal amusia found in patients with unilateral damage in the right hemisphere.) However, there were great individual differences varying from attempted singing to no attempts to sing at all. And the investigators noted that while tonality in singing was impaired, no such impairment was present for speaking. The current overall view of the brain's control in singing is that the right hemisphere plays a greater role in rendering the melody, particularly in non-musicians, but the left plays a crucial role as well so that in balance each hemisphere makes a contribution to the total production (Altenmuller, 2001).

The critical role of the frontal lobes in singing in professional musicians becomes apparent after reviewing several reports on neurological patients. A. Jellinek described the rare case of a professional singer who lost singing skills following removal of a glioma tumor in the left frontal lobe in 1933 (described in Benton, 1977). After surgery the patient suffered from Broca's aphasia as well as from dyslexia, dysgraphia, and from impairment in comprehension of spoken language. He became unable to sing familiar melodies and he had great difficulties applying the correct pitch. He also became unable to sing the notes of a scale, could not perfectly reproduce rhythmic patterns, and completely lost the ability to read music. Another trained musician, not a professional singer, was described in 1926 and 1927 by P. Jossmann (see Benton, 1977). He had an aneurysm in the right bifurcation of the common carotid artery, and the aneurysm was removed surgically. After surgery he was unable to sing or whistle previously familiar tunes, and he lost the ability to read musical scores. At the same time, he retained his ability to recognize pitch (highlighting the dissociation in brain localization of music components). Other neurological cases reported in the literature seem to point to the frontal lobes as a brain region that modulates the control of singing (Basso, 1999; Benton, 1977), showing that expressive components of music are under fine cortical motor control and may be dissociable from receptive circuitry that could include cortical and subcortical structures. If singing were a mere extension of an early biological form of animal communication, subcortical regions would have controlled singing. The fact that cortical regions, particularly in the frontal lobes are critically involved, suggests otherwise.

Brain representation of musicians' hands

Imaging studies of the brain have revealed clues about neuroanatomical representations in musicians. In addition to the left planum temporale being larger in people with perfect pitch compared to those who have normal pitch perception (Zatorre, 2003), other musically related neuroanatomical findings have been uncovered. Adults with musical training that began earlier than age 7 have a larger region in the corpus callosum than people who were not musically trained; that region is in the trunk of the callosum (the middle section) (Schlaug, Jancke, Huang, & Steinmetz, 1995). The motor cortex is bordered on one end by the central sulcus. The depth of this sulcus is significantly deeper in professional musicians who play on the keyboard than in non-musicians, and this is true in both the left and right hemispheres (Amunts, Schlaug, Jaencke, Steinmetz, Schleicher, & Zilles, 1996). Among the musicians, the depth of the sulcus is greater the earlier the age at which the training began. In musicians playing string instruments from an early age (the left hand typically presses on the strings and the right modulates the bow) the postcentral gyrus, which is the somatosensory cortex, in the right hemisphere is larger than normal (Elbert, Pantev, Wienbruch, Rockstroh,

& Taub, 1995; Elbert & Rockstroh, 2004). These results demonstrate alterations in brain structure that address the issue of brain plasticity.

At the same time, they do not indicate whether or not there is an alteration in neuronal networks, or, at the very least, they do not indicate the nature of the alterations. Large cortical size could mean large neurons with long axons, or it could mean greater density of neurons than normal. So neuronal networks could vary in size across different individuals. The advantage of greater density is that there is increased ability to control particularly fine finger movements or increased sensitivity in the tips of the fingers. In balance, the results show that professional musicians have slightly different brains than non-musicians, especially in music execution regions, and the thicker section in the corpus callosum implies some sort of increased connectivity between the hemispheres in a region critical for music processing. It is not obvious that the connectivity enhances inter-hemispheric transfer of information; it could reflect the fine regulation of unilateral hemispheric control, for example. The function of the corpus callosum is to allow transfer of information between the two hemispheres but that does not mean it is a "highway bridge" on which pieces of information flow back and forth. Instead, the callosum may serve as a neural system that transmits inhibitory as well as excitatory neural messages of one hemisphere over the other.

Alternatively, consider the findings involving a professional organist who suffered from temporal lobe epilepsy and the implications of his condition for the brain's control in musical manual coordination (Wieser, 2003):

> We studied the recorded organ performance of a professional musician with right temporal lobe epilepsy during a right temporal lobe seizure. While playing an organ concert (John Stanley's Voluntary VIII, Op. 5), he suffered a complex partial seizure. Music analysis of the recorded concert performance during the seizure and comparison with other available exercise recordings and with the composition itself indicated seizure-induced variations. At the beginning of the seizure, the left hand started to become imprecise in time and deviated from the score, whereas the right hand remained faultless at this time. With increasing duration of the seizure discharge, the dissociation of both hands from the score increased, but the right hand compensated for the errors of the left hand in a musically meaningful way, that is, aiming to compensate for the seizure-induced errors of the left hand. The case illustrates untroubled musical judgment during epileptic activity in the right temporal lobe at the onset of the seizure. Whereas the temporal formation of the performance was markedly impaired, the ability of improvisation, in the sense of a "perfect musical solution" to errors of the left hand, remained intact . . . the left hand performs with imprecise tone lengths, whereas the right hand performs perfectly. Deviations from the notation are evident in both hands, but the right hand (directed by the "healthy" = unaffected

left hemisphere) compensates for the errors of the left (affected) hand in a musically meaningful way.

(Wieser, 2003, pp. 85–86)

Music brain activation in fMRI and PET studies

The findings from some neuroimaging studies have uncovered several regions that illuminate some of the neural substrates of music. In 2003 a review of forty-four functional imaging studies (fMRI and PET) in non-musicians discovered a great deal of overlap (but not perfect consistency) in regional brain activation for musical sequencing tasks and music perception (Janata & Grafton, 2003). The bilateral areas found to be active during reading and playing music involve maximal activation of the primary motor cortex, premotor cortex, the superior parietal lobe, lateral prefrontal cortex, and the cerebellum. Musical score interpretation activates the superior parietal lobe and intraparietal sulcus. In tasks where subjects were required to discriminate or detect the parts played by different instruments, or disembeded target from a background with music, the premotor region in the prefrontal lobe was maximally active as were the parietal lobe, cerebellum, and the basal ganglia. If subjects were required to imagine in their mind's ear a specific melody after being given a cue, the maximal activation areas were seen in the parietal, ventrolateral prefrontal area, and the premotor area. These same regions appeared especially active during the perception of musical stimuli. When the inferior and superior portions of the parietal lobe were activated, there seemed to be asymmetry in activation, while in other regions the asymmetry was not so consistent. Figure 6.1 illustrates brain activation areas in music perception.

Using PET scans in non-musicians, Halpern (2001) discovered that the right temporal lobe and the right supplementary motor area in the prefrontal cortex were maximally active in musical imagery (imagining a tune in the head) or in perceiving music, but that the left prefrontal regions were active when the music had lyrics. Also with PET, while subjects listened to pieces of music, Platel and colleagues discovered that maximal activation in the left hemisphere was associated with familiarity, pitch, and rhythm, and maximal activity in the right hemisphere was uncovered for timbre identification (Platel et al., 1997). Specifically, familiarity of melodies recruited the left inferior frontal gyrus and the anterior region of the superior temporal gyrus. The rhythm task maximally activated Broca's area as well as the insula (which is buried deep inside the Sylvian fissure). These findings clearly reveal that several widely spread brain regions are activated when subjects (non-musicians) listen to music, as is confirmed by numerous studies (Meister et al., 2004).

A particularly revealing study investigating brain activation upon hearing musical tones in non-musicians, found maximal recruitment of neuronal activation in several bilateral regions, but when laterality was detected it

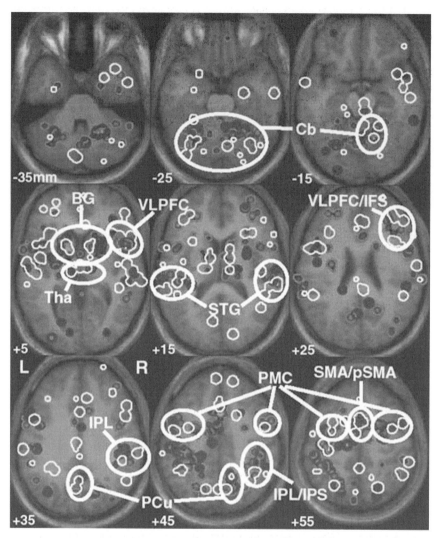

Figure 6.1 Music and the brain. Combined results from forty-four neuroimaging studies of musical sequencing (Janata & Grafton, 2003). The brain areas that were most active during performance of the music tasks are encircled and labeled as follows: BG = basal ganglia; Cb = cerebellum; IFS = inferior frontal sulcus; IPL = inferior parietal lobule; IPS = intraparietal sulcus; PCu = precuneus; PMC = premotor cortex; pSMA = pre-supplementary motor area; SMA = supplementary motor area; STG = superior temporal gyrus; Tha = thalamus; VLPFC = ventrolateral prefrontal cortex. (Printed with permission from Nature Publishing.)

was associated more clearly (but not exclusively) with the right rostromedial prefrontal cortex (Janata, Birk, Van Horn, Leman, Tillmann, & Bharucha, 2002). It is in this region of the brain that an unusual activation pattern occurred as different tones were played to the subjects:

> we found that the mapping of specific keys to specific neural populations in the rostromedial prefrontal cortex is relative rather than absolute. Within a reliably recruited network, the populations of neurons that represent different regions of the tonality surface are dynamically allocated from one occasion to the next. This type of dynamic topography may be explained by the properties of tonality structures. In contrast to categories of common visual objects that differ in their spatial features, musical keys are abstract constructs that share core properties. The internal relationships among the pitches defining a key are the same in each key, thereby facilitating the transposition of musical themes from one key to another. However, the keys themselves are distributed on a tonus at unique distances from one another.
>
> (Janata et al., 2002, p. 2169)

Critical factors that influence such dynamic activity involve rhythm and tempo, to name but a few, and motoric cognition and control involving the motor cortices in both hemispheres as well as the cerebellum maximally (Popescu et al., 2004). The wide reaction in the brain to music highlights the challenge of understanding the neuropsychology of music and at the same time contributes to realizing the complex coordination of the involved neural substrates.

Summary

Widely spaced brain structures are activated in musical artists and no single "music center" has thus far been identified. Early on, neurologists did not fail to observe that music disorders followed both left and right hemisphere damage. The temporal lobes are predominantly involved with musical perception and the frontal lobes in musical output and expression. The attempt to distinguish between music and language stemmed from observations that patients with language deficits can sometimes have spared musical abilities. The general hemispheric picture is that while the left hemisphere specializes in the perception of timing and rhythm, the right hemisphere specializes in pitch and timbre perception. However, previous training in music shapes memory and reactions to music. Musical training plays a crucial role in hemispheric involvement, with the left hemisphere being maximally involved in trained musicians while the right hemisphere is maximally involved in the non-musicians. Cases of trained musicians with right hemisphere damage are exceptionally rare. Neuroimaging results reveal that professional musicians have slightly different activated brain regions than non-musicians, especially in music execution regions. Imaging studies of non-musicians and musicians alike suggest that music triggers multiple neural regions, and this further complicates pinpointing responsible neural regions ("centers") while at the same time highlighting the broad spectrum of musical reactions. A spatial map of the brain's reaction to music as function of tempo, rhythm, context, format, contour, and other identified "primitives" of music listening and performing can potentially help in forming a neuropsychological picture of music perception.

Further readings

Chen, R., Cohen, L. G., & Hallett, M. (2002). Nervous system reorganization following injury. *Neuroscience*, *111*, 761–773.

Elbert, T., & Rockstroh, B. (2004). Reorganization of human cerebral cortex: The range of changes following use and injury. *Neuroscientist*, *10*, 129–141.

Frost, S. B., Barbay, S., Friel, K. M., Plautz, E. J., & Nudo, R. J. (2003). Reorganization of remote cortical regions after ischemic brain injury: A potential substrate for stroke recovery. *Journal of Neurophysiology*, *89*, 3205–3214.

Hyde, K. L., & Peretz, I. (2004). Brains that are out of tune but are in time. *Psychological Science*, *15*, 356–360.

Peretz, I., & Zattore, R. J. (Eds.). (2003). *The cognitive neuroscience of music*. Oxford: Oxford University Press.

Polk, M., & Kertesz, A. (1993). Music and language in degenerative disease of the brain. *Brain and Cognition*, *22*, 98–117.

Popescu, M., Otsuka, A., & Ioannides, A. A. (2004). Dynamics of brain activity in motor and frontal cortical areas during music listening: A magnetoencephalographic study. *NeuroImage*, *21*, 1622–1638.

Raffmann, D. (1993). *Language, music, and mind*. Cambridge, MA: MIT Press.

Sloboda, J. A. (1985). *The musical mind: The cognitive psychology of music*. Oxford: Clarendon Press.

Swain, J. (1997). *Musical languages*. New York: Norton.

Trevarthen, C. (1999) Musicality and the intrinsic motive pulse: Evidence from human psychobiology and infant communication. Rhythms, musical narrative, and the origins of human communication. In *Musicae Scientiae*, special issue, 1999–2000, European Society for the Cognitive Sciences of Music, Liège, pp. 157–213.

Zbikowski, L. (2002). *Conceptualizing music: Cognitive structure, theory, and analysis*. New York: Oxford University Press.

7 Artists and viewers

Components of perception and cognition in visual art

Introduction

Some features in visual art have been gleaned from non-artists with neurological damage through standard neuropsychological tests and experiments. Other features can be interpreted in terms of perceptual, cognitive, and mnemonic concepts worked out by cognitive psychologists. In order to gain insights into the neuropsychology of art we need to discuss art-relevant features straddling neuropsychology and cognitive psychology as well. This is the approach adopted in this chapter.

How is a visual artist to depict a cup, car, flower, slice of orange, chair, bed, rug, or a stove, given the ever changing perspective views under which these objects are seen? Regardless of the artist's mind or intentions, pictures are meant to communicate with others, and the observer has to respond somehow to what is being shown. What distance to adopt, what type of scaling, what colors, shadows, or texture? For example, despite the fact that in the real world we typically see objects from various perspective views, we know what they are conceptually, with or without the aid of language. Because of perceptual constancy, size and orientation end up not interfering with our basic knowledge of the shape of things in the world. A cup is a cup even though we repeatedly view it from the side, top, 30 degree, or 90 degree angles. How we define pictorial realism is a philosophical question whose answer lies partly in perceptual constancy.

At the same time, it is because of perceptual constancy that non-artists have a hard time rendering an object from a model. The image that forms on the retina is two-dimensional, same as on the drawing surface. The brain combines visual signals from both eyes to produce the perception of depth and the three-dimensional nature of the real world, as well as constancy. We do not see the parts of our modeled object that are close to us as being much larger than the farther parts. Such gross disparities are evened out by the constancy principle. Artists are trained to "see" the disparities nevertheless and to render them through exaggeration on a two-dimensional surface. They may even have perceived them prior to receiving training through some exceptional ability that they posses.

Concepts stored in long-term memory enable us to recognize the same object regardless of perspective view. Even when that viewpoint is remarkably extreme we nevertheless know what we are looking at: consider being on top of the Eiffel Tower in Paris or on top of a skyscraper looking down at the street below. While people and cars appear very tiny, a size which we are not accustomed to seeing, we nevertheless know and recognize their shapes. Yes, context plays a major role in our knowledge of objects. The wiring diagram of the mind in the brain requires storage of concepts each of which represents many different details extracted from reality.

Blind children's ability to draw real objects, scenes, or human interactions in pictorial ways that are highly similar, if not identical, to drawings by sighted children and adults confirms that representations of knowledge are organized through concepts, and need not depend on visual input alone (Heller, 2002; Kennedy, 2003; Kennedy & Igor, 2003). Once these concepts are formed, it is not difficult to render them. It is a uniquely human ability to draw spontaneously. In rendering objects, people with normal vision have at their disposal checks and balances from their sight, they can correct their drawings to appear more realistic or to alter them in a number of creative ways. They can test their pictorial theories more readily than blind people. The fact that a blind human can draw spontaneously while a sighted ape cannot shows that this capability is neuronally wired selectively into the human brain.

Art, perceptual constancy, and canonical views

Artists' sketchbooks are replete with drawings of objects from multiple viewpoints. Leonardo da Vinci's anatomical sketches and Michelangelo's drawings of human faces are a couple of examples. A sketchbook is ubiquitous among artists. They study their subjects, whether still life, landscape, or the human body, by depicting an object from multiple perspectives. These sketches are not mere practice exercises, although they may sometimes serve as that. Comparing their sketches to the final product clearly demonstrates that while they can accurately render different perspectives of the same object in the end they opt for a particular view. Looking at such sketches, one is struck by the available possibilities, the absence of aesthetic appeal of some views, and the artist's wisdom in choosing the view with the greatest impact or appeal. How do they decide what is aesthetic, how do they know what is best? Henri Matisse, for example, made eighty drawings of one model:

> From his model, the future Soeur Jacques, he made about eighty drawings exploiting all the plastic possibilities of her face: in one, he accentuated it in the form of a square; in another, all the round features were strongly exaggerated; in another, the eyes were small and very close together; another was sharply linear; another, very softly modeled with charcoal. And yet those eighty drawings, which were all very different,

one from another, expressed complete unity; throughout, one had the sense of art embroidered on the same feeling.

(Gilot & Lake, 1964, p 267)

In fact, the basis of the final artistic decision regarding what to represent in the actual painting is not clear. Artists probably end up choosing the view that they assume has the greatest aesthetic appeal and simultaneously the view that will convey meaning; that is, a view that matches stored representations of the object in the viewer's mind. If subjected to an empirical investigation, however, that view preferred by an artist may not correspond to what the public prefers. In one related empirical study of the relationship between the artistic decision and the viewer's preference for a perspective view, there was a discrepancy – the viewers preferred a view opposite to the artistic decision (Zaidel & FitzGerald, 1994; see also Chapter 9).

Canonical views represent the concepts of objects. Figure 7.1 is an illustration of various views of a cylinder. Which one is more typical? In real life, objects have many identifiers – various forms, shapes, textures, colors, contexts, perspective views, sizes, functions, and more than one name. Many things matter about objects, things such as functionality, age at which we first encountered them, frequency of use in daily life, or emotional attachment. What ends up being depicted pictorially is the stored concept. Asked to draw a picture of a car we typically draw a side view, and when asked to draw a cup we also choose a side view and include a curved handle (despite a multitude of shapes for cup handles). A human is depicted frontally, as are hands, computers, or eyeglasses. These are canonical representations of familiar objects. What makes artists so special, in my view, is that they can "transcend" the canonical concept and through their talent can pictorially represent objects from a variety of perspective views.

When participants in an experiment were asked to name single objects photographed from various perspectives, their accuracy level depended on which hemisphere of the brain received the stimulus (Burgund & Marsolek, 2000). The study concluded that the right hemisphere stores concepts of objects in a manner that relies on the view-dependent representations whereas the left hemisphere strategy relies on view-independent representation of objects. The findings of this study support notions of whole versus part cognition in the right and left hemispheres, respectively. So according to the study the right hemisphere specializes in remembering the concept of the whole object and subsequently recognizes objects as function of their viewpoint, not their parts. The left hemisphere was found to be cognitively more flexible by comparison since the perspective view did not matter in the recognition. In identifying objects from pictures, each hemisphere of the brain makes its own contribution to the process and together a unified perception emerges.

The issue of recognition despite multiple viewpoints is a subject of much discussion in the cognitive psychological literature. The most original and

Figure 7.1 Different views of a cylinder. Which one of these cylinders represents your concept of a cylinder? Which one would you have drawn had you been asked to draw a cylinder? Despite multiple views of a single object, we store only a single concept of the object and the concept has a view that is common across many people. Canonical views represent concepts of objects. Many things matter about objects, things such as functionality, age at which we first encountered them, frequency of use in daily life, or emotional attachment. Furthermore, despite our familiarity with actual objects we nevertheless can recognize and identify them in two-dimensional representations, that is, pictorially. So what ends up being depicted pictorially is the stored concept. Asked to draw a picture of a car we typically draw a side view, and when asked to draw a cup we also choose a side view and include a curved handle (despite a multitude of shapes for cup handles). What makes artists so special is that they transcend the canonical concept and through their talent can represent pictorially objects from a variety of perspective views. Indeed, the extent to which an artist can manage not to depict the canonical view evokes an aesthetic reaction from the viewer. This is largely because an uncommon view draws attention. Regardless of the artist's mind or intentions, pictures are meant to communicate with others, and the observer has to respond somehow to what is being shown.

influential explanation came from Marr (1982) in the late 1970s. Basically, he proposed that the brain computes signals from the retina that inform the brain on edges, angles, juxtapositions, and many other local features in objects. The computation produces three-dimensional concepts of objects so that they are always recognized regardless of the shifting views, sizes, distances, lighting effects, and so on, that that their images create on the retina. In the ensuing years, Marr's ideas were developed and expanded further by others. Unfortunately, he died at a very young age. Currently, one school of thought proposes that shape constancy arises from recognition of invariant properties in objects, properties that do not change regardless of the viewpoint. These serve as anchor points in our stored concepts and schemas. So even if the object is pictorially misshapen, distorted, or partially hidden, we will still recognize the object for what it is providing at least some of those anchor point properties in the stored concept become active. What matters in the structural geometry of objects? This is the view-independent theory of object recognition (Biederman, 1987; Biederman & Gerhardstein, 1993; Hummel & Biederman, 1992). It is contrasted with the view-dependent theory (Ullman, 1996), which proposes that knowledge of objects depends heavily on the common view of the object in reality. The theory assumes that concepts of objects represent the whole object, as a self-contained entity, rather than its parts, something that the view-independent theory assumes. Thus, when inspecting pictures of an object drawn from an atypical perspective, the observer would have difficulties in deciphering the identity of the object. In fact, both theories are true of everyday recognition of pictorial objects.

Despite object constancy, not all viewing angles are conducive to efficient or preferred object recognition. In a study that compared 0° rotation to 120° and 240° of the same familiar objects, it was found that verbal responses to 120° and 240° were slower than to the no rotation at all condition (Lawson, 1999). On the other hand, 30°, 90°, 150°, and 180° rotations produced less slowness in responding. This finding supports the notion of preferred view representation in the brain. Possibly there is interference between the newness of the rotated view and the known elements of the figure that match the canonical representation. An insight into why certain rotated views are more difficult than others is suggested by a study that examined the effect of depth rotation on speed of verbal labeling (Newell & Findlay, 1997). Pictured common objects were shown from many different perspective views and the task to the subject was to name the objects. The investigators measured the number of naming errors and discovered that certain views were more difficult than others. Specifically, upside-down and end-on produced many naming errors. They conducted five separate experiments in their study and concluded that there is no single canonical view of a given object but rather several canonical views are possible, at least for objects that are typically elongated and that we are used to seeing in an upright position. Thus, such objects have a range of canonical views that emanate from stable views of the objects (Newell & Findlay, 1997). In short, the represented image of an object in the brain is an average, a prototype that can be used to match several different newly seen perspectives of the object.

Hemispheric categorization and perspective views in pictures

There is more to recognition than just the viewer-centered versus viewer-independent issue. The mind in the brain interprets pictorial representations by tapping several layers of previously stored knowledge. The hemispheric status in processing perspective views depending on the object's level of membership in a natural superordinate was investigated as well (Zaidel & Kosta, 2001). Pictorial stimuli depicting three-dimensional views of single objects were rendered with computer software. Six different views for each object were created: front (F), front-right (FR), front-left (FL), side (S), back-left (BL), and back-right (BR). The F and S views depicted objects as they would appear with the center of the object at viewer's eye level. The off-center views (FL, FR, BR, and BL) were rotated 33.75° from center on the vertical axis and 45° from center on the horizontal axis. BR and BL views were rotated as described from the back view while the FR and FL views were rotated from the front view. The rotations represented the view as seen from an individual viewing the center of the object (from the back or front) at eye level and moving to the left or right 45° then up 33.75°. The task for the subjects participating in the experiment was to decide whether or not a given stimulus object was a member of a pre-designated natural superordinate category. There were two categories, Furniture or Carpenters' Tools. The different views were presented in the left or right visual half fields, that is, in the right or left hemispheres, respectively. Independently of this study, it is known which objects are typical, medium, or low exemplars of their respective category. Thus, the main question was whether or not there will be an interaction between viewpoint, typicality level, and cerebral hemisphere. The findings revealed a strong triple statistical interaction, suggesting thereby that our visual knowledge of objects is processed through multiple cognitive levels. Moreover, the results indicated that right hemisphere processing was more heavily influenced by the typicality level of the object, responding much faster to objects with high typicality than to those with low typicality, regardless of the perspective view. The left hemisphere reacted evenly to the various stimuli, regardless of their typicality level (Zaidel & Kosta, 2001).

Unilateral damage and pictorial object recognition

The investigation of neurological patients with unilateral focal brain lesions helps understand the underlying mechanism of pictorial object recognition. An early investigation, published in 1917 by Friedrich Best, described soldiers with gunshot and missile wounds in the brain during World War I (Ferber & Karnath, 2003). He described their performance on various visual tests (he was an ophthalmologist). One particular patient that he identified as "Case Z" is of interest here. The patient had a behavioral dissociation between object recognition and object orientation. Specifically, he had no problems identifying objects in pictures but at the same time he was unable to say what their perspective view was. He also had no problems in identifying colors, in recognizing objects despite size differences, in recalling his house in his mind's eye or his relatives' faces. He did, however, have problems in visualizing certain spatial features in his mind's eye: he could not visualize specific points in the layout of his hometown, nor the geographical location where he had been wounded. Similarly, he had problems with egocentric localization, that is, he could not say where an object was located with respect to the position of his body. So if an object was placed above his head, he could not say where it was. He was also unable to determine the direction of object motion. At the same time, he had no problems with auditory localization with respect to his body or with localizing parts of body to which pressure had been applied. The dissociation interesting to our discussion here is this: shown pictures of familiar faces upside down or sideways, he was able to recognize the person but when asked what orientation he was looking at, he was unable to do so. This inability extended to letters as well. He was thus unable to distinguish between *n* and *u*. The brain damage caused by the bullet was bilateral, in posterior regions of the parietal lobes including the border of the occipital and parietal lobes. Unfortunately, he developed fever and abscesses in his right hemisphere four days into Best's testing. Despite medical treatment, a few days later Z died (Ferber & Karnath, 2003). Z's performance on the visual tests supports the view-independent theories described above, since he was able to recognize objects independently of their perspective orientation.

Additional neurological cases have been reported since then supporting the idea of dissociation in the control of object knowledge versus object orientation. A patient with bilateral frontal brain damage due to abscess also showed difficulties with perspective views. While he could identify individual letters, he could not say whether or not they were presented to him upside down or right side up. This is despite the fact that the patient could read them in the inverted orientation (Solms, Kaplan-Solms, Saling, & Miller, 1988). Another published report described a neurological patient, RM, who displayed a similar behavioral dissociation (Robertson, Treisman, Friedman-Hill, & Grabowecky, 1997). The damage in this patient was bilateral, in the posterior region of the brain, specifically in the parietal-occipital lobes. The case of KB has also been described (Karnath, Ferber, & Bulthoff, 2000). Again, this patient could recognize objects, letters, pictures of animals or of faces, regardless of perspective orientation (four different orientations were used, 0°, -90°, +90°, and 180°) but was unable to determine the orientation itself. There was damage bilaterally in the parieto-occipital regions and unilaterally in the left frontal lobe. Other cases in the literature who had correct object recognition abilities in the face of poor recognition of perspective views suffered from damage in the right hemisphere, in regions involving the parietal lobe (either alone or together with the temporal lobe). Thus far only the right hemisphere has been implicated in those cases where the damage had been unilateral. In all of these studies canonical views of objects were used. It would have been helpful to determine the patients' performance with different perspective views of the same object.

In an elegant experiment utilizing fMRI and a paradigm based on neuronal adaptation to repeated stimulation, the findings revealed that object size and position are invariant features whereas illumination and viewpoint perspective are important features to which neurons do not easily become adapted (Grill-Spector, Kushnir, Edelman, Avidan, Itzchak, & Malach, 1999). The idea of repetition suppression was first described for single cell recording in monkeys in the early 1990s (E. K. Miller, Li, & Desimone, 1991). This newly recognized neurophysiological phenomenon reflects the fact that neurons become less active with repeated stimulation, that is, they become adapted. The stimuli in the Grill-Spector et al. (1999) study were pictures of common objects as well as of faces. Different orientation views and illumination and size features were manipulated. The investigators looked for stimulus conditions under which changes in neuronal activation occurred particularly after repeated stimulus presentation. In other words, they looked for recovery from adaptation. Conditions with no adaptations provided clues to regional brain specialization and to what parameters in objects are salient. The caudal-rostral portion of the lateral occipital region was relatively immune to adaptation (that is, was not passive during repeated exposure of the stimuli) while the posterior fusiform region became adapted (that is, displayed less activity during repeated exposure). In addition, there was more activation response to face stimuli, not surprisingly given known specialization in the fusiform gyrus for faces.

From the foregoing it emerges that the brain stores structural information about objects in the real world, represents them as concepts and schemas, and when it is time to retrieve the information, as when we need to obtain meaning from visual input, we match between what is seen in the real world and the previously stored concept. Apparently, the different orientations in which we see objects are not critical visual features for gaining meaning from pictorial representations. On the other hand, object identity is critical since we see a multitude of objects from various angles. In any case, orientation knowledge is more sensitive to brain damage but not to object knowledge.

Disembedding in pictures and the left hemisphere

Isolating a single figure from a confusing cluttered and complex background consists of a process known as disembedding (see Figure 7.2 for an example of overlapping figures). In psychology, disembedding is also known as closure flexibility (Thurstone, 1944). In digital imaging it is a process similar to segmenting. The process is akin to what is required for seeing through warfare camouflage. Another example is picking out single bad apples in a tree full

Figure 7.2 Overlapping figures. This is a good illustration of a type of a figure–
ground relationship problem. The ability to tease apart these objects despite a confusing background involves disembedding, a function specialized
in the left hemisphere. It taps the ability to focus on details and parts.

with good apples, the sick tree in a forest in an aerial view, diseased coffee
beans on a moving belt carrying all the picked coffee beans, and so on. In
tests designed to tease apart this ability, common objects or geometrical
shapes are hidden, concealed, or camouflaged through partial overlap and
superimposition by other figures and the task is to find specific, designated
objects or forms. Several visual disembedding tests have been constructed
since 1917 when a German neurologist, Poppelreuter, first started to require
soldiers suffering from head injuries in World War I to visually isolate single
figures from a confusing background (Poppelreuter, 1917). The test that he
designed is known as the Overlapping Figures Test. An example of the type
of task required by Poppelreuter is shown in Figure 7.2. The task was to
name the figures in tangled pictorial arrays. He found that brain damage in
any cortical area contributed to poor performance. Now, there are two main
types of disembedding tests: one type consists of realistic figures while the
other has straight lines and geometrical shapes. The idea is to see through the
entanglement. This is a figure–ground problem that confronts visual artists
and observers alike.

In her book about Picasso, Françoise Gilot describes a classic figure–
ground problem that plagues artists (and also provides insight into Cubism
before 1914). Picasso is telling Françoise the following story about his friend
and collaborator Georges Braque:

I remember one evening I arrived at Braque's studio. He was working on a large oval still life with a package of tobacco, a pipe and all the usual paraphernalia of Cubism. I looked at it, drew back and said, "My poor friend, this is dreadful. I see a squirrel in your canvas." Braque said, "That's not possible." I said, "Yes, I know, it's a paranoiac vision, but it so happens that I *see* a squirrel. That canvas is made to be a painting, not an optical illusion. Since people need to see something in it, you want them to see a package of tobacco, a pipe, and the other things you're putting in. But for God's sake get rid of that squirrel." Braque stepped back a few feet and looked carefully and sure enough, he too saw the squirrel, because that kind of paranoiac vision is extremely communicable. Day after day Braque fought that squirrel . . . Finally, after eight or ten days, Braque was able to turn the trick and the canvas again became a package of tobacco, a pipe, a deck of cards, and above all a Cubist painting. So you see how closely we worked together. At that time our work was a kind of laboratory research from which every pretension or individual vanity was excluded.

(Picasso, quoted in Gilot & Lake, 1964, p. 76)

An additional figure can be formed unintentionally from a combination of intentional patterns. This would explain what happened to Braque. It is very difficult to extract one detail given existence of a background full of information. Have you ever had to meet a friend in a crowded restaurant, bar, classroom, or concert-hall? Picking out the one face is not an easy task. Visual search mechanisms suffer from interference by the presence of a multitude of visual information. The attention system is required to inhibit the excess visual load. Subconscious mechanisms are at work in the disembedding process: do they influence our perception of the whole composition? On some level they must do so since perception means filtering irrelevant information and the brain must decide what is irrelevant. In viewing art works, what we see typically is the whole, not the details. If we paid attention to brush strokes we would not see the whole design.

Research has revealed some underlying brain mechanisms in visual disembedding. Patients with unilateral focal damage in the left and right hemispheres were administered a hidden figures test developed by Ghent. The test consisted of seeing overlapping common figures and the task was to identify each figure in the entangled array (De Renzi, Faglioni, & Scotti, 1969). The results showed that both left and right hemisphere patients performed worse than control subjects. Another study measuring the performance of left and right hemisphere damaged patients on the same type of Ghent hidden figures test revealed that patients with damage in posterior regions of the brain performed worse than those patients whose damage was in frontal regions (Masure & Tzavaras, 1976). Moreover, given damaged posterior areas, patients with left damage performed much slower than those with right hemisphere damage. When hidden figures tests consisting of geometrical figures were used on groups of neurological patients with hemispheric damage, the investigators found that those with left hemisphere damage who also had aphasic language disturbances performed particularly poorly (Russo & Vignolo, 1967; Teuber & Weinstein, 1956). Indeed, severity of the language disturbance had a particularly detrimental effect on test performance (Russo & Vignolo, 1967). In all, the fact that deficits are seen after damage to either hemisphere suggests that such disembedding tasks tap at least two perceptual abilities: one is right hemisphere-dependent and relies on visuo-spatial cognition and the other is left hemisphere-dependent and relies on detailed, analytic, and piecemeal cognition.

Finding that a perceptual task consisting of non-verbal material is sensitive to damage in the left hemisphere was surprising, given left hemisphere specialization in language-related deficits. One would initially think that disembedding requires solely a spatial skill, the type that depends on right hemisphere specialization. Additional evidence for hemispheric superiority in disembedding was tested in two complete commissurotomy patients on the Embedded Figures Test devised by Spreen and Benton (1969); the results revealed left hemisphere superiority (E. Zaidel, 1978). This test requires tracing with a pencil a designated geometrical figure embedded in a complex design. Similar results were obtained on another test where real-life scenes are shown: Using the Visual Closure (actually a disembedding test despite its name) subtest of the Illinois Test of Psycholinguistic Abilities, with the same commissurotomy patients confirmed left hemisphere superiority in disembedding (E. Zaidel, 1979). This subtest consists of five separate realistic pictures, and the task is to point to all the portions where a designated object is located. For both tests a special visual technique was applied, the Z-lens (designed by E. Zaidel, 1975), that allows each hemisphere at a time to scan and view the visual information presented to it. The results obtained with the use of this lens technique are thus both important and revealing about hemispheric specialization.

Figure–ground and visual search in art works

What the background consists of has an effect on the speed with which a figure can be visually isolated. In several experiments it was found that visual search strategies are affected by the relationship of figure and ground. The search process is slowed down substantially when there is great similarity between the target and background (Wolfe, Oliva, Horowitz, Butcher, & Bompas, 2002). The more the ground and figure are alike, the more likely we are to observe difficulty in disembedding. The process of visually extracting a form in a cluttered background is influenced substantially by attention (Wolfe, 1998). In order for the search to be successful, the guiding process has to steer the eyes away from irrelevant features and the cognitive system has to eliminate unnecessary form information. It should be mentioned that there is discussion on whether or not the guiding process, known as preattentive, works in parallel with the cognitive system during the visual search event. Some of the factors in the relationship between figure and ground that are likely to affect speed of visual search and accuracy in disembedding are size of items in the background, their color, shade, form familiarity, texture, orientation, spatial juxtaposition, and context familiarity versus random association.

> If guidance were perfect, search would never be required. Attention would be deployed to the target item, first time, every time. This is roughly what happens in a simple feature search. If the target is a red item and the distractors are green items and all these items are clearly delineated on a blank background, then it will be possible to guide attention to a red target, if it is present, without ever selecting a green distractor.
>
> (Wolfe et al., 2002, p. 3001)

When people visually scan an array, they quickly learn what items are present there so that it is hoped that some could be eliminated from the search to save time. This "knowing the old" notion has been linked to memory, that is, we remember the items we have seen and ruled out as targets of interest. It has been suggested that there is a process of prioritizing what to look at in an array and that there is a sort of visual-attentional "marking" of objects already scanned. In one carefully constructed laboratory experiment, one designed specifically to determine memory's role in this process, the investigators found that subjects re-scanned items and their location in the array, thus memory for the old items was not a major guiding search principle (Olivers, Humphrys, Heinke, & Cooper, 2002). Memory formed during a visual search for a specific target may not be very strong but rather designed to play a minor or collaborative role in identifying targets. It may be a special-purpose type of memory, one heavily subjected to attentional and inhibitory brain processes.

In a segmenting task where rod orientation is demanded, some people are more affected by the nature of the background than by the target rod (see Figure 7.3). This issue, known as field-dependence and field-independence (Witkin, Moore, Goodenough, & Cox, 1977), was discussed in the 1960s and 1970s. The test used to determine the extent to which a person is influenced by the background is the rod-and-frame test. It is used in a dimly lit room. If when viewing a tilted square inside of which there is a single rod the person judges the rod to have the same tilt as the square, when in fact there is a discrepancy, then the person is said to be field-dependent. The field is the background, and it interfered with the orientation judgment of the figure. If, on the other hand, the person can judge the tilt of the rod regardless of the tilt of the frame, then the person is said to be field-independent. The way the subject indicates judgment of the rod's tilt is by aligning it relative to the frame. Now, judgment of line orientation set against a blank background is associated with right hemisphere specialization. Based on a number of

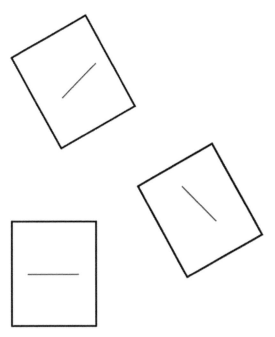

Figure 7.3 Rod-and-frame. In a segmenting task where rod orientation is demanded, some people are more affected by the nature of the frame in the background than by the target rod. This issue is known as field-dependence versus field-independence. The test used to determine the extent to which a person is influenced by the surrounding background is the rod-and-frame test. If when viewing a tilted square inside of which there is a single rod the person judges the rod to have the same tilt as the square, when in fact there is a discrepancy, the person is said to be field-dependent. The assumption is the background (the field) interfered with the orientation judgment of the rod. If, on the other hand, the person can judge the tilt of the rod regardless of the tilt orientation of the frame, then the person is said to be field-independent.

studies, personality-types have been inferred from the susceptibility to the position of the frame. Field-dependent people were found to be attuned to social cues, being interested in people, social situations, open emotionality, and choosing careers that help others. By contrast, field-independent people were said to have diminished sensitivity to others or to social cues, to be less interested in being with others, and to choose careers that emphasize science, math, and impersonal professions. It is likely that those individuals in whom there is strong field-independence are good in right hemisphere tasks since the rod-and-frame test is strongly related to visual-spatial skills (Lezak, 1995). Some research has shown an increase in field-dependence compared to field-independence as people grow older, an outcome consistent with reduced spatial abilities in old age (Spreen & Strauss, 1998).

Global–local, wholes, and details in art works

The visual arts often confront us with complex compositions. In visual arrays where the background itself has a large form, the enclosed details can be hard to detect on first sight. This phenomenon is known as the "global prece-dence" effect. If we see a city's skyline, our perception of it dominates over our perception of the individual buildings (Navon, 1977). We see the forest before the trees. Similarly, at first we see the building not the individual win-dows, nor the balconies, nor the plants on the balconies. Examples of part-wholes (global–local) are shown in Figure 7.4 a, b, c, and d. Not only do we see the global form first, but also the global interferes with our perception of the details that make up the whole. This phenomenon has been repeatedly shown in laboratory experiments. Looking at a painting, our perception is dominated by the whole spatial layout. It is difficult for us to see the details within. With effort and purposeful scanning we overcome the attraction to the conglomerate presentation and in the end do see the local features in the painting. Experts are particularly good at achieving such perception, being guided by their knowledge and expectations to a greater extent than non-experts. Pictorial art forms are multifaceted with respect to wholes and parts, but the whole may be more salient than the parts and thus attract our attention at the outset.

In neuropsychology, the distinction between the whole and its parts was first discussed in the context of patients with unilateral damage who drew real life objects in distinctly different ways depending on the laterality of damage. Those with left-sided damage drew global features, emphasizing the contour and layout while excluding the details normally encompassed within. Patients with right hemisphere damage drew the same objects with the details within the global layout but left out the global frame (McFie &

Figure 7.4 a, b, c, d Global–local perception. Several illustrations of the global–local, whole–detail issue are shown here. What is the first thing you see when you look at the letter *A*? Do you see the small *W*s? In contrast, upon viewing the letter *W*, people typically see the *W*, not the small *A*s, because global (the whole) perception dominates over local (the details) perception. And with "art", do you see the word "art" or the small ducks in the letters? In which one of the "art" words are the ducks less visible? The visual arts often confront us with complex compositions. In visual arrays where the background itself has a large form, the enclosed details can be hard to detect on first sight. This phenomenon is known as the "global precedence" effect. If we see a city's skyline, our perception of it dominates over our perception of the individual buildings. We see the forest before the trees. Looking at a painting, our perception is dominated by the whole spatial layout. It is difficult for us to see the details within. With effort and purposeful scanning we overcome the attraction to the conglomerate presentation and in the end do see the local features in the painting.

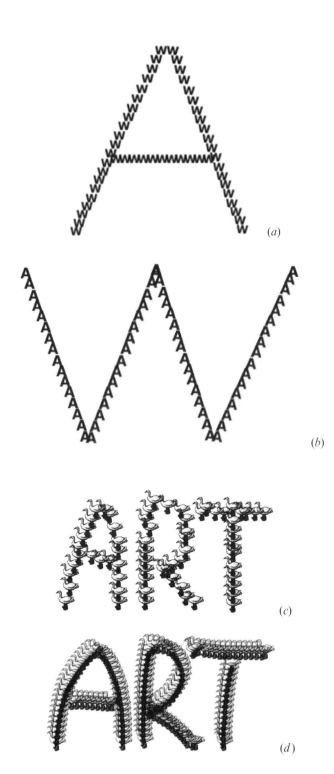

(a)

(b)

(c)

(d)

Zangwill, 1960; Paterson & Zangwill, 1944; Warrington & James, 1966). Many subsequent studies have shown that the right hemisphere specializes in wholes whereas the left hemisphere specializes in details. Since the early 1980s or so there has been much discussion about global–local perception in the cognitive and neuropsychological literature. The factors that seem to have an effect on processing global–local and influence the outcome are visual angle, relative size, perceptual salience, and number of local units. Moreover, hemispheric effects have been uncovered in designs that incorporate global–local composites: the right hemisphere is reportedly superior to the left in processing the global features whereas the left specializes in processing the local features. The right posterior temporo-parietal region controls global perception while the homologous area in the left hemisphere controls perception of local perception (Robertson & Lamb, 1991). By and large, numerous studies on normal subjects have confirmed the hemispheric asymmetry findings, as have fMRI and physiological experiments (Evert & Kmen, 2003; Yovel, Yovel, & Levy, 2001). Together, the behavioral and anatomical results suggest that global features can interfere with local details but that within the local details there is global–local dissociation as well.

Why do global features dominate our perception? One answer lies in the size of the visual field that is occupied by the global aspects of the array. Some of it is outside foveal vision (see Chapter 3). Global features activate several visual systems, including those that are active in subcortical areas, not just in the primary visual system. The subcortical systems are sensitive to global features and are not sensitive to detailed, focused elements in the environment. They are designed to take in as much as possible of the visual world in order to detect deviations within it such as sudden irregular motion, light–dark changes, and motion that can potentially signal danger. The global array, then, may be linked to biologically old visual mechanisms meant to alert and thus protect us. Speed in transfer of global information to the left hemisphere, in order to engage the left in attention to the local features is critical. We could speculate that the rate of interhemispheric transfer may be asymmetrical, with right hemisphere information about global arrays being transferred much faster than the left hemisphere's information to the right about the details. This is a scenario that is currently difficult to ascertain but it is an appealing notion.

Unconscious influences on perception of art works

It is widely accepted in cognitive psychology that meaningful interaction with the world reflects a match between what is already mentally stored and what is newly sensed and perceived (Zaidel, 1994). Painting landscapes, the human figure, or still life, all draw upon what was already experienced in the artist's mind. For the observer, looking at a painting for the first time there is a similar interaction between the visual input and the stored collection of experiences. A similar process is underway when listening to a piece of music for the fist time, or watching a film, reading a story, and so on. The mind becomes modified with new experiences and the alteration occurs without conscious awareness. What we look at is subject to constraints imposed by what we have already experienced and retained in long-term memory. Similar constraints are imposed on the expressing artist.

The first analysis of subconscious influences on art production was by Freud (1947, first published in 1910); he analyzed Leonardo da Vinci's *Mona Lisa* painting (Blum, 2001). Observers interact with a painting on multiple levels, conscious and unconscious, their judgment summing the interlocking influences of these awareness levels (Leader, 2002). The same would be true for all forms of art expression. (If previous non-art experience plays a major role in art enjoyment, pleasure, cognitive appraisal, acceptance, and understanding, then the typical perceiver of art is not a completely naïve observer.) In an experiment, Seitz and Watanabe (2003) show that when an unconscious event becomes paired with a conscious stimulus, the unconscious/conscious pair is nevertheless learned and remembered. Conscious judgment can be affected by unconscious perception, and vice versa. The unconscious effect on the brain can be seen in experiments that tap subliminal perception; that is, when we perceive something without our subjective awareness (Zaidel, Hugdahl, & Johnsen, 1995b). On a physiological level, the brain's reaction to stimuli perceived unconsciously is highly similar to consciously perceived stimuli (Shevrin, 2001). One particular type of physiological brain wave known as the P200 has been elicited for unconscious perception, although its amplitude is smaller than for conscious perception. The very presence of P200, however, is physiological evidence for neurally processed information. Even more interesting is the recent demonstration that when a sudden event occurs, at least in the laboratory, of which the subject is unaware, a unique wave response is recorded, namely the P300 (Bernat, Shevrin, & Snodgrass, 2001). This type of evoked potential is elicited by rare, novel, unique events and not associated with sensory experience. Thus, finding that unconsciously we have brain reactions similar to consciously perceived information is important for understanding the influence of everything that is present in a visual array. There is even P300 evidence that unconscious and the conscious cognitive systems interact: the amplitude of the P300 wave changes when the experimental stimulus becomes partially available to the conscious system, and the cognitive process requires an interaction between unconscious levels and conscious levels (Bernat et al., 2001).

The hippocampal complex is widely accepted as a critical neuroanatomical structure for memory consolidation, particularly for explicit memory (Nadel & Bohbot, 2001; Nadel & Moscovitch, 2001), and asymmetrical functions are associated with the hippocampus in each hemisphere (Beardsworth & Zaidel, 1994; Milner, 1958, 1968). Some studies have shown that the structure is involved in unconscious perception as well. A good example is an fMRI study in which subjects were exposed to subliminal stimuli without their conscious knowledge (Henke et al., 2003). The experimenters observed activation in the hippocampus, bilaterally. There is also evidence from neuropathology and neuronal density counts for a relationship between hippocampus and implicit memory (Zaidel, Esiri, & Beardsworth, 1998). The implication is that exposure to external stimulation can trigger memory formations over which we do not have conscious control but which can influence our decisions, observations and assessments of art works, as well as production of art works at some future time. Indeed, artists are not always able to explain explicitly why they have chosen to depict what they depicted in the particular way that they did. Unconscious memory likely plays a role in their compositions, and this is not easily available to verbal explanations.

Right hemisphere specialization, representation of space, and art history

Visual understanding of depth and space extends to building up mental images from fragmented realistic figures in order to match with pre-existing stored knowledge of the figures (Corballis, 1994; Sperry, 1974; Warrington & Taylor, 1973). In the majority of people, the right hemisphere specializes in spatial perception, in memory for the topography in which we navigate, graphic displays of layouts, the relative positions of the parts in the whole, in mentally visualizing physical space, and obtaining different perspective views of the same object or topography through mental manipulation of the mind's images (De Renzi, 1982; McCarthy & Warrington, 1990). Examples of right hemisphere-type tasks are shown in Figures 7.5, 7.6, and 7.7. Damage in the right parietal lobe is frequently associated with topographical agnosia – the loss of knowledge of previously familiar routes and surroundings extending to personal and extra-personal space (De Renzi, 1982). The inability to copy a Necker Cube drawing (Figure 7.5), which represents three-dimensional depth, is commonly seen in patients with right parietal damage. Assuming that visual artists generate complete images of their compositions in their mind's eye and that they depend on visuo-spatial cognition a great deal, Winner and Casey (1992) studied adult artists' ability to generate mental

Figure 7.5 The Necker Cube. This representation of depth relies largely on intact right hemisphere functionality. Neurological patients with right hemisphere damage in the parietal lobe commonly are unable to copy the Necker cube correctly, leaving out diagonal lines that characterize the three-dimensionality feature. The problem lies in the inability to understand the spatial representation rather than in the motoric execution of the copying.

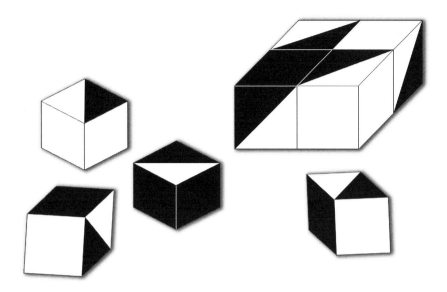

Figure 7.6 Kohs Blocks. Being able to create a three-dimensional model with these blocks from a two-dimensional diagram taps the visuo-spatial capabilities of the right hemisphere.

images and measured their visuo-spatial skills. They found that their subjects were superior in many visual skills and some mental imagery tasks, but that these skills were not much higher than in math and science students. The difference between the two groups of subjects was in verbal skills, where the artists showed a large discrepancy between the visual and verbal (low performance on the verbal skills) and the other group did not.

Spatial perception is not all there is to visual art. What distinguishes cultures that exercise veridical representation of space in pictures from those that do not is essentially a distinction in artistic style: whereas European artists have from the end of the thirteenth century until the end of the nineteenth century been interested in depicting as closely as possible the real visual world, and society valued such depictions (for a variety of reasons), artists in most other cultures depicted compositions consisting of what they saw plus what they knew conceptually (Kemp, 1990) – hence, the expressed conceptualization and symbolism in the art of East Asia, Africa, Native America, aboriginal Australia, and in most of Western twentieth century art. The same non-Western artists probably could, if given the cultural opportunity, produce pictorial representations of space. Chinese and Japanese art works are replete with human and animal figures shown from different perspective views other than just sideways even while representation of depth of the physical environment is largely missing (see further discussion on Chinese

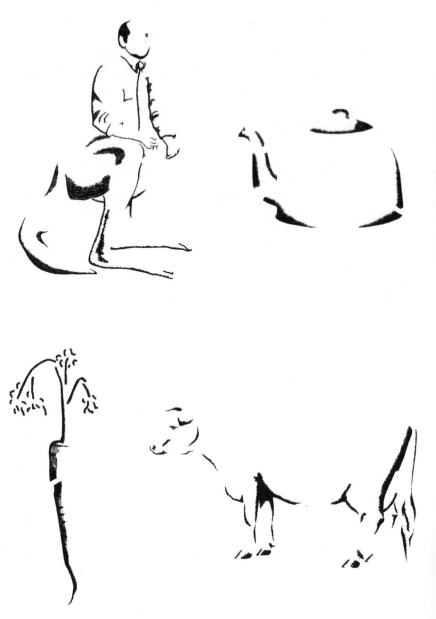

Figure 7.7 Being able to complete these figures in the mind's eye taps right hemisphere specialization. The ambiguous figure on the upper left is a chimera of a man and a kangaroo. The reason it is difficult to identify is that the mental dictionary of pictorial objects includes previously seen objects. New forms such as man/kangaroo are not stored in that dictionary. Target figures in a visual array are sometimes partially occluded. In visual closure what is required is identifying the whole from only partial information. This can be accomplished by mentally "closing" the gaps in the contour of the

art later in the chapter). Similarly, prehistoric cave art in Europe shows accurate physical depictions of animals including the use of depth cues such as foreshortening, overlap, three-quarter views, and color patches. All of these examples suggest the intact functioning of the right hemisphere's specialization in spatial cognition.

Depth perception in pictures

Stereoscopic visual information of the world provides the most accurate view of depth and three-dimensional space. It is also possible to get information about depth space through monocular vision, but such information can be less accurate. However, since we learn how the world looks from babyhood onward, we can still see depth in the real world through a single eye.

With two-dimensional pictorial space we obtain visual information about depicted space through several cues, including texture gradient, aerial views, shadows, linear perspective, overlap, relative size, and foreshortening (Kalat, 2002). Texture gradient is where the farthest elements in a scene are depicted with density that is greater than the closest elements; the bunching of the details implies distance. Objects in the scene that are bathed with light imply closeness relative to those that are covered with a shadow. The ones in the distance are fuzzier and darker than close-up objects. The technique of introducing the use of shadow in art is credited to Leonardo da Vinci (1452–1519) (Shlain, 1991). He observed in his writings that artists should be sensitive to the effects of light under different lighting conditions: diffused light and horizon light, light emanating from a specific source, such as the sun, light reflected off objects, and light that can be seen through it, i.e. translucent. He also spoke of shadow as being of different shades. Another two-dimensional cue that mimics depth is linear perspective, that is, convergence of a line of sight with another parallel line, even when the other line is the bottom edge of the canvas gives the impression of distance and depth. Overlap is when interposing figures give the impression of the figure on top being closer to the viewer and the partially hidden figure being farther from the viewer. Relative size means that larger sized objects are interpreted by the viewer as being closer than smaller sized objects, which are interpreted as being far.

---

figure, spaces interposed between the fragments. A standard test is the Street Completion Test. It contains fragmented figures and the task is to identify the whole from mentally aligning the fragments together. Partial information is not created by overlap, superimposition, concealment, and so on, as is the case in embedded and hidden figures. Rather, entire single figures are shown but in separate components that need to be put together in the mind's eye. There are different levels and extents of fragmentations. The right hemisphere is considered to be superior to the left in visual closure (De Renzi, 1982; De Renzi & Spinnler, 1966; Nebes, 1971; Sperry, 1968, 1974, 1980; Warrington & Taylor, 1973; Wasserstein, Zappulla, Rosen, & Gerstman, 1984; Wasserstein, Zappulla, Rosen, Gerstman, & Rock, 1987).

Foreshortening aids the impression in the viewer of rotation in space, and consequently in relaying the message of depth. Through these various illusionistic techniques, artists have been able to convey space, depth, and realism.

The interpretation of real space in planar space stems from experience with the seen world where we have learned that faraway objects are fuzzier than close-up objects, that the closer an object is to us the bigger it appears, and the reverse is true when the object is far (see Figure 7.8). Our observation of shadows enables us to interpret pictorial representations that use bright versus dark pigments. Context is also a feature of the seen three-dimensional world that enables us to implement the various depth cues present in pictures.

Convergent and linear perspective in the history of art

A consistent art trend that began at the end of the thirteenth century, with the early start of the Renaissance in Italy, was the emphasis on illusionist pictures in which a unified perspective point, including showing receding horizon lines in the background was implemented (Bellosi, 1981). In addition, at that historical turning point, single pictorial scenes started to show an event and an occurrence frozen in time. The eyes of the viewer now focused on a single

Figure 7.8 Convergent railroad lines and linear perspectives, taking into account the way things look at a distance versus close-up, is what interested artists from the very start of the Renaissance in Italy. Convergent and vanishing point perspectives, which seem to be reduced to a tiny point in the distance, where objects can no longer be seen with normal sight, enabled artists to depict three-dimensional space on canvas. This approach has become the norm in Western art.

pictorial theme rather than on multiple events, as was the case in the preceding historical period. To enable the new conceptualization in paintings, European artists applied highly worked out geometrical representations of space through linear, convergent perspective. Indeed, the vanishing point perspective was introduced and developed further through mathematical and geometrical formulas by many Renaissance artists (Panofsky, 1991).

The art historian Martin Kemp (1990) suggests that acceptance of visual perspective with its closeness to the appearance of reality in Western art stemmed from prevalent cultural and religious realization, namely that how things really appear is all right and desirable. The latter need not interfere with devotion to God.

A key stimulus in determining that a precisely proportional system was used, rather than the highly effective but essentially non-mathematical method of Jan van Eyck in the Netherlands was the annexing of classical aesthetic values, particularly the proportional system of architectural design and town planning. By contrast, mediaeval surveying or optics can be seen to provide available resources, but these resources only became relevant to the painter within a framework of new assumptions about the functions of what we call art. The fact that Brunelleschi's demonstrations stood so far outside the normal function of painted panels helps explain the delay in the implementation of his methods in a standard context. It took artists of real insight, Donatello and Masaccio, to extend the mental ends of their art so that the new means became accessible. In a sense, the whole of this study has been concerned with the legacy of their insight, as successive generations of artists, adjusted the parameters of art in such a way as to convert varied aspects of optical science into grist for their mills. The theme has its own special history, not in the sense that it is autonomous or has a uniquely privileged value in explaining the works of art, but in as far as it came to be recognized as an essential and codifiable component in the artist's intellectual and visual equipment. This recognition and codification was, in keeping with my gross hypothesis, characteristic of Western art during the period 1400 to about 1880 at a level, which was not shared with other periods and cultures.

(Kemp, 1990, pp. 335–336)

In Western art, realistic pictorial representations made their major beginnings when the vanishing point principle was discovered (Panofsky, 1991). The interest in linear perspective became an intellectual pursuit, opened up new possibilities for experimentation in art, and initiated an approach that applied drawing skills with systematic pictorial logic and incorporated detailed analytic thinking. Figuring out the desired perspective from a vanishing point principle required planning and analytic thinking as well. A single converging point on some imaginary horizontal line receives all the lines of sight from a particular viewpoint. In a given painting, there may be only a single point while in others there may be double or triple vanishing points, all arranged on the horizontal plane. Prior to the development of this perspective, depth was depicted through axial perspective, a technique in which parallel lines converge on multiple points along the vertical axis.

This illusionistic approach assumed that art is aesthetic when it represents the world as realistically and figuratively as possible. In art in which there is dearth of space and depth emphasis, indeed often ignored, other considerations are applied without sacrificing aesthetic reaction. Time, for example, is important in Chinese art and the way this is depicted is by avoiding emphasis on fixed, stationary objects; geometrical representation of depth implies a fixed, rigid, and static world (Thorp & Ellis, 2001). The permanence of geological forms notwithstanding, humans interact with them through fluid life experiences, an interaction that is heavily embedded in temporal sequences (Barnhart, 1997; Cahill, 1997). Chinese artists must rely on spatial cognition nevertheless. While the intact functioning of the right hemisphere in spatial rendering is essential, this alone should not imply that all other elements in artistic productions, particularly those requiring analytic strategies and deliberation, are subserved by this cerebral hemisphere alone.

Summary

Some aspects of visual art have been gleaned from non-artists with neurological damage through the use of standard neuropsychological tests and experiments, and some experiments in normal subjects. Insights into the neuropsychology of art require consideration of art-relevant features straddling neuropsychology and cognitive psychology, particularly when data from physiological experiments are available. Those include perception, cognition, and memory. Our basic knowledge of the shape of things in the world is based on perceptual constancy, object size, and orientation. Canonical views of objects and scenes reflect perceptual constancy and play an important role in art making. Unilateral damage and pictorial object recognition suggest that the brain stores structural information about objects in the real world, and represents them as concepts or schemas. Hemispheric asymmetries in canonical perspective views suggest a continuum of representation in the brain where the right hemisphere has "rigid" concepts of objects compared to "flexible" concepts in the left hemisphere. Such a continuum has implications for creativity in the visual arts. Disembedding, the isolating, or segmenting, of a figure from a confusing background in pictures, has a left hemisphere cognitive component. In viewing paintings and other visual arts, global–local, wholes and details, functions enter into the visual search process. Global or whole features are detected earlier than the local or detail features. In addition to conscious understanding of art, by both the artist and the viewer, unconscious memory likely plays a significant role in compositions and interpretation.

The invention of convergent perspective provided artists with a tool for depicting depth and space two-dimensionally. Depicting realism in painting could be drawing heavily on right hemisphere cognition. But dearth of depth depictions in paintings, as in ancient Egyptian art or classic Chinese or Japanese art, should not be interpreted as lack of right hemisphere involvement in the production or perception of the art.

Further readings

Arnheim, R. (1974). *Art and visual perception: A psychology of the creative eye.* Los Angeles: University of California Press.

Bearden, R., & Holty, C. (1969). *The painter's mind: A study of the relations of structure and space in painting.* New York: Crown Publishers.

Chalupa, L. M., & Werner, J. S. (Eds.). (2003). *The visual neurosciences.* Cambridge, MA: MIT Press.

Goldstein, E. B. (2001). *Sensation and perception* (6th ed.). New York: Wadsworth.

Hockney, D. (2001). *Secret Knowledge: Rediscovering the techniques of the Old Masters.* New York: Penguin Putnam.

Johnson, P. (2003). *Art: A new history.* New York: HarperCollins.

Kemp, M. (1990). *The science of art.* New Haven, CT: Yale University Press.

Panofsky, E. (1991). *Perspective as symbolic form.* New York: Zone Books.

Shlain, L. (1991). *Art and physics.* New York: William Morrow.

Westen, D. (2003). *Psychology: Brain, behavior, and culture.* New York: John Wiley.

Zakia, R. D. (2002). *Perception and imaging* (2nd ed.). Boston, MA and Oxford: Focal Press.

8 Neuropsychological considerations of drawing and seeing pictures

Introduction

Pictures are commonly used as stimuli in neuropsychological tests. Since left hemisphere damage often leads to language impairment, pictures are used to assess the extent of impairment through such non-verbal means. Similarly, damage in the right hemisphere can result in loss of previous knowledge, of familiar faces, objects, maps, and spatial layouts, so pictures are used to determine what knowledge is preserved. In a wide range of neurological brain disorders there is no apictoria (a selective loss of the ability to understand any pictorial representation). With visual object agnosia there may be an impairment in deriving the meaning of pictured objects but the same patient may not have problems with recognizing pictured faces, pictures of scenes, of geometrical shapes, or of nonsense shapes. Primates, birds, and rats can be trained to respond to pictures. But, unlike humans, they cannot produce them. The production may be unique but the communicative value of pictures, on a certain level, is not unique to humans.

Meaningful symbolic drawings by non-artists can be executed in ways that convey concepts, knowledge, past memory, and emotions. Simple, figurative line drawings with colored pencils were produced by a 70-year-old man with probable fronto-temporal dementia, verified by CT scan, conveying appropriate events in his life, even while he was unable to communicate through language or overt emotions (Thomas Anterion et al., 2002). He was not an artist; his occupation was working in metallurgy. At that time he was in the end stages of the disease; his symptoms consisted of mutism, apathy, hyperorality, lack of volition, poor language comprehension, flat affect, and lack of appropriate responses. His wife presented him with colored pencils and he picked up drawing. For the next six months he drew intensively on a daily basis. The drawings were simple, resembling those of young children. He depicted faces, houses with appropriate depth perspective, landscapes, and objects. The drawings sometimes depicted events from long ago in his past. Many were self-portraits. Importantly, around that time his mother died and in response to the news, he drew a church as well as a death head (four bones sticking out of a live face). His wife reported that he did not seem to react behaviorally upon receiving the news, and yet he understood the message well as evidenced by appropriate drawings depicting concepts associated with death. What is the significance of preservation of symbolic communication through drawings? That this ability was spared while specialized functions such as language, emotional social skills were absent suggests the obvious inference, namely, that intact regions in the brain, particularly the parietal lobes and posterior temporal lobes mediated the drawings. Other brain regions may have been involved as well, of course. However, symbolic communication of concepts, knowledge of the world, emotions, and personal memory, was spared here and that is not a function subserved by language specialized regions alone (see also Chapter 4).

Drawings by professional artists with aphasia address the issue of language and art production. Dissociation between drawing and language is demonstrated in professional artists who suffered left hemisphere stroke and aphasia (see Chapter 2). One such case is of an 82-year-old art professor who suffered from Wernicke's aphasia. Despite the inability to communicate verbally, he was nevertheless able to draw cartoon strips (Gourevitch, 1967). Another case is that of French graphic artist, Sabadel (Pillon, Signoret, van Eeckhout, & Lhermitte, 1980). Following a left-sided stroke, he had severe aphasia and right hemiparessis. Not long afterward and still experiencing aphasic impairments he began to draw again. He had to train himself to use his left hand. But the realistic objects that he managed to depict, he was unable to name correctly. Eventually, he went on to draw a whole series of cartoons depicting his life in a published book. The dissociation between acquired language deficits and spared creative artistic skills supports localization of language functions in the brain without directly resolving the issue of functional localization for art production.

Handedness in artists

At the heart of neuropsychological research is hemispheric specialization. Starting with the middle of the nineteenth century it became clear through systematic study that the human brain is organized according to the principle of hemispheric specialization, that is, that the left hemisphere mainly controls language functions and specialization in visuo-spatial functions is controlled mainly by the right hemisphere. The emergence of handedness in humans is linked to the development of cerebral lateralization of language, and, particularly, the evolutionary expansion of the frontal cortex (Ambrose, 2001). The pattern now is estimated to be 90 percent right-handed and 10 percent left-handed, across all cultures (Annett, 2002). This ratio is genetically determined and assumed to have existed as long ago as biblical times, and even earlier as can be seen from handprints on cave walls and rock shelters. There is consistency in hand use after ages 3 to 5 years. The relationship between language dominance and handedness originally came from Brenda Milner's studies in the Montreal Neurological Institute in which neurological patients experiencing intractable temporal lobe epilepsy undergo the Wada test (intracarotid sodium amytal injection resulting in hemispheric anesthesia) prior to unilateral anterior temporal lobectomy (Branch, Milner, & Rasmussen, 1964; Milner, 1958). It was determined that 96 percent of right-handers have left hemisphere specialization for language, 4 percent have right hemisphere specialization; with left-handers, 70 percent have language in the left hemisphere as well, 15 percent in the right hemisphere and 15 percent bilaterally. Inferring to the general population, the majority of people, including left-handers, have left hemisphere dominance for language. But within the group of left-handers there is greater variability than in right-handers possibly because left-handedness is not always inherited and can sometimes arise because of perinatal trauma that compromises the right hand area in the left hemisphere (Knecht et al., 2000, 2002).

A large survey study by Philip Lanthony in 1995 estimates that the rate of left-handedness among established and exhibited artists is 2.8 percent (Lanthony, 1995). This is way below the estimated left-handedness rate of 10 percent in the general population. The study consisted of works by 500 painters. The direction of hatchings were analyzed. Hatchings made by a right-handed artist typically proceed from upper right to lower left of the canvas, whereas those made by a left-handed artist go from upper left to lower right. (The hatchings have to be consistent across many paintings by the same artist, since some artists switch the painting hand in order to introduce some sort of change.) Another method was to look at photographs of artists in the act of painting. Typically, when artists make self-portraits, they base the image of themselves as reflected in a mirror. The painting hand may be reversed and thus handedness cannot be determined with certainty. Thus, self-portraits were not included in the study. Another source about handedness in artists is published reports, and this information was researched and included in Lanthony's study. Some of the artists determined to be left-handed were Raoul Dufy, M. C. Escher, Hans Holbein, Paul Klee, Leonardo, and Alexandre Regnault. Some of the artists reputed previously to be left-handed but who in fact had been found to be right-handed were Albrecht Dürer, Raphael, Michelangelo, and Picasso. In sum, there are many more right-handed than left-handed artists.

Drawings and the parietal lobes

The notion that the right hemisphere specializes in interpreting visual input in gestalt configurations was first inferred by British neuropsychologists (McFie & Zangwill, 1960; Paterson & Zangwill, 1944; Warrington & James, 1966). They asked their patients with lesions in the right parietal and occipital lobes to draw a bicycle from memory, and discovered that they omitted the contour frame, emphasizing instead the details of bicycle parts. The parts were organized in a recognizable configuration. In contrast, their patients with left hemisphere damage in the homologous regions drew the contour frame of the bicycle while omitting many of the parts contained within a bicycle. This suggested to Paterson and Zangwill (1944), and later to other neuropsychologists, that the right hemisphere stores global and gestalt concepts of the world while the left stores details. The damage in the right hemisphere allowed the expression of the intact left hemisphere while damage in the left hemisphere allowed the expression of the right, so went the thinking at the time. They proposed the idea of piecemeal and analytic thinking in the left hemisphere and gestalt thinking in the right hemisphere. The important lesson from the British experiments was that both hemispheres could control the act of drawing, albeit in asymmetrically characteristic ways. It was not as if the right brain-damaged patients lost all ability to draw, and that the left-damaged group drew perfectly complete figures. Subsequently, confirmation for this distinction between the human cerebral hemispheres was observed in studies with complete commissurotomy patients in Roger Sperry's psychobiology laboratory in Caltech, Pasadena, California (Levy-Agresti & Sperry, 1968; Nebes, 1971; Zaidel & Sperry, 1973). That work added the further characterization of cardinality, logical, and step-wise thinking to the cognitive style of the left hemisphere. Note that the distinction between the hemispheres was not along the verbal versus non-verbal cognitive axis.

Drawings in neurological patients

Kirk and Kertesz (1993) investigated the drawings of 125 stroke patients with focal, unilateral lesions. They administered the drawing subtest of the Western Aphasia Battery (WAB) to 78 left-sided cases and 47 right-sided cases. Cortical and subcortical damaged patients were identified. They were shown samples of six figures, including a cube, circle, square, clock, tree, and a house, and asked to draw each one after the samples were removed. In addition, the patients were asked to draw a picture of a person. All drawings were scored independently by two raters (one of the raters was an artist while the other was not). The results revealed a significant difference between the two patient groups.

> While patients with right hemisphere lesions displayed neglect and impairment of spatial relations between components of drawings, left-sided strokes resulted in simplified drawings with fewer lines and fewer details. Drawings by patients with left hemisphere lesions also tended to be more tremulous and to be displaced toward the left side of the page. Overall impairment was significantly greater in the left hemisphere patients.
>
> (Kirk & Kertesz, 1993, p. 63)

This finding is consistent with findings by others (McFie & Zangwill, 1960; Paterson & Zangwill, 1944). The tremulous effect was ascribed to presence of hemiparessis in many cases with the left-sided lesions and the need to use the left hand for drawing in these right-handed individuals. What was interesting in their study, and something that was investigated previously, is that they did not find a significant difference between those with cortical versus those with subcortical damage, regardless of laterality of lesions.

Using the same modified administration of the WAB subtest, analysis of the drawings by thirty-eight patients with Alzheimer's disease (AD) has revealed dissociation between language and memory functions (Kirk & Kertesz, 1991). That is, while those functions were severely impaired, drawings of the seven figures were not. However, compared to a control group, AD patients were worse. The AD patients' drawings were characterized by poor spatial relations and distorted perspective. There was, in addition, a reduced number of angles compared to the control group. Kirk and Kertesz (1991) noted that distorted perspective is seen in both left-sided and right-sided stroke patients. The simplified drawings of the AD patients and the spatial relations deficits are not unlike the drawings of left-sided and right-sided stroke patients, respectively.

Hemi-neglect and attention

As is widely known in neuropsychology, hemi-neglect of left half of space is seen mostly in patients with right parietal-occipital damage (also with right thalamus damage); hemi-neglect is very rarely seen in patients with left hemisphere damage. The neglect consists of inattention to left personal or extra-personal space. One factor that seems to correlate with speed of recovery is presence of insight regarding the disorder. Federico Fellini, for example, did have insight into his neglect (see Chapter 2). The neuroanatomical underpinning for such insight is not yet clear.

An emphasis on functional neuroimaging techniques since the mid-1990s has revealed important clues that might explain the relationship between hemi-neglect, knowledge of the topography, and spatial perception. Specific areas within the right parietal lobe may be under the modulated control of attention in order to direct eye movements to environmental layouts, not only for perceiving new information, but also in order to compare against previously stored layouts (Shipp, 2004). Such control facilitates the pick-up of information from the surroundings, both personal and extra-personal. Parietal neurons may be particularly sensitive to the action of attention (Behrmann, Geng, & Shomstein, 2004). Knowing how to get from one place to another requires systematic perception of the environment, accumulation of data, consolidation of the information, and encoding and storing for future use. This should apply to both personal and extra-personal space. It would seem that where to look is controlled by cortical events in the right parietal lobe. In addition, it is highly likely that there is a dedicated neural circuitry between the right parietal lobe and the posterior hippocampus on the same side (Maguire, Valentine, Wilding, & Kapur, 2003). There is MRI evidence from professional route-finders and navigators such as taxi drivers in London, professionals who need to undergo continuing education training in navigation in order to renew their licenses, that the volume of the posterior right hippocampus is strongly correlated with years of professional driving experience (Maguire et al., 2000), the larger the size, the greater the experience.

The left parietal lobe is also involved in attentional mechanisms concerning the environment (Assad, 2003). The attention sensitive neurons may be tuned to the details in the environment, not to the global layout. In fMRI studies, the right superior and inferior parietal regions were selectively active in transient relocation of attention, while the neurons in the left parietal lobe, in the intraparietal sulcus, were selectively active in sustained attention (exactly what we do when we attend to details, examining them). The same region was found to be maximally active when subjects were required to switch quickly between two visual tasks, and this result suggests that the left lobe is involved in dictating when to switch between tasks as a function of the information that comes in (Assad, 2003; Platt & Glimcher, 1999). The importance of these findings is not that specific attention dedicated regions were found in the parietal lobes, but rather that regions that are part of the attention circuitry are active in the parietal lobes, asymmetrically so depending on the task at hand.

Pictorial scenes: simultanagnosia

A typical pictorial scene consists of several objects and figures positioned in a way that denotes an interaction that can give rise to a meaning, a single theme. The pictured objects are like words in a sentence. Alone the words would mean one thing but together they form a grammatical sentence that has a particular meaning. The inability to derive the theme of a scene is known in neuropsychology and neurology as simultanagnosia (Levine & Calvanio, 1978). Patients suffering from this disorder are nevertheless able to name single objects appearing in the scene. Their difficulty lies in the inability to understand the whole picture. The difficulty does not lie in blindness, paralysis of gaze, or difficulties in speaking. The first published classification of the symptoms of simultanagnosia was by Wolpert, in 1924. Since Wolpert's publication, faulty attention has been commonly blamed as the cause of simultanagnosia because the patient fixates gaze on each pictured object at a time, instead of rapidly taking in the whole display (Wolpert, 1924). Clearly, however, attention cannot explain the inability to relate the meaning of the picture as a whole.

If neurological patients do see single objects in the scene why are they unable to relate them to each other in their mind's eye, or in their conceptual system, given their co-occurrence, their juxtaposition in the pictorial layout? Surely if they have already seen an object, identified it and moved on to the next object they would remember what they have seen. In daily life we frequently see disparate objects and later connect them in our minds into a single meaningful unit. No global short-term memory impairments have been documented in simultanagnosia cases. The crux of the difficulty lies in the inability to form the theme; that in essence implies an inability to derive meaning. This is not unlike the inability to get the theme of a long sentence, a paragraph, a literary composition, or a published scientific paper. The failure may reflect an inability to integrate a particular kind of visual information, complex scenes. In unilateral cases, the left hemisphere is typically damaged. Rarely do we hear of right hemisphere damage alone giving rise to simultan-agnosia. The localization within the left hemisphere is the junction of the posterior temporal lobe and anterior region of the occipital lobe (Kinsbourne & Warrington, 1962; Levine & Calvanio, 1978). (This is reviewed in Farah, 1990.)

The question of memory and simultanagnosia was tested early on by Kinsbourne and Warrington (1962) because of their supposition that there is a refractory period during which disparate objects blend into a unified theme. They discovered that there is an element of "memory" in the simultanagnosia problem since the length of time that it takes to unite objects in the mind was longer in these cases than in control subjects; this is regardless of whether they viewed two related objects, or two geometrical figures, simultaneously or sequentially. It would appear that in order to derive the meaning of multi-object scenes, the details need to be perceived rather rapidly, because taking in one object at a time slows the integration process. Contact was made between the individual objects in the scene and the semantic system where knowledge of the meaning of objects is stored. What has gone awry is the further higher-level unification into a single concept. Left hemisphere cognition, then, is particularly critical for integration of pictorial information into a meaningful entity.

Scenes, eye movements, and the frontal eye fields

Two areas in the frontal lobes controlling exploratory eye movements are the frontal eye field and the supplementary eye field (see review by Paus, 1996). The frontal eye field controls exploratory eye movements in search of specific targets (Fukushima, 2003; O'Shea & Walsh, 2004). The neuroanatomical area in each hemisphere involves Brodmann's 8 (labeled frontal eye fields in Figure 1.4), situated in the precentral sulcus (and also possibly Brodmann's area 6, labeled premotor area on Figure 1.4). The supplementary eye field area, first discovered in monkeys (Schlag & Schlag-Rey, 1987) is localized in the dorsomedial prefrontal region known as the supplementary motor cortex and has been localized to the superior portion of the paracentral sulcus (Grosbras, Lobel, Van de Moortele, LeBihan, & Berthoz, 1999; Schlag & Schlag-Rey, 1987) (see medial view of the cortex, Figure 3.2). These two areas were hard to distinguish in humans before the fMRI technique, and even now their separation as distinct functional zones remains to be clarified since there is individual variability in their size. For a long time it was known in neurology that deficits in exploring scenes and complex visual arrays follow damage to the frontal eye fields. Visual search tasks in which a single target is sought take an enormous amount of time to execute or the search results in failure. The problem is neither blindness nor paralysis of gaze but rather a failure to explore insofar as visual exploration involves attention: both sustained attention needed to maintain the search as well as oculomotor movements are defective in such disorders (Grosbras & Paus, 2003). Scanning a meaningful visual array requires perceiving the spatial layout, a function that can be mediated successfully by the parietal lobes. However, once immediate perception has occurred, understanding the whole requires deliberate and systematic taking in chunks of details, and this consistent attention, motoric in nature and internally generated, requires the intact activity of the frontal eye fields. Damage results in unsystematic exploration, erratic, and non-purposeful searches. These behavioral patterns are exaggerated in non-meaningful arrays.

A neurological case of a 55-year-old man with highly localized damage (stemming from a stroke) in a small area in the left prefrontal lobe, specifically, in the supplementary eye fields, has been reported (Husain, Parton, Hodgson, Mort, & Rees, 2003). Such cases with highly circumscribed lesions are rare and their brain activity in fMRI behavioral studies is highly valuable. This patient had difficulties shifting the direction of his eye gaze in order to accommodate a new intention or a new mental set. At the same time, he was able to detect and monitor his errors and correct them quickly. This result supports the role of the left prefrontal cortex in shifting and changing mental set, but adds to the understanding of error monitoring in that it shows that at least this left area eye field is not critical for error monitoring and correction. Areas in the prefrontal cortex implicated in error monitoring are considered for now to be the anterior cingulate gyrus and the dorsomedial region. The laterality in this type of behavior, and similar ones, is not well delineated yet. Several fMRI studies of people without brain damage have also reported a preferential activation of the left supplementary frontal eye area and a distinction has been revealed between internally generated eye movements versus voluntary eye movements to external stimuli (Grosbras et al., 1999). The left area appears to be particularly active in the former, in the internally generated eye movements. In contrast, no laterality of general activation was found in the frontal eye fields. Grosbras et al. (1999) note that the selective role of the left area cannot be attributed to eye dominance since one of his subjects was left-eye dominant.

Eye gaze could be paralyzed and prevent efficient searching of visual scenes for reasons other than prefrontal damage. In Balint's syndrome there is an inability to shift eye fixations from one point to another due to bilateral damage in the parietal and occipital lobes, particularly in areas controlling eye pursuit movements (Hausser, Robert, & Giard, 1980). Normally, pursuit eye movements are designed to be smooth and rapid despite the fact that pursuit consists of multiple saccades. In Balint's syndrome eye saccades are prolonged and the patient is unable to disengage fixations. The control of the eye movements engages both the frontal and parietal lobes. The critical cortical oculomotor-related regions are thought to be the frontal eye field, supplementary eye field, and lateral intraparietal cortex (Shipp, 2004).

Summary

Communication through pictures and drawings is observed in neurological patients who have lost the ability to communicate verbally or emotionally. Pictures are commonly used as stimuli in neuropsychological tests, following left or right hemisphere damage. In some patients with visual object agnosia there may be impairment in deriving the meaning of pictured objects but agnosic patients are not impaired across the board in deciphering pictorial representations (of faces, maps, diagrams). Drawings by patients with lesions in the right parietal and occipital lobes lack the contour frame, emphasizing instead the details of the drawn objects. Drawings by left hemisphere damaged patients shows the reverse, that is, of contour frames lacking in inside details. The idea of piecemeal and analytic thinking in the left hemisphere and gestalt thinking in the right hemisphere was initially derived from observations of the drawing patterns by patients with different laterality of damage. Subsequent studies of drawings revealed distorted perspective in both left-sided and right-sided stroke patients. Drawing is accomplished when language and memory are severely compromised: patients suffering from Alzheimer's disease can go on drawing even as their language and memory fail. Drawings by professional artists with aphasia address the issue of language and art and further highlight dissociation between the two modes of expression; drawings can be achieved even in the presence of aphasia. But this does not have to imply accomplishment through right hemisphere control. The role of the left hemisphere in deriving pictorial meaning, particularly with regards to scenes, is evident in simultanagnosia. Even with characteristic techniques of representing objects, drawing can be conceptualized and executed with the control of neural substrates in each hemisphere. When viewing scenes, pictures, or external environment, exploratory eye movements are controlled by the frontal eye field and the supplementary eye field. The frontal eye field controls exploratory eye movements in search of specific targets.

Further readings

Annett, M. (2002). *Handedness and brain asymmetry: The right shift theory* (2nd ed.). Hove, UK: Psychology Press.

De Renzi, E. (1982). *Disorders of space exploration and cognition*. New York: John Wiley.

Fuster, J. M. (1997). *The prefrontal cortex: Anatomy, physiology, and neuropsychology of the frontal lobe*. Philadelphia, PA: Lippincott-Raven.

Goldberg, E. (2001). *The executive brain: Frontal lobes and the civilized mind*. Oxford: Oxford University Press.

Heilman, K. M., & Valenstein, E. (Eds.). (2003). *Clinical neuropsychology*. Oxford: Oxford University Press.

McCarthy, R. A., & Warrington, E. K. (1990). *Cognitive neuropsychology: A clinical introduction*. San Diego, CA: Academic Press.

McManus, I. C. (2002). *Right hand, left hand: The origins of asymmetry in brains, bodies, atoms, and cultures*. Cambridge, MA: Harvard University Press.

Medin, D. L., Lynch, E. B., & Solomon, K. O. (2000). Are there kinds of concepts? *Annual Review of Psychology, 51*, 121–147.

Wilson, F. R. (1999). *The hand: How its use shapes the brain, language, and human culture*. New York: Vintage.

Zaidel, D. W. (1993). View of the world from a split-brain perspective. In E. M. R. Critchley (Ed.), *Neurological boundaries of reality* (pp. 161–174). London: Farrand Press.

Zaidel, D. W. (1994). Worlds apart: Pictorial semantics in the left and right cerebral hemispheres. *Current Directions in Psychological Science, 3*, 5–8.

Zaidel, D. W. (2000). Different concepts and meaning systems in the left and right hemispheres. *Psychology of Learning and Motivation, 40*, 1–21.

9 Beauty, pleasure, and emotions
Reactions to art works

Introduction

Aesthetic taste emanates from neural activity but its representation is mysterious. There are several directions of inquiry. What are the cytoarchitectural and excitatory principles on which aesthetic responses might rest? What role do aesthetic standards play in the neural response? What is the biological purpose of aesthetic taste in the first place? No easy neuroscientific answers are currently available although the topic is debated in evolutionary circles (Aiken, 1998; G. Miller, 2000). Humans react to perceived visual beauty regardless of its format in nature or on canvas. The former is three-dimensional while the latter is two-dimensional. The latter does not have to faithfully represent reality in order to elicit beauty-related reactions. We respond to the beauty we perceive in paintings by the Cubists, modern abstract painters, or Surrealists as well as to classic Chinese and Japanese art where there is little attempt to depict three-dimensional space. So beauty reactions are independent of the degree to which reality is represented. It is quite remarkable that photographic close-ups of a hand, a glass, and a variety of visual images can elicit beauty reactions, and at the same time so do wide-angle vistas such as what we see from mountain tops, high-rises, driving in the desert, and sitting on a beach. Visual angle is not crucial here. And there are specialty scenes in films that are relevant, described by a leading film critic, Roger Ebert (2002):

> three films [the Apu Trilogy] were photographed by Subrata Mitra, a still photographer whom Ray [the director] was convinced could do the job. Starting from scratch, at first with a borrowed 16mm camera, Mitra achieves effects of extraordinary beauty: forest paths, river vistas, the gathering clouds of the monsoon, water bugs skimming lightly over the surface of a pond.
>
> (Ebert, 2002, p. 46)

It seems that words alone cannot convey the range of visual events giving rise to beauty-related impressions that Ebert is describing.

Exploring these responses empirically has been complicated by several considerations. First, scientists have attempted very little systematic study of the concept of beauty. Consequently few direct experiments have been designed to delineate its characteristics. For example, is beauty of a face the same as the beauty of a painting, or of a sunset over the Pacific Ocean viewed from a cliff in southern California? Second, beauty seems to exist in many formats and domains of everyday life, even if we are not directly conscious of it being there and teasing them apart is a daunting task. Third, beauty's anchor in biology may make untangling difficult from other basic biological reactions. Nevertheless, some limited empirical work has been done, showing that aesthetic judgments have a neuroanatomical underpinning, and this will be explored in subsequent sections of this chapter.

Beauty and aesthetics

Alterations in aesthetic preference following brain damage

Neurological cases displaying changes in artistic taste after brain surgery or injury are remarkably few. Their very existence shows that there is a neural basis for aesthetics. Sellal and associates described a right-handed man with circumcised surgical excision who suffered from epilepsy since age 18 years (Sellal, Andriantseheno, Vercueil, Hirsch, Kahane, & Pellat, 2003). Left temporal lobe seizures were indicated with EEG recordings. The seizures were attributed to a tumor identified as ganglioglioma situated in the left third temporal gyrus (T3). At age 21 he underwent left temporal lobectomy to alleviate drug resistant epilepsy. The surgery consisted of resection of the anterior temporal pole, as well as other temporal lobe regions (T2, T3, T4, and T5). The hippocampus, the parahippocampal gyrus, and the amygdala were not removed. The seizures disappeared following surgery. Neuropsychological tests prior to surgery revealed worse verbal than visual memory and presence of a mild anomia. Following surgery, the tests indicated that verbal memory was at normal level, but the mild anomia remained unchanged. Both verbal and performance IQ (intelligence quotient) increased by a few points. Auditory tests showed deficits in pitch and tone discrimination without there being a hearing loss. Here is the interesting outcome to our discussion here: he reported in the year following surgery that he had developed new musical, visual art, and literary preferences.

> Formerly a "fan" of rock music, he found that the music he used to listen to before the operation sounded "too hard, too fast, and too violent." He now had a preference for Celtic or Corsican polyphonic singing and was unable to listen even to one of his rock songs. In literature he completely lost his taste for science fiction books and now preferred novels, e.g., the novels from Buzzati [an Italian author]. In paintings, he showed

increasing interest in realistic works, in which he liked the fine detail he was formerly unable to appreciate.

(Sellal et al., 2003, p. 449)

In contrast to all of this artistic-related preference, food, dress, or face preferences remained unaltered, nor were personality changes noted (based on informal observations as well as on a standardized personality test).

> The patient was surprised by his taste changes, did not find that they were the mere consequence of maturation, and complained about them: he now had difficulty staying with his old friends, since he could no longer share his musical preferences and hence his topics of discussion.
>
> (Sellal et al., 2003, p. 449)

The significance of this case is that limbic structures normally associated with emotions were not removed by the surgery and yet attributes associated with feelings and pleasure were altered. One would have logically expected to see preference changes with limbic structures resections but not with cortical resections, given the assumed associations between the limbic reward system and pleasure from art. With this rare case we see that there is a relationship between artistic preference and a neocortical region. It implies that there is a very strong cognitive component in art preference, that, as has been proposed, art is a communicative system for concepts. What remains to be determined, with a larger group of patients, is whether or not the laterality of tissue resection contributes asymmetrically to artistic preference changes.

An exceptionally brief report about a change of musical taste in a dementia patient was published in 2001: "A man exhibited typical features of semantic dementia, with onset at age 52. At age 55, he became infatuated with polka music. He would sit in his car in the garage and listen to polka on the radio or on cassettes, often for as long as 12 to 18 hours" (Boeve & Geda, 2001, p. 1485). The obsessive interest in polka was a new development, presumably not observed prior to illness onset. MRIs taken at ages 53 and 55 years indicated progressive amygdala and temporal cortex atrophy, bilaterally. Here we do have involvement of a limbic structure. What is not clear here, because of the brief nature of case description, is whether what was new was the infatuation itself or the interest in polka. Preference and taste for art could have "obsessive" qualities and the infatuation with polka may be an example of this.

Two neurological cases diagnosed with fronto-temporal dementia had alterations in musical taste (Geroldi, Metitieri, Binetti, Zanetti, Trabucchi, & Frisoni, 2000). In both there was bilateral atrophy of the frontal and temporal lobes as well as enlargement of the lateral ventricles, particularly of the frontal and temporal horns. In case 1, a 68-year-old lawyer, there was slightly greater right-sided atrophy while in case 2, a 73-year-old housewife, the atrophy was symmetrical. With case 1 the pre-morbid musical preferences had been directed to classical music, and he used to define pop music as "mere noise." About 2 years after his diagnosis, he started to listen at full volume to a popular Italian pop music band – "883." During the following 2 years, apathy worsened, spontaneous speech production was reduced, and the patient lost emotional contact with his family. However, he kept listening to 883 for many hours daily, actively looking for tapes, and using the recorder. Three years after onset, the patient developed motor neuron disease. He died 4 years after initial diagnosis.

(Geroldi et al., 2000, p. 1935)

With case 2, prior to disease onset she did not have a particular interest in music or its enjoyment. About a year after disease onset this changed: she began to show excessive interest in pop music, the same music that interested her 11-year-old granddaughter. She now listened to and enjoyed Italian pop bands as well as pop singers, noting their beautiful voices and pleasant rhythms. The brain alterations associated with the dementing process are clearly implicated in these aesthetic changes. Unfortunately, in the normal population, alteration in aesthetic preference across several domains throughout the lifetime has hardly been studied. There is only a general assumption that aesthetic preference is stable. In the cases with preference alterations discussed above, the temporal lobe was affected, and this implies a relationship with a particular neural substrate for aesthetic leanings. The cases thus offer us a tantalizing window into neuro-aesthetics. Additional neurological cases would be needed in the future in order to clarify this issue further.

Brain activity and aesthetics

Using the method of magnetoencephalography (MEG), Cela-Conde and colleagues (2004) have measured brain activity in eight female subjects in an aesthetic judgment task. While viewing a wide range of colored pictures, subjects were asked to indicate whether a picture was beautiful or not. Half the subjects responded by raising a finger if they thought the stimulus was beautiful and the other half responded with a raised finger if the picture was not beautiful. The pictures were carefully selected not to include close-up views of faces, and they represented art works of many genres (Classic, Abstract, Impressionist, and Postimpressionist), photographed scenery, landscapes, and objects. In all, there were 320 pictures, which were carefully controlled for complexity, color range, luminosity, and light reflection. The results of the MEG recordings showed significant preferential activation in the left prefrontal dorsolateral area when stimuli were judged beautiful, regardless of whether or not the material consisted of art works. As would be expected, there was simultaneous activation in the visual cortex. On the whole, beautiful stimuli triggered more cerebral activation than non-beautiful stimuli. Moreover, more left hemisphere sites were active than right hemisphere sites regardless of the nature of the stimulus (beautiful or not). This study used the most extensive range of pictorial stimuli, and most controlled stimulus selection procedures, applied to date. No breakdown with regards to art movement style is provided, but with time, we may learn about additional cortical correlates of aesthetic judgment of the different movements. It may, however, turn out that aesthetic judgment is uniform across all art genres. For now, it is clear that there is no distinction between painted art works and photographed nature, and that the left hemisphere is more active in aesthetic judgment than the right (although the reasons why this should be so are subtle).

With fMRI, Kawabata and Zeki (2004) studied brain activation of subjects who viewed paintings representing a variety of categories (faces, landscapes, still life, or abstract). Unlike the MEG study above where the subjects did not view the stimuli prior to brain recording, the subjects here saw the paintings between three and six days prior to actual brain scanning. There were ten subjects (five females, five males). In the fMRI procedure, 192 paintings were exposed twice (altogether 384 presentations) and the task was to indicate by pressing a button whether each stimulus painting was beautiful, ugly, or neutral. The authors found activation in several cortical areas including the visual cortex, motor regions, anterior cingulate, and orbitofrontal regions, largely for beautiful works. As in the MEG study, they also found that no separate specific area engaged when stimuli were perceived ugly. However, because of multiple stimulus presentations to the subjects, interpretation of the results is muddied by the mere exposure effect and familiarity effects (Kunst-Wilson & Zajonc, 1980). These effects alter responses in that they increase the likelihood of positive preference. Moreover, the portraits elicited strong activation in the fusiform gyrus as would be expected if photographs of faces were used. Measurement of the aesthetics of the portrait as a painting was complicated by its very depiction of a human face. Thus, it is difficult to interpret the reactions as distinct from aesthetic judgments.

In another fMRI and aesthetics for paintings study, the investigators showed their subjects abstract and realistic paintings and measured brain activation while aesthetic judgments were provided (Vartanian & Goel, 2004). There were twelve subjects (ten females, two males); only 40 stimulus paintings were administered. The original 40 stimulus paintings were altered in three different ways so that in the end subjects viewed 120 presentations. The task for the subjects was to rate each stimulus presentation on a 0–4 scale, where 0 represented very low preference while 4 represented very high preference. In general, subjects preferred representation over abstract paintings. With regards to brain activation, the significant results showed increased activation in the left cingulate sulcus, particularly to paintings with the highest ratings. There was a similar association in the occipital gyrus (bilaterally). The latter is not surprising, given visual stimulation. What is remarkable, and in agreement with the MEG study, is the selective activation of the left hemisphere for beautiful ratings. Further, there was a decrease in activation in the right caudate nucleus as stimuli were judged very unbeautiful. However, this experiment, too, is subject to the criticism that the mere exposure effect masked aesthetic judgments.

Considered together, it would thus seem that "beautiful" engages direct processing while "ugly" is a passive process. In the brain, then, the aesthetic decision uses beauty as a target associated with potential pleasure and reward while non-beauty is not a significantly stimulating event, at least as can be inferred given the type of stimuli used in the experiments.

Aesthetics, the oblique effect, and properties of the visual cortex

Gombrich (1968) proposed that the attraction to forms and shapes in art, or in nature, lies in their biological relevance. Stebbing (2004) has further argued that the grammar of art is an extension of existing organic forms that play an important role in biology, evolution, and survival. Such basic art-organizing principles are contrast, rhythm, balance, and symmetry. These units, Stebbing argues, are the elements in the grammar of art used by artists to communicate and by the viewer to understand.

Along the same line, it has been suggested that aesthetic interpretation of two-dimensional rendering in art is directly related to the elemental features in the art that the visual and perceptual systems are wired up to detect (Latto, 1995; Latto & Russell-Duff, 2002; Washburn, 2000). The greater the neuronal excitation upon viewing visual art, the greater the aesthetic response (Latto & Russell-Duff, 2002). Insight into this idea originated with the notion of anisotropy and the oblique effect. The oblique effect refers to inferior perception of patterns oriented obliquely as opposed to horizontal or vertical orientations (McMahon & MacLeod, 2003). The effect has been found in human children and adults as well as in cats, monkeys, and other animals (Appelle, 1972; Baowang, Peterson, & Freeman, 2003). It has been suggested that the locus of the effect lies in the visual cortex rather than in the retina (Baowang et al., 2003; McMahon & MacLeod, 2003). One explanation for greater sensitivity to the preferred horizontal and vertical orientations rests on the early visual exposure to structures in the environment and the plasticity of the visual system. According to this view, there is greater prevalence of horizontal and vertical content in the environment than of oblique content, and consequently, the experiential events sculpt the visual system to be more sensitive to horizontal and vertical orientations. The superior detection and recognition of these orientations over the oblique has been shown in both simple laboratory stimuli consisting of line gratings and in pictures of natural scenes (Coppola, Purves, McCoy, & Purves, 1998). Neuronally, more cells tuned to detecting horizontal and vertical patterns have been found than those responding to oblique orientations (Baowang et al., 2003). But inconsistencies in such findings have also been reported. On the whole, however, researchers agree that the oblique effect arises from cortical computations rather than retinal processing.

Oblique lines as opposed to non-sloping horizontal and vertical lines are not as aesthetically appealing (Appelle, 1972; Latto, Brain, & Kelly, 2000). Latto and associates have found that orientation of lines in paintings contributes greatly to aesthetic preference; component lines parallel to the frame were preferred over those that were not parallel. Piet Mondrian and the Dutch art school of De Stijl espoused the predominance of horizontal and vertical lines in eliciting aesthetic reactions (White, 2003a). Latto and others have argued that the strong appeal in those orientations stems from a close match with what the visual and perceptual systems are tuned to detect, and the consequent level of neuronal activity. Thus, while abstract paintings by the De Stijl school do not depict figurative art, they do evoke strong aesthetic reactions. At the same time, Washburn (2000) points out that simple forms and shapes, not necessarily representational, and not necessarily emphasizing horizontal and vertical lines (or orientations), are recognized and liked as well. To sum up, the visual system reacts to components of form primitives in perceived shapes and the match between what is seen, form edges, say, and visual feature detectors explain reactions to art on two-dimensional space.

Left–right perception and aesthetic preference in pictures

The left–right organization of a pictorial layout has an influence on aesthetic preference as well. In photographed scenery, Levy (1976) has shown that observers prefer scenes where the most informative focal portion is in the right half. One group of observers first judged the most important portion in asymmetric vacation scenes. Then, another group of subjects, the raters, viewed these scenes and provided a preference judgment. Levy was interested in comparing performance between right-handed and left-handed subjects. She found that right-handed subjects aesthetically preferred the scenes where the informative locus was on the right half, regardless of whether or not the viewed scene was in the original orientation or mirror-reversed. With left-handed subjects there did not seem to be a significant left–right locus differ-ence. The findings with right-handed subjects have been supported by other experiments that also used vacation scenes (Banich, Heller, & Levy, 1989). Beaumont used simple drawings to test the same idea, that of left–right organization and focal importance, and confirmed the right side aesthetic preference (Beaumont, 1985). He proposed that what lies at the core of this preference bias is the movement of the gaze to the right side of the picture and the stimulation of the left visual half field: when a subject moves the eyes all the way to the right side, this results in more of the picture falling in the left visual half field and consequently to preferentially engage the right hemi-sphere. According to this interpretation, specialization in visuo-spatial cogni-tion in the right hemisphere and the notions of aesthetic judgment of pictorial representations are thus wedded. An alternative explanation for the right side locus and aesthetic judgment is that it is the left hemisphere that becomes preferentially activated, and the aesthetic response is a reflection of that hemisphere's cognitive apparatus (Heller, 1994). A further study found that side of emphasis in content of photographs interacts, thus complicating conclusions regarding the involvement of the right or left hemisphere alone in aesthetic decisions (Valentino, Brown, & Cronan-Hillix, 1988).

While the foregoing described photographed vacation scenes, landscapes, and simple drawings, the right side bias does not square with established art works. Paintings in which the information emphasis was in the left side received aesthetic preference over those in which the emphasis was located in the right side (McLaughlin, Dean, & Stanley, 1983). Similarly, paintings in which the emphasis was in the right side did not necessarily receive greater aesthetic preference over those in which the emphasis was in the left side (Freimuth & Wapner, 1979). The role of either the left or the right hemisphere in aesthetic judgment is currently uncertain. There is no convincing evidence, owing largely to scarceness of data on and lack of valid studies.

Grusser has studied the lateral depiction of light source in 2124 museum paintings from the fourteenth to the twentieth centuries (Grusser, Selke, & Zynda, 1988). Grusser was interested in whether or not there is a left–right bias in light source depictions. He found that while most paintings in the fourteenth century had diffuse illumination, a few showed clear left side bias, that is, the light source originated in the left segment of the painting. This bias progressed consistently until it reached a peak in the seventeenth and eighteenth centuries, where about 70 percent of his sampled paintings showed this bias. In the nineteenth and twentieth centuries there was a major decline in this bias without a rise in a right bias. However, in the nineteenth century there was a steep rise in middle or diffuse light illumination so that 60 percent of his sample showed this trend. Grusser points out correctly that this marks the time when artists began to question the convergent perspective and depth depictions; lateral light source highlights the illusion of depth on a two-dimensional surface. And, he goes on to emphasize that ancient wall paintings from Pompeii and Herculaneum, and Byzantine mosaics in Ravenna churches had a left light source bias. However, the left–right light source bias in paintings can be explained in terms of balanced composition where the most important information is placed in the right half with the light shining upon it originating in the left half. Together, the laterality of the light source and the weight of important information in pictorial representations complement each other and give rise to a coherent creation.

Hemispheric aesthetic preference

Aesthetic preference for a stimulus presented in the left or right visual half field is complicated by interaction between the cognitive and perceptual components on the one hand, and the aesthetic requirement, on the other. Regard and Landis (1988) tested subjects in a hemi-field study that required an aesthetic decision between pairs of simple perceptual forms. They found an interaction between sex of subject and hemi-field of presentation for the preference judgments; women did not show a hemi-field difference for these figures while men showed a left visual field dominance for certain figures. Specifically, men seemed to prefer the figures that did not obey the gestalt law of simplicity and completeness (Pragnanz). The authors concluded that hemispheric aesthetic judgments were difficult to tease apart from inter-actions between sex of subject and cognitive/perceptual demands. In another hemi-field and aesthetics experiment in which subjects saw faces in each vis-ual half field the results were ambiguous with regard to hemispheric aesthet-ics (Regard & Landis, 1988). The authors agree that cognitive and aesthetic requirements interact with hemispheric specialization factors in ways that complicate conclusions regarding cerebral laterality of aesthetics.

Indeed, there have not been satisfactory studies of hemispheric aesthetics largely because the nature of aesthetic taste is obscured by interactions between several components some of which are hemispheric functional specialization, emotional reactions, cognitive features, and unconscious influences.

Beauty as an emergent property of art

Beauty itself could be viewed as an emergent property of art. That is, the beauty feature of a work of art is something that the observer who did not create the art sees. The neuroanatomical underpinning of beauty may apply only to perception and its interpretation but not to the building blocks in the creating of the work, perhaps in much the same way that consciousness is seen as the emergent property of neural activity (Sperry, 1980). Picasso commented on the moment of realization that art production is not infused for aesthetics for its own sake but rather a way to represent what is on the mind. "Painting isn't an aesthetic operation; it's a form of magic designed as a mediator between this strange, hostile world and us, a way of seizing the power by giving form to our terrors as well as our desires" (quoted in Gilot & Lake, 1964, p. 266).

Biological nature of beauty in faces

Beauty reaction to art could be viewed as an extension of responses rooted in biological human needs, such as attachment and care giving. Generalizing to parents and babies, most parents think their own babies are beautiful, more beautiful than the baby next door, more beautiful than their older brother's baby, whom they originally thought was beautiful, and even more beautiful than they were when they themselves were babies. In fact, such tiny babies can have wrinkled faces, their skulls slightly misshapen (unless born by cesarean section); they grimace a great deal, keep their eyes closed, have some skin discoloration, and so on. Babies' faces have what Konrad Lorenz has termed the "kewpie-doll" effect on adults (Kalat, 2002). The biology of the beauty response is further apparent in anecdotal observations, when parents judge their own infant's pictures many years later, when the infant has grown to be an adult. The love and attachment attitude remains, but the original beauty judgment of that very early period has been altered. There might be a biologically active window for beauty responses in the period in which the child needs the greatest care.

Beauty reactions in the brain are likely not to be uniform. A range of reactions could possess a narrow or a wide band, and the reactions may be format, domain and material specific. Given beautiful words, for example, some may trigger one level of brain activity while others trigger another level. The intensity of the reaction may be individual-specific or not.

Painted portraiture

What about beauty in painted portraits? For hundreds of years in Western art, starting with the Renaissance, artists have painted sitters' faces with a slight turn of the head where a left–right asymmetry in extent of side exposure was created, rather than with a head on symmetrical view. Previously, artists depicted sitters in profile views. With women's faces, the reason for the profile can be explained against prevailing society's attitudes at the time, namely that virtuous women did not look directly at men (Brown, 2001). The new artistic, societal, and intellectual developments in the Renaissance somehow contributed to the introduction of a slight turn of the head in sitters that ranged from a three-quarters view to only a quarter view, and even less than that. Ever since the early to mid-1400s there seems to have been in portraits of single sitters a bit of a turn resulting in an asymmetrical face side emphasis. (Holbein's head-on portrait of Henry VIII of England is highly unusual for that period.)

In a study of painted portraits of single sitters displayed on exhibit in the National Portrait Gallery in London, a sex difference in the side of the face that was emphasized was revealed (McManus & Humphrey, 1973). Women's faces had a greater proportion than men's faces of a left side emphasis (68 percent versus 56 percent, respectively). There is no a priori reason why artists should favor women's left side more than the right and why they would want to emphasize the left significantly more often in women than in men. An empirical attempt to understand the basis for the side bias in Western portraiture was launched many years after those results were first published (Zaidel & FitzGerald, 1994). The first key conjecture was that the principal determinant in the bias was a preference by the observer, particularly the paying observer (for hundreds of years, artists made a living through commissioned portraits). The working hypothesis was that observers liked to view women's left side of the face more than the right, and that artists wanted to accommodate them. They wanted their works to be liked. They spent days, weeks, months, and even years on a given portrait (e.g., Leonardo's *Mona Lisa*). The bias could not have been some random and haphazard event. Thus, it was important to find out what viewers think by way of liking a portrait.

Subjects in a laboratory were shown painted portraits of single sitters and asked to judge on a five-point scale the degree to which they liked the painting as a whole. A separate group of subjects were shown these portraits and asked to judge them on a five-point scale according to how attractive they considered the sitter. In each type of judgment requirement, one group of subjects saw the original orientation of the paintings and another group saw a mirror reversal version of the paintings. The unexpected findings were that in each type of judgment, regardless of whether the original orientation or its lateral reversal were shown, women sitters whom the artist originally painted with a right side emphasis were preferred: the painting was preferred as a whole and the sitter was considered much more attractive than paintings where the left side was emphasized. Moreover, no significant left emphasis versus right emphasis was found for the men sitters, in each type of judgment. One would have expected at the very least that portraits of women with left side emphasis to be the most preferred, since this is the Western trend in painted portraits. But the fact that sex difference emerged in the portrayed face indicated that the subjects picked up (unconsciously) an artistic bias after all. (There was no statistically significant sex difference in the judging subjects.)

These remarkable findings have led to a natural question regarding functional asymmetries in the face particularly as they relate to face sex. The next study examined this question directly by photographing head on views of people's faces, then dividing the photographs down the vertical midline and creating two faces from each, one showing the left-left face and the other showing the right-right face (Zaidel, Chen, & German, 1995a). This was accomplished on a computer by creating a mirror image of a given half and aligning it with the original half so that together, the original and its mirror image, looked like a normal face (albeit perfectly symmetrical). Subjects in the laboratory were then asked to decide which one of the two faces, the left-left and the right-right, was more attractive or there was no difference between them. The results indicated that subjects preferred right-right over left-left in women's faces and no distinct preference between the right-right and left-left of men's faces was found. These results with current photographed faces were consistent with the results of the portraits; together they suggest presence of asymmetry in the appearance of beauty in the human face.

Going back to the artist's studio, in making the artistic decision regarding the head turn in sitters, Western artists were influenced somehow by reactions and responsivity in their sitters' faces (to them, the artists) during small chat and conversation in the studio. The left side of the face is more reactive expression wise than the right side, particularly in women. Men are more expressive in the left facial half than in their right half as well but the asymmetry is less striking than in women, possibly because men do not show strong facial expressions as readily as women do. Women smile more than men, for example (LaFrance, Hecht, & Paluck, 2003). The smile has been found to be strongly asymmetrical, being more salient in the left than the right facial half (Zaidel et al., 1995a). The right side of women's faces, the attractive side, is not similarly reactive, and perhaps artists, most of whom were men, resonated to the smile and entered that unconscious perception into their conceptual artistic formula, and in so doing painted the essence of a positive reaction (reaction to the artist). This is what they wished to capture in their creation.

Facial asymmetry and art

Human faces are in fact structurally asymmetrical and this has long been known from anatomical and craniofacial research (Ferrario, Sforza, Pogio, & Tartaglia, 1994; Ferrario, Sforza, Ciusa, Dellavia, & Tartaglia, 2001; Peck, Peck, & Kataia, 1991; Scheideman, Bell, Legan, Finn, & Reisch, 1980; Vig & Hewitt, 1975; Woo, 1931). Ancient Greek artists were aware of the asymmetry since they depicted it in sculptures of the human body and head. Ancient Roman artists copied Greek statues and were not observant enough to notice anatomical asymmetry details or else chose to ignore them (Peck, Peck, & Kataia, 1991). In neuropsychology, functional asymmetry in the face was known for happy and sad expressions, both being more salient in the left side of the face (Borod, 1992; Borod, Haywood, & Koff, 1997). Smiling was found to be particularly salient in the left half of the face (Zaidel et al., 1995a). But the question of facial beauty and its asymmetrical organization, let alone any sex-related difference in that regard, had not been investigated until the question arose following the empirical studies with preferred depictions in painted portraits discussed above (Zaidel et al., 1995a). Contrary to the symmetrical appearance of animals and prevailing biological views on the relationship between symmetry and quality of genes, in humans asymmetry in the face (and skull, body, limbs) is the norm. Left–right directional asymmetry has a genetic and molecular underpinning and can be the basis for various physical abnormalities in humans (Levin, 2004; Varlet & Robertson, 1997). While animals can display body asymmetry, in humans this takes on significant value particularly because of the association of the asymmetry to hemispheric specialization and handedness (see especially Bradshaw & Rogers, 1993; Hiscock & Kinsbourne, 1995). Consequently, finding sexually dimorphic functional asymmetrical organization for beauty in humans should perhaps not be surprising particularly if we view it from an evolutionary adaptive perspective, as has been proposed (Chen, German, & Zaidel, 1997; Zaidel et al., 1995a). The theoretical explanation lies in the signals relayed by the two sides of the owner's face and the brain hemispheres of the observer; signals from each side are meant to be processed by two separate hemispheres of the observer so as to minimize interference in interpretation of the signals and increase efficiency of input processing. It is possible that attractiveness/beauty and emotional expressions represent mutually exclusive facial properties, that they represent opposite ends of the facial signals spectrum.

In face-on interactions, the right half of the owner's face lies in the observer's left visual and attentional field, which projects initially to the observer's right hemisphere (the face specialization hemisphere), while the left half of the owner's face lies in the observer's right visual and attentional field, which projects information to the left hemisphere. So signals emanating from women's right facial half are biologically meant to be processed by the functional specialization of the right hemisphere of the observer (a male, if considered from a biological advantageous perspective) while the left half of the face (which relays communicative signals through expressions) is processed by the left hemisphere as a sort of a communicative signal. Anthropological studies do not place facial attractiveness in men on top of the list of considerations by women choosing a mate while facial attractiveness in women is on top of the list for men choosing a mate (Buss, 1998). Left–right facial attractiveness asymmetry in men may not be an important biological factor for predicting health and survival potential of offspring.

Facial asymmetries, with greater salience of the expressions in the left facial half have thus far been noted in rhesus monkeys (Hauser, 1993), in marmosets (Hook-Costigan & Rogers, 1998), and in chimpanzees (Fernandez-Carriba, Loeches, Morcillo, & Hopkins, 2002). It is proposed that the selective adaptive pressures shaping the primate's brain to a brain supporting hemispheric specialization in humans also shaped facial functional asymmetry; the face evolved to signal asymmetrical expressions and display not only for the purpose of communicating verbal and non-verbal emotional expressions but also for the coordination of the whole body with a preferred hand dominance, as in the process of carrying babies, holding tools, and throwing stones, as well as in coordinating bimanual activities. The extent of facial anatomical asymmetry is critical since too much asymmetry borders on deformity. However, the thickness of the line dividing normal directional facial asymmetry and deformity has not been studied systematically. Normally we are not conscious of these facial natural asymmetries in daily interactions. Those asymmetries emerge only under controlled laboratory conditions.

Beauty in colors: the film

We react to the beauty of blobs of color regardless of where we view them. Perhaps the reason we think sunsets in the great American Western skies or over the Pacific Ocean as viewed from a California hilltop are beautiful is not because of the colors in those sunsets, but rather because of their unique luminance. There is very little color in gray, foggy days on rocky sea sides, and yet such scenery elicits beauty-related reactions. There is no color in most of

Ansel Adams' photographs but they appear very beautiful to us. White marble statues from ancient Greek and Roman eras as well as from Renaissance times are three-dimensional art works, they have volume and depth, but no colors, and many of us consider them fantastically beautiful, even though they are at times disproportionately large. Stories told in black and white films appear just as beautiful as those told in color. Currently, the reasons for why this is so remain a mystery.

As stated previously in different sections of this book, color adds yet another dimension to art. In nature there is plenty of color everywhere, even in deserts. However, color is only one feature of the visual world that can convey meaning. To wit, color-blind people interact meaningfully with the world, and some can be first-rate artists (see Chapter 3). Film is an exceptionally good example of art that does not need color to convey meaning and aesthetic pleasure.

> The spectator experiences no shock at finding a world in which the sky is the same color as a human face; he accepts shades of gray as the red, white and blue of the flag; black lips as red; white hair as blond. The leaves on a tree are as dark as a woman's mouth. In other words, not only has a multicolored world been transmuted into a black-and-white world, but in the process all color values have changed their relations to one another: similarities present themselves which do not exist in the natural world; things have the same color which in reality stand either in no direct color connection at all with each other or in quite a different one.
>
> (Arnheim, 1958, p. 15)

The viewer of art works is not shocked by many representational things, nor should there be shock when watching a movie in black-and-white. It is an art form that conveys remarkable meaning and aesthetics. Art represents concepts and humans deal with concepts every single minute of their existence. Humans can separate the representation of a concept from actual reality of their existence. The time when this distinction breaks down is in mental illness, in psychosis, for instance. In any case, before color film was invented, black-and-white films were the norm.

For many years, even after color film stock became available, well-known film artists preferred to continue shooting film for motion pictures in grayscale. In 1964, Ingmar Bergman, the film director, and Sven Nykvist, the cinematographer, made their first color film, *All These Women*, after years of making first-rate, highly acclaimed non-color films (see Chapter 3). This is what happened before they embarked on making it, as Nykvist (2003) tells it:

> When Ingmar was going to make his first film in color, we made it a point to learn everything there was to know about color film. We even set up a color film school at the Swedish Film Institute in cooperation with Eastman Kodak. I shot over 6000 metres of Eastman color film in a

series of tests. But, as I mentioned, technology is not all. Much of what I have studied comes from painting and still photography. In the preparation for *Pretty Baby* (1978), Louis Malle and I spent a lot of time studying Vermeer's paintings, especially the way he uses light. The still photographer Ansel Adams is an idol of mine and I once made a pilgrimage to meet him. He too is known for waiting hours for the right light.

(Nykvist, 2003, p. 11)

In the end, *All These Women* was not received well by the critics (not necessarily because of the color), but the next color film that Bergman and Nykvist made, *Passion of Anna*, in 1969, was widely acclaimed; interestingly, the colors were muted, appearing in some sense to be monochromatic.

What the foregoing shows about beauty and aesthetic reactions to art is that the subject matter is not one of the elements in the reaction equation. Some other features in the art elicit the beauty. Real life situations depicting illness never elicit such reactions. But illness in art, is a different matter. The art itself is what gives rise to the evocation.

Neuropsychology and emotional reactions to art

Emotions of the creating artist

Art reflects the inner life of the artist not only by displaying talent, skill, creativity, experience, psychology, and cognition, but also by mirroring emotional states. If art is an expression of the mind, then it is reasonable to wonder about the influence of emotional states on the final product. But emotional states can consist of moods, short or long term, for which there are cognitive strategies to overcome or to enjoy. Several moods can coexist at the same time. When artists compose a happy and exuberant musical piece, is this because they are happy and elated? We could argue that the opposite is true; the artist's emotional state was down and depressed but in order to extricate themselves, they produced a happy piece. Paul Hindemith (1895–1963), the German composer and musician, is reported to have said that just because a composer works on funeral music it is no indication that he is in a melancholic mood throughout the composing (Trethowan, 1977). At the same time, there is no reason to assume that in order to create such music, composers do not try to re-create a solemn mood within themselves, much as actors do when they apply the Lee Strasberg method to acting a character. Naturally occurring emotions and mood states in the composer, however, may enter into the formula of creation anyway. Hindemith offered a clue to this question: he claimed that when composers write, they know based on previous experience how to match the musical notes with mood evocation in the listener. He also pointed out that emotions invoked in the listener have different characteristics from emotions invoked by real life situations, since emotions invoked by music are short-lived, beginning with the onset of the music and terminating when the music no longer plays. In real life situations, it is rare that we experience a timed beginning and ending of emotional states aroused by an external source. To some extent Hindemith is right. The strong emotions invoked by music are sustained while the music is playing. But some emotions remain afterwards, albeit at much reduced levels.

Pleasure and the reward system

What is the anatomical underpinning of enjoyment upon reacting to art? What is the underlying neurophysiological reaction of "dislike" or "like" to art? Where in the brain is the activity the greatest? What processes in the brain give rise to aesthetic judgment, appreciation, enjoyment, and evaluation? If several brain systems are involved, which one acts first? What parallel processes are active? Viewing an art work and liking and enjoying what is in front of us without knowing why exactly does not mean that our reaction is emotional. The absence of words does not necessarily mean emotion. The not-knowing-exactly-why state could be intellectual. Even with things that are purely intellectual, not all are understood with words or can be expressed with words. The sensation of liking a painting involves both cognitive (conscious and unconscious) and visceral reactions. Just because we are more aware of visceral changes does not mean that this is the only reaction we have, and it certainly does not mean that the reaction to art originates in the viscera. What we are aware of concerning the viscera is due to the action of the brain. Both emotional and cognitive responses originate with the brain computing what the senses perceive. Feeling visceral responses – tightening of the stomach, relaxed breathing – is possible because the viscera are represented in the somatosensory cortex. The awareness of feeling something in one way or another, as in reacting to an event or a stimulus, reflects multiple actions of the general arousal system, the reticular activation formation, the system involved in attention (because we are aware of how we are feeling), to name but a few. When it comes to assigning words to the "feeling something," this would involve the left hemisphere and the language centers localized there. This does not mean that when we do not have words for feelings that the right hemisphere is "doing the feeling" and the left does not.

The hypothalamus is strongly associated with the "pleasure center" through its extensive connections to the septum, a structure located just in front of it. The pleasure center is now considered to be part of a neuronal network known as the reward system. James Olds and Peter Milner accidentally discovered it in 1954 while searching for a completely different brain mechanism, one that is associated with learning (Olds & Milner, 1954). When an electrode was accidentally inserted into the rat's septal area, and an electric current stimulated the area, the rat continued to press the lever (which was supposed to stop the electrical current) non-stop in order to receive this stimulation, going without food or drink for hours. They pressed the lever to get more and more of the electrical stimulation even when they were near starvation. Later experiments replicated the response in monkeys as well. In humans, a medical doctor had the idea that this procedure of self-stimulation through brain-implanted electrodes could bring relief from intractable pain (Milner, 1991). Since the discovery by Olds and Milner (1954), other scientists have worked out what other regions are connected to this hypothalamic region (Neill, Fenton, & Justice, 2002; Schultz, 2000).

The reward pathway consists of the medial forebrain bundle (MFB), which goes through the hypothalamus, along with the mesolimbic dopamine system, synapsing on the nucleus accumbens (NA). Stimulation of the MFB releases the neurotransmitter dopamine by the outer shell of the NA. Importantly, the NA sends numerous axons to dopaminergic neurons in the frontal and temporal lobes (including the hippocampus). The NA also receives projections from the cortex, amygdala, and hippocampus, and this implies that secretion of dopamine by the NA occurs with information arriving from regions other than the MFB. Prefrontal neurons are particularly sensitive through their specialized receptors to the action of dopamine. Cocaine, for example, allows the release of enormous quantities of dopamine in the brain by acting on specific neuronal receptors that normally inhibit the release of dopamine, thereby tricking the brain into responding as if there is pleasure-related activity. It does it by blocking the reuptake of dopamine in the postsynaptic gap, thereby increasing dopamine's circulation in the brain. Cocaine also works on the sympathetic nervous system by influencing blood pressure and heart rate. The sympathetic part of the nervous system controls the dilation and constriction of blood vessels. The pleasure-related activity in turn becomes part of a neural self-regulating loop, creating a brain dependence and behavioral addiction. In order to operate, the brain requires more and more of the dopamine, and this is how the physiological and chemical underpinning of addiction become entrenched (Schultz, 2004).

An exciting discovery in monkeys (Liu et al., 2004) links obtaining goals and rewards to the genetic underpinning of the D2 receptor (dopamine) in the primate rhinal cortex.

While the reward system offers an appealing explanation for brain underpinning of addiction, many issues concerning the mechanisms of this pathway as well as its relationship to the subjective feeling of pleasure are under debate. Research has not clarified yet whether addiction works in conjunction with learning mechanisms. Subtle interaction with additional neurotransmitters may be critical as well. Moreover, with regards to pleasure, it is difficult to ascertain whether relief from pain is the same as sexual pleasure, the pleasure that comes from enjoying art works, successful accomplishment, reading cartoons, watching film tracks of the Marx Brothers or Eddy Murphy, or relaxing on vacation. The pleasure that the rats experienced when Olds and Milner (1954) stimulated their brains could have just triggered a sensation of relaxation. In any case, the reward system is currently associated with pleasure-related responses, and dopamine in particular is associated with reinforcement of behavior in learning situations.

What is interpreted to be pleasure-like responses does not have to be related to liking something. Dopamine could be the underpinning of wanting something in order to receive reward rather than of liking something. That is, dopamine is involved in craving and seeking to be satisfied (Schultz, 2002). A relationship between exploratory and novelty-seeking behavior in experimental rats has been linked to levels of dopamine secretion by the NA, and this is likened to curiosity-motivated behavior in humans. There is also evidence for a genetic link in sensation seeking in humans (Limosin, Loze, Rouillon, Ades, & Gorwood, 2003). The repeated seeking includes being attached to something, crucially involving dopamine in its actions in the reward system (Wise, 2002). The attachment, in this case, is the reward. There is addiction to the repetition itself.

Emotional reactions in the brain to films

There has been some discussion about the role of the amygdala in deciphering emotional expressions on faces (Somerville, Kim, Johnstone, Alexander, & Whalen, 2004). In fMRI studies, subjects had increased activity in the amygdala when shown pictorial stimuli where emotional expressions were depicted on faces. People with damage in the amygdala have difficulties in judging fearful facial expressions in others while not being impaired in judging other facial expressions. Greater activation in the amygdala was recorded when subjects viewed photographed faces and had to decide automatically (while consciously doing so) whether or not they appeared trustworthy (Winston, Strange, O'Doherty, & Dolan, 2002). A study measuring amount of cerebral blood flow during film viewing by female subjects revealed bilateral activation of the amygdala (Aalto et al., 2002). The stimuli consisted of twelve movie clips taken from *When Harry Met Sally*, *Kramer versus Kramer*, *The Champ*, and *Bean: The Ultimate Disaster Movie*. Together, the clips represented neutral, amusement, and sadness emotional categories, based on independently collected data from a separate group. Each clip lasted an average of two and a half minutes. The study indicated that several brain regions were involved in amusement and sadness reactions, including the temporal-occipital region, the anterior temporal lobe, and the cerebellum. Specifically, the researchers found for both amusement and sadness that the right temporal pole was active, as well as the amygdala bilaterally, and the cerebellum. They found little evidence for subcortical activation, except for the amygdala. Other studies using imaging techniques of brain activations are currently being used to delineate brain areas involved in emotional processing, but there is not always consistency among them and much work remains to be done. The current consensus is that several brain regions become active during emotionally related tasks.

The various functional brain imaging techniques overlook the fact that although the experiments are designed to measure emotional reactions, they also recruit cognitive components. It is not trivial or simple to separate emotions from cognition. The regions that have been found to be active to date in emotion experiments are localized in the neocortex as well as in subcortical regions; the cortical regions are known to be active when non-emotional cognitive tasks are administered. If all the activity seen in the brain during emotion-related experiments were restricted to subcortical structures alone, it would be reasonable to deduce that the experiments truly tapped emotional reactions. Since this has not been so, one needs to assume that the emotional content of the stimuli have cognitive components. It is only logical to infer the involvement of cortical regions in emotional reactions. One of the theories of emotions, known as the James–Lange theory, presupposes a rational, conscious reasoning for being in a particular emotional state (Lang, 1994): verbal labels determine the conscious awareness of the emotion. For example, sensations of trembling are interpreted to mean fear, sensations of quickened heart pace are interpreted to mean being happy in anticipation of seeing someone special, smiling interpreted to mean happy, and so on. The body may react before the conscious verbal label is assigned but the name of the emotion and the interpretation imply involvement of cognitive cortical centers. This situation may be unique to humans and suggests an interactive cognitive loop for emotional reactions.

Hemispheric laterality of emotions

Since art represents the context and environment of the artist, the perceptions, experiences, ideas, and insights, it is reasonable to expect similarity or, at the very least, a natural continuum in the brain between emotional reactions to non-art stimuli and art. Separate emotions are evident with unilateral hemispheric damage. Following right hemisphere stroke there is preponderance of euphoria, indifference reactions, and denial of illness, whereas damage to the left hemisphere is often accompanied by depression (Gainotti, 1972). These opposite types of emotional valances indicate that emotion is not a unitary process, and this is consistent with the notion that there is a cognitive, cerebral component to its expression. If emotions were controlled solely by subcortical structures, the evolutionarily old brain parts, we may not see the coloring of the emotions through the neocortex, through human cognition. As an example, a study on 141 patients with unilateral stroke in the left or right hemispheres revealed that the preponderance of depression reactions were in the left hemisphere group (Paradiso, 1999).

The fact that humans interpret their emotional reactions in terms of their contextual source attests to the fact that cognitive features play a role in emotions. The interaction of the two can serve as a theme, a guiding principle for future behavior. Extending the discussion to what humans describe as "feeling guilty" illustrates the interaction of morality and society's rules and emotions. There is a developmental sequence to empathy, which suggests that cognitive features of yet another non-verbalized reaction are a component of emotional reactions (Leslie, Johnson-Frey, & Grafton, 2004). Reactions to facial expressions are processed in brain areas similar to those modulating face identification and recognition, namely the fusiform area in the right hemisphere. The right hemisphere specializes in processing faces for recognition and identification (LaBar, Crupain, Voyvodic, & McCarthy, 2003; Posamentier & Abdi, 2003). But there is some evidence that this lateral specialization changes in older adults (Gunning-Dixon et al., 2003) and there is a suggestion that not all emotional reactions to facial expressions are uniform, that is, hemispheric-selective activation co-varies with type of expression (Kilts, Egan, Gideon, Ely, & Hoffman, 2003). In any case, both hemispheres are characteristically involved in emotional reactions albeit the reactions take on different "colors" depending on the nature of the emotion.

As described earlier, art productions commonly express social, political, and personal happenings. Capturing responses to such surroundings in images is meant to convey meaning and thereby elicit reactions. This reaction is initially in the emotional domain but does not have to imply not understanding the symbolism, whether the art is realistic, impressionistic, or abstract, despite not immediately being available to logical or linguistic analysis.

Summary

This chapter reviews responses to art that concern the issues of beauty, aesthetics, and emotions. Beauty reactions are independent of the degree to which reality is represented, thereby suggesting beauty's anchor in biology and neuroanatomy. Despite scarcity of empirical investigations into the brain's underpinning of beauty responses to pictures, a few results emerged. With magnetoencephalography researchers have found that more left than right hemisphere sites were active regardless of the nature of the stimulus (beautiful or not). No distinction was found between painted and photographed nature. With fMRI, brain activation of subjects who viewed paintings representing a variety of categories (faces, landscapes, still life, or abstract) found multiple, widely spread activated cortical areas, mostly activated in conjunction with beautiful works; the painted portraits elicited strong activation in the fusiform gyrus, as would be expected if photographs of faces were used. There is some evidence that reactions to facial expressions are processed in brain areas similar to those modulating facial identification and recognition. Another fMRI study revealed decrease in activation in the right caudate nucleus as stimuli were judged very unbeautiful. Together, it would seem that stimuli judged beautiful elicit stronger activation than ugly stimuli. Other neuroimaging studies showed increased activity in the amygdala when subjects looked at pictorial stimuli consisting of emotional expressions in faces, and looking at amusement and sadness recruited activation in several additional brain regions, including the temporal-occipital region, the anterior temporal lobe, and the cerebellum.

One notion regarding art works is that the brain's reaction to visual aesthetics arises from the visual system's search for components of form primitives in perceived shapes. Presumably, a good match between what is seen, form edges, say, and visual feature detectors, explains reactions to art. Findings and discussions in the literature regarding the oblique effect lay bare this notion and future work has the potential for finding fine and subtle differences among aesthetic stimuli.

The left–right organization of viewed images plays a role in aesthetic reactions. Focal components in the right half of photographed landscapes have greater influence on aesthetic judgment. On the other hand, paintings, rather than photographs, in which the information emphasis was in the left side received aesthetic preference. Facial beauty is asymmetrically organized on the face with the emphasis being located in the right half, but this is so only in women's faces; in men's faces there is no left–right difference in appearance of beauty. Research on painted portraits and photographed faces seems to concur on this sex difference with regards to the organization of beauty in faces.

Color adds yet another dimension to art but it is not a critical aesthetic component of art. Film is an exceptionally good example of art that does not need color to convey meaning and aesthetic pleasure. For many years, even after color film became available to filmmakers, well-known film artists preferred to continue creating motion pictures in grayscale. Ingmar Bergman, the film director, and Sven Nykvist, the cinematographer, provide examples that are discussed in this context.

Emotional reactions to life events are not diametrically opposite of reactions to art. Since art represents the context and environment of the artist, it is reasonable to expect a great similarity or, at the very least, a natural continuum between emotional reactions to non-art stimuli and art stimuli.

Further readings

Cupchik, G. C., & Laszlo, J. (1992). *Emerging visions of the aesthetic process: Psychology, semiology, and philosophy*. Cambridge: Cambridge University Press.

Eco, U., & Bredin, H. (1988). *Art and beauty in the Middle Ages*. New Haven, CT: Yale University Press.

Gardner, H. (1997) *Extraordinary minds: Portraits of exceptional individuals and an examination of our extraordinariness*. New York: Basic Books.

Halgren, E., Raij, T., Marinkovic, K., Jousmaki, V., & Hari, R. (2000). Cognitive response profile of the human fusiform face area as determined by MEG. *Cerebral Cortex, 10*, 69–81.

Miller, A. I. (2000). *Insights of genius: Imagery and creativity in science and art*. Cambridge, MA: MIT Press.

Miller, A. I. (2002). *Einstein, Picasso: Space, time, and the beauty that causes havoc*. New York: Basic Books.

Moller, A. P., & Miller, A. P. (1994). *Sexual selection and the barn swallow*. Oxford: Oxford University Press.

Sabelli, H., & Abouzeid, A. (2003). Definition and empirical characterization of creative processes. *Nonlinear Dynamics in Psychological Life Science*, 7, 35–47.

Sacks, O. (1995). *An anthropologist on Mars*. New York: Alfred A. Knopf.

Schenk, R. (1992). *The soul of beauty: A psychological investigation of appearance*. Lewisburg, PA: Bucknell University Press.

10 Human brain evolution, biology, and the early emergence of art

Introduction

How can one analyze the significance of the findings on artists with localized brain damage, neuropsychological clues to art from non-artists, or the role of sensory loss in art production, without a discussion of art's origin against the background of human evolution and biological influences? Exploring these origins sheds light on the brain's control in human art production and appreciation. One form of cognition on which art relies, as does language, is abstraction and symbolic representation. The biological and neural mechanisms supporting cognitive abstraction are assumed to have provided the underpinning for the practice of art. However, anthropologists, biologists, archaeologists, and evolutionary scientists are not clear on the acquired sequence of traits leading to the appearance of art. This is largely due to varied interpretations of the available fossil record and archaeological findings. Still, despite controversies, debates, and myriad of opinions, a pattern of agreement does emerge. A synthesis of this pattern is presented here and additional views on the origins are introduced.

The debate centers on the emergence of the ability for symbolic representation in human brain evolution. First, it is doubtful that the ability did not have a slow course of evolving (Flinn, Geary, & Ward, 2005). Second, the cognitive underpinning of symbolic thinking need not express itself necessarily as language or visual art. It could be expressed in a variety of ways that do not leave behind object artifacts – music making, dancing, praying, social clustering, and other clever ways.

One of the unique features of human societies is the prolonged teaching through demonstration and communication (Johnson & Earle, 2000). Humans purposefully teach their young, molding and shaping their behavior according to the rules of society, teaching them how to communicate and interact, which in turn allows the young to be fully integrated into the society (G. Miller, 2000). This practice goes on for an extended time compared to other primates. Caregivers teach their children to speak, to pronounce words, shaping their mouths in particular ways so as to accentuate the visual appearance of the face for the infant to see clearly and mimic correctly

(Holden, 2004). Adults universally modify the natural pitch of their voice to accommodate infants' hearing, presumably comprehension, capability; they typically raise the pitch and speak slowly with exaggerated speech inflection. Adults also hand over to their young preshaped tools and teach them how to use them. All of this active and direct teaching and learning creates an enriched environment for shaping behavior. Doing things socially, in a group, could have served as a selective adaptive stage for creating art by modern humans.

Of all other animals, humans have the most varied social groupings. There is the family, and there is the group of all women, of all men, the shamans (the religion), warriors and soldiers, the working women, the non-working women, and so on. Now, one of the important theories about the origin of human art is that it began with body decoration, and this is related to the social grouping idea (Lewis-Williams, 2002). The body decorations by early humans are known from burial sites. One notion is that it was used to designate group membership. Those who were decorated in a certain way belonged to one group, possibly a family group, while those decorated somewhat differently belonged to another group, another family, another association. Beads and jewelry highlighted and emphasized distinctions, and also united individuals. Adding feathers and furs to their body decorations made humans feel more at one with animals, which they particularly considered to be powerful, capable, and challenging. Early use of body decorations could also have reflected a separation according to rank, even within a family group.

Biology and display of art

Roots of exhibiting talent and skills and sexual selection

Humans share with other animals many biological features including the basic biological need to propagate the species through procreation. Extending this biological need to the ubiquitous practice of art, in all societies, in all epochs of modern Homo sapiens, and even before, in early hominids (White, 2003b), suggests a need for a type of expression that has roots in biology. One proposal is that the desire to create art in the first place is an extension of mate selection strategies wired into our brain as part of a biological scheme directed at reproduction and procreation (G. Miller, 2000). Art is normally produced for display, whether to a small elite group, or for everyone to see and hear. The display aspect is what makes art not unlike the biological need to display physical characteristics to the potential mate in the ritual of mate selection. Miller proposes, then, that human art and courtship animal displays are related and rooted in biology. In particular, the biological roots are embedded in the evolutionary concept introduced by Darwin, namely sexual selection (Cronin, 1992).

The view that human art has roots in biology and sexual selection strategies is shared by other scholars (Aiken, 1998; Coe, 2003; Dissanayake, 1988,

1995; Kohn, 2000). One challenging idea is that humans are driven to create art works for the same exhibitory reasons that animals display in courtship rituals (G. Miller, 2000). For humans, art is tied to the judgment of the other; art is tied to the judgment of one's potential as a mating partner. It is used to assess others' fitness. In nature, the best display, the one that gets to be chosen for mating, or the one that leads to choosing, represents quality genes that hopefully will be reproduced in the offspring, and promote survival. Thus, art creation is a more peaceful and profitable way of attracting the judgment of the other than head-on, physical, aggressive fights. It is also less energy consuming than some animals' aggressive fights meant to win positive evaluation of the mate. In this sense, then, human art is consistent with Freud's sublimation notion, redirecting biological aggressive drives in order to be aesthetically gratified and exercise symbolic representations. These are shortcuts that the cognitive apparatus is equipped to handle.

What animals do to survive is controlled by their central nervous system and the specific way in which it is neuronally wired and controlled by genetic material (Gould & Gould, 1989). With the famous example of the peacock, there has always been a need to explain its long elaborate tail, since he cannot use it for flying; it gets in the way when attempting to run very fast, and it can get stuck in the underbrush. In order to procreate, the peacock must attract a peahen, and in order to succeed in attracting her, he must exhibit his health and genetic fitness through his plumage. The ability to spread his tail feathers into a gigantic fan signals to the potential peahen that he has strong muscles, that they can support his ability to parade back and forth in front of her while the fan is still spread, upright, and vibrating further informs her of his prowess. The peacock is interested in revealing himself to the best that his brain will allow him to do so since he is neuronally wired up to pursue a mate in order to procreate and propagate his species. The peahen, in turn, has a brain that is wired up to interpret the signals sent in her direction.

Birds known as bowerbirds, after the bowers that the males create, live mostly in Australia and New Guinea (Diamond, 1982) and provide a biological model for the idea that art can have its roots in mate selection strategies (G. Miller, 2000). The bowers are constructions ranging from the simple to very fanciful, complex, and elaborate, created from materials in the forest (and if close to human habitat include artifacts used by humans). The male bowerbird builds his constructions solely for the purpose of attracting a female. Once attracted, they do not mate in the bower nor do they raise their young there. The purpose of the bower is to show off talent and skill in constructing the design, which must be maintained in the mind while the bird executes and assembles the individual components. Indeed, it has been found that the size of the brain in bowerbirds correlates with the architectural complexity of the bower (Madden, 2001)! This is true in both members of the species, in the male who builds and the female who observes. In those species where bower design is not very elaborate the brain is not as large as in those that build very large, elaborate, complex, and sophisticated bowers. So the mental power to create and observe such constructions has neuroanatomical underpinnings.

The functionality of some early hand axes fashioned by humans, principally in the Upper Paleolithic period in Western Europe, is not questioned, but what is interesting is their elaborate handles. It is suggested that they were artistic and meant for exhibition (G. Miller, 2000); exhibiting the bodily strength required in shaping them, as well as the cleverness, intelligence (possibly aesthetic sense), and creativity; all of which add up to having genes that promote successful survival, even if they were designed just to call attention to group belongingness. Along the same lines, body decoration and ornamentation are thought to have emerged when early human societies became stratified and were used to show membership in a social group. In so doing they were also advertising the quality of genes that their fellow group members have. In this sense, art is not only for advertising oneself, the quality of clever inherent abilities, but also of the people with whom one is associated. A competitive arena is created in stratified structures, and art works help seal the layers. So at a crucial time for brain development as realized in the anatomical modern humans, the Homo sapiens, art expression extended to the display of genes of relatives, friends, and allies (Lewis-Williams, 2002).

Pleasure of art and its roots in biology

One feature of art whose roots are reasonably to be found in biology is the pleasure that both the creators of art and the observers of art sense with art works. The professional creators enjoy improving on previous productions and innovations. They enjoy the actual production, the reaction of others (particularly if favorable), their special status in the society, and their success. Humans throughout the world enjoy some manifestations of art (Dissanayake, 1995). The care, attention to form, details, persistence, and energy that go into art making is not incidental (Winner & Casey, 1992). It is a purposeful, integral activity representing evolved cognitive features of the human brain; it must activate the rich representation of the hands as opposed to the legs, for example, in the motor cortex, modulating fine finger motor control as well as precise hand grips (Tattersall, 2001). The Action Paintings of Jackson Pollock, for example, require restrained and planned flinging of paint on horizontally placed canvas, something that demands just such refined wrist–hand control. Whatever energy is invested in producing human art, it is the culmination of how human needs and biology sculpted the brain.

Visual arts

Initial appearance of many artistic productions

Archaeological evidence indicates that anatomically modern humans emerged around 100,000 years ago, but, critically, there is a gap between that time and the emergence of abundant representational art (Appenzeller, 1998; Bahn, 1998). The anatomically modern humans are believed to have come out of Africa, migrating outward through the Middle East (their remains have been found in Israel) and to continue their migration through Eastern Europe toward Western Europe (Balter, 2001). The Neanderthals are people who well preceded Homo sapiens in Europe and even overlapped with them by 10,000–15,000 years (Clark, 1999; Finlayson, 2004; Lewis-Williams, 2002). They seem to have disappeared around 30,000–35,000 years ago (Klarreich, 2004; Klein et al., 2004); some argue they are not related to Homo sapiens and some do support their genetic relationship to anatomically modern humans (Wolpoff et al., 2004). David Lewis-Williams (2002) proposes that art first appeared on the human scene when fine hand tools, small statuettes, beads, and pendants appeared about 35,000–45,000 years ago in Western Europe, in a period known as the Upper Paleolithic. The technology associated with that period is Aurignacian and it is distinct from the technology of the Middle Paleolithic, which is known as Mousterian technology. Anatomically modern humans started to appear in Europe around 45,000 years ago (Mellars, 2004). Thus, the period between 45,000 and 35,000 years ago is called the Transition, signifying the big change, sudden in the archaeological record, in what humans began to produce in addition to mere tools. The new developments were in the categories of adornments and symbolic art, and the use of plastic materials such as bone, antlers, ivory, and stone (Balter, 2001). The thrust of the argument is that the fine hand tools had decorative handles which were not necessary for functionality. This is viewed as initial signals of visual art (the fact that they were decorative but not functional).

In addition, Homo sapiens, the anatomically modern humans, decorated their bodies with paint and jewelry. Lewis-Williams (2002) proposes that the appearance of those early signs of visual art correspond to the development of human social groups and status. Not that the Neanderthals did not have social groups. There is a possibility, however, that they did not have stratified social status. The issue of rank and of fine social layers within the group may be a key to understanding the nature of modern humans' society and art practices. Such differentiation is coupled with the definition of a single person in relationship to the rest. Designation may be necessary; there are the prepubescent boys, the prepubescent girls, the brave and courageous, the young and the old, the wise and the clever, the leaders and the led, the specialists, the artisans, and so on with various social distinctions. Body adornments (a form of art) may have been done in order to help in the visual identification of who belonged where in the hierarchy.

However, it should be mentioned that in 2004, radiocarbon dating of bones suggested that the bone remains of anatomically modern humans found in close proximity to the Aurignacian art and technology could represent burial sites that slipped somehow into Aurignacian soil levels but actually originated in a later period. Such findings have raised the possibility that Aurignacian artifacts may not have been produced by the anatomically modern humans after all (Conard, Grootes, & Smith, 2004; Mellars, 2004).

In the gradual course of evolution where sometimes there seem to be leaps and sometimes bounds, but almost always with adaptation to the environment (and genetic mutations), it is highly likely that what happened in Western Europe about 45,000 years ago had its precursors elsewhere, specifically in Africa (McBrearty & Brooks, 2000; Tattersall, 2001). The evidence from Africa indicates that

> the making of blades and pigment processing using grindstones date back to 250,000 years ago. Long-distance exchange and shellfishing started about 140,000 years ago. Bone tools and mining are about 100,000 years old. Ostrich eggshell bead making started between 40,000 and 50,000 years ago, but present evidence suggests that the species of art that we call representational images may date back to between only 30,000 and 40,000 years ago. Most astonishing of all is the recent find that Chris Henshilwood and his colleagues made in the southern Cape cave known as Blombos. A piece of ochre, carefully engraved with crosses with a central and a containing line has been dated to approximately 77,000 years before the present. [The cave also contained carved bone tools and fishing materials.] Though not a representational image this is now the oldest dated "art" in the world. It shows indisputable modern human behaviour at an unexpectedly early date. While there may be some debate about the details of all of this evidence, it now seems clear that modern human behaviour was appearing piecemeal in Africa before the Transition in Western Europe.
>
> (Lewis-Williams, 2002, pp. 98–99)

To all of this must be added the discovery in Schöningen, Germany, in 1995, of highly preserved long wooden spears, each about 6 feet, dating to 400,000 years ago (Dennell, 1997; Thieme, 1997). The skill, planning, and intelligence that went into shaping the javelins, although many would say is not art, can be viewed as skillful early know-how for eventual full-blown artistic technology of forms.

Art as an extension of clever survival strategies

Another view that is proposed here is that body decorations first became useful to humans and early hominids in conjunction with camouflage, possibly even before the desire to delineate group membership. It is not unreasonable to propose that not wanting to be spotted from above by birds that could give them away through screeching or overhead circling, modern humans realized that camouflaging their bodies with body paint and artifacts (furs, feathers, skins) increased their ability to catch prey (to eat it, and use its skin). They had to have had a cognitive apparatus to keenly observe that some animals blend well into their surroundings. They could have symbolically wanted to match their own skills against the animals by showing who is the cleverer of the two, the human or the animal. Throughout human history people have had the tendency to mimic animals, to even create chimeras known as *therianthrope images* in which half is human and half is animal. (The earliest evidence comes from Germany in the shape of a 32,000 years old statuette depicting a human male with feline head.) Of course, they may later have realized that they could use camouflage to win wars and gain territory, and other precious things with a cognitive apparatus that supported cunning, deviousness, treachery, and guile.

The idea behind body decorations, for adornment or for deception, as in camouflage, is that it is symbolic; it stands for something else, something that is in the mind. It does not have to be a faithful facsimile but rather an idea that can be further used to enhance survival. Lewis-Williams (2002) argues that even if the Neanderthals used body decorations for symbolic reasons, they did not extend that notion to carvings or making pictures. The reasons remain a mystery at this point. Thus, he said, body painting itself did not extend to making images (pictures and statuettes). Instead, he proposes, image-making was possible with the highly evolved mind of Homo sapiens, those humans that showed up in Europe long after the Neanderthals had established themselves there. So even though one thing led to another, painting on two-dimensional surfaces other than the body itself, as well as the fashioning of figures in ivory, stone, antlers, or bone, human or animal, both signal a highly evolved brain, able to support cognition, and that expresses itself on extra-personal space material. The consensus is that representational art began with pictures, three-dimensional figures, and with carvings. These followed something else, namely, adornments on the body. However, with regards to the absence of evidence for Neanderthal art, of the type created by the Homo sapiens, the possibility that they had symbolic thoughts, beliefs, and actions not expressed in art should be entertained. Indeed, some scholars believe that there is more morphological brain similarity between the Neanderthals and Homo sapiens than is commonly believed (Wolpoff et al., 2004).

The archaeological evidence for the period extending from 35,000 to 45,000 years ago in Western Europe is of fine stone tools, shaped over and above mere functionality; body decoration and ornaments; elaborate burial grounds for some members of the society (wherein the graves contain various goods); and images in the form of carvings, statuettes, pictures, and markings (G. Miller, 2000). The elaborate graves reflect the symbolic representation of attachment and love for the deceased (Bahn, 1998). This, in turn, signifies symbolic belongingness to someone who ceases to exist in real time. The materials used for tools varied for the first time in this period – it included flint, bone, antlers, ivory, shell, and wood. It is meaningful that there developed a wide variety of tools alongside the different materials exploited for making them. By comparison, the tools of the Neanderthals were less varied and had uniformity to their designs, although they did shape musical flutes from bones (Fink, 2003). Some scholars believe that whatever was fashioned by the Neanderthals so as to be symbolic could have been borrowed from Homo sapiens (Appenzeller, 1998). The jewelry of the Upper Paleolithic consists of different animal teeth (fox, wolf, and bear). Holes were made so that the teeth could be strung together and hung on parts of the body. Moreover, seashells were found in places that were far from the point of origin and this implies trade or travel across great distance (which, in turn, implies good spatial orientation and spatial cognition). The combined juxtaposition of these events and artifacts in time suggests a change in human behavior compared to what hominid brains expressed previously (Mithen, 1996, 2004). The precursors for this activity probably already existed in Africa but it seemed to fuse and coalesce into a high level of symbolic activity in Europe. Indeed, in 2003, 75,000-years-old shell beads were discovered in the Blombos cave in South Africa (Henshilwood, d'Errico, Vanhaeren, van Niekerk, & Jacobs, 2004).

The juxtaposition of the art-related events in Europe may have been crucial. One can debate, argue, and speculate about the reasons for the particular abundant appearance of art in Europe. Weather climate and habitat are important to consider, for example (Calvin, 2003). Another strong possibility that needs to be considered is the very interaction with Neanderthals, the successful group of people who had lived in Europe for over 200,000 to 300,000 years (Tattersall, 2001). They did not leave behind the equivalent in terms of quantity and range of symbolic and representational art but the Homo sapiens may somehow have benefited from interactions with these people who successfully managed to live in the European environment for so long. In a speculative scenario, the interactions with them, positive and negative, have challenged further development of the anatomically modern humans, through war, dominance, and deception. A triggering phenomenon could have been the combination of war and attachment. Protection of those to whom we are attached can motivate war, which in turn, results in the destruction of attachment bonds (through death), an event which may have further inspired the reinterpretation of the same art-like rituals used for war.

In many societies existing nowadays we see the tendency to mimic animals through body wrappings and decorations, in special ceremonies and celebrations, as well as in daily life. Using elaborate head gears made of feathers assembled from exotic birds, is one example. The killing of animals requires a great deal of cognitive skill – it requires cunning, meticulous observation, planning based on knowledge of when animals come to a specific site, where the trap is set out, or being able to divert animals to the trap: knowing when they need to drink, and waiting there to catch them. "Being at the right place at the right time meant a great harvest of fish that they could dry and store. Upper Paleolithic people thus tended to concentrate on a single species, especially at certain times of the year; these included reindeer, wild horse, and salmon" (Lewis-Williams, 2002b, p. 78). Thus, what may have started as a practical means of survival (animal skins for protection and meat and fat for food) may have naturally developed into the notion of body adornments (display of prowess, physical and cognitive, quality of genes, fitness indicator, and so on). Given the highly developed brain that came up with clever strategies to survive, it is not unreasonable to suggest that the next step was to rationalize the advantage of body adornments.

Fortuitous juxtaposition of early conditions

The delay differential in the emergence of fashioned art work between the period 100,000 years ago when modern humans emerged and the period between 45,000 and 35,000 years ago in Western Europe when art was practiced in quantities might be explained against the background of warfare. In Europe, certain conditions were in place that were not present elsewhere. One of the factors that I am suggesting has triggered increased art production is warfare, and that the early representational art consisted of simple diagrams denoting location of the enemy and landmarks crucial for a successful plan of attack. It may even have been three-dimensional at first: small stones represented people, hills, plants, and shelters of the enemy and of one's own society. The stones could have been fashioned to represent people symbolically, with lines that resemble stick figures. From there the practice of representation would have been a very small step to elaborated figures and to realize the advantage of image representations, everything else being equal. Pictorial war diagrams may have been the first expressions of art form (even if none has been discovered yet). Successful battles needed consultation, discussion, pulling together of brain resources, and the quickest way to communicate perhaps was to draw diagrams.

The young of many mammals play with each other, practicing and exercising their muscles, preventing atrophy, promoting development of brain synapses and neuronal networks. Preparing children for their future roles in society through symbolic play and games with instruments and tools fashioned for their little hands, keeping a protective eye on them and encouraging the natural tendency of the young exercise something they do naturally, namely play, is not that unlikely a scenario. Early hominids and humans could not have been blind to activities of chimps, a species that uses twigs (purposefully stripped from their leaves) for extracting termites from a cavity. Play activity of children of the early humans could have become a watershed for creation of art works, since finger agility, strong wrists, and bimanual coordination are all essential for artistic expression (visual or musical). By the time the Upper Paleolithic period rolled in, games could have been practiced.

Safety and comfortable time for art creations

Producing art works reflects the well-being of the society. It takes time to create bone tools with lovely handles and figurines out of ivory or antlers, or to create pendants and necklaces, puncture careful holes in shells, and grind color pigments, as well as figure out what pigments will last the longest (Henshilwood et al., 2004). The humans who were interested in doing so must have been well fed and in control of their environment. Being able to exercise good judgment in obtaining food and providing protection from the elements and wild animals left time for other things, namely for making images. The period of the Transition included very cold spells. Modern humans may have discovered the notion of refrigeration for keeping foods safe for eating. So the appearance of art around 45,000 years ago and its development in the next 10,000 years reflects a brain with a mind that was developed enough to occupy itself in times of isolation, to control and enjoy the immediate surroundings when travel was difficult. (Sort of like "snow days" when modern-day adults and children alike are forced to stay indoors and occupy themselves.) The early people could turn their attention to experimentation and symbolic representations of what was in their minds. There was time to mull over and think through doodling, possibly, since food was now not a major issue for concern.

In those early times, some individuals in the society may have had more talent than others due to genetic variations in the population, and those talents were entrusted to depict ideas and the real world. The following scenario may have transpired: time was set aside for them and the rest of the society provided support. Some of the discovered artifacts may have been fashioned by those artists, others by everyone else. Necklaces, for example, could have been fashioned by everyone. But to carve a bone or a piece of ivory in the shape of a human or an animal requires a great deal of skill today, and probably even then not everyone possessed that skill. It is not unreasonable to suggest that early humans living in small groups and bands functioned along divisions of labor, not only for men versus women, but also within the group as a whole; the ones who had more artistic talent than others may have spent time on their crafts. The notion of sticking together, supporting each other, identifying with members, all existed before image making appeared on the scene in human existence.

Origins of music in human brain evolution

Music as a communicative tool

Just as visual arts are ubiquitous in human societies, so is music. Cultural traditions distinguish the melodies of one culture from another, accentuating some sub-components more than others, while sharing a few universal features, such as the size of the octave (Hauser & McDermott, 2003). Music is ever changing even in our Western society. The human brain everywhere is designed to support and interpret musical sounds despite that fact that the ability to carry a tune may have a genetic basis (Trevarthen, 1999). The ability to sing or compose is independent of hearing level since people who have progressively lost their hearing continue to sing correctly, and some have gone on to compose (e.g., Beethoven, Smetana, Fauré; see Chapter 5).

In attempting to understand the origins of music we must consider that patterns of sounds uniting into meaningful wholes are not unique to human societies (Gray et al., 2001). Patterned sounds have a key role in animal communications; they vary widely in scope, extent, and intended purpose. Humans have even learned to imitate animal sounds, and some animals, notably certain parrots and mynah birds can learn to imitate human sounds, including singing. The chief difference between humans and animals is that the human brain can control various sources of musical expression, while with animals this is not so: most use their vocal cords; some birds do use their wings and feathers as well. Very few use instruments to make sounds, and in such rare cases this is part of a direct mate selection courtship display. There is another major difference and that is that the repertoire of humans' music is potentially infinite while this is not so with animals. There is a strong relationship between the diversity of human music and the grammatical flexibility of human language (Patel, 2003). Yes, some birds have remarkably rich and elaborate song repertoires, but this is unusual and still limited by biology and probably rarely if ever changes in the species. The fact that acoustic energy has patterns that can be converted into neuronal signals in many species inhabiting the earth, and interpreted to mean specific things, suggests a very early origin to human audition, music, and language.

As with animals, human music is a communicative tool. It has evolved to be performed in groups (Benzon, 2001), more so than in animals (although in some birds there is group vocalization by the males in a lek for the benefit of the observing females in courtship displays). Humans are highly social and music constituted a type of cohesiveness signals or alternatively, signals of distinctiveness (G. Miller, 2001). The evolutionary and adaptive origin of music in cohesiveness and bonding can be traced to a member of the great apes: in the group of the great apes, only the white-handed gibbons use songs to communicate. Specifically, they do so in order to cement social bonds between individual female–male pairs. The practice of chorusing could have preceded language (Merker, 2000). Music, because of its form and tempo, triggers rhythmic dancing movement and enables the group to engage in the response as a whole unit. Whereas in early times, and even now in non-Western societies, people continue to make music and dance in groups, in present-day Western societies this is not so to the same extent; the advent of radio and TV enables people to listen to music when no one else is around, and disco dancing usually involves only two partners. Although in some ways, listening to music alone is still a vicarious social event. It serves as a link to others, whether the other is nature or humanity. Either way, we experience this link upon listening to music. It makes us feel connected. Even when music evokes feelings of loneliness or smallness in the vastness of the world, that is in itself an acknowledgment of others.

The pleasure derived from producing music, through instruments or the voice, is hard to pin down, and to uncover its neural underpinnings. Why would there be universal pleasure associated with music? The energy that goes into producing it in some societies is enormous (Benzon, 2001). Music creates an emotional high that can be felt physically. A plausible explanation is that the pleasure is driven by some innate biological need, specifically the biological need to reproduce; it could be related to mate selection strategies and courtship displays (G. Miller, 2001). The louder the song and the music, the longer it can be emitted and played, the more it indicates fitness and good genes with a potential to produce healthy offspring. It would indicate very strong lungs, for one thing. Strong lungs predict endurance, perseverance, energy, robustness, and health, all of which are extremely desirable traits for survival. Similarly, strong arms and fingers are implied in sustained instrument playing. Thus, the pleasure associated with music is likely to have biological adaptive evolutionary precursors.

Mimicry of animal sounds, deception, and language

It is not unreasonable to propose that early humans learned to mimic animals in order to deceive and successfully hunt them. While most animals heard human sounds, they lacked the brain capacity to mimic them. The early humans could not have failed to notice that animals use deception in a variety of ways and manners, not only to hunt their prey but also for their own protection. A change in the location, shape, and capacity of the larynx is widely believed to signal the birth of human language (Holden, 2004). However, the unique shape of the larynx in humans compared to primates and early hominids does not necessarily have to signal the beginning of language. It could equally reflect the long-term use of the larynx for subtle and superb mimicking of animal sounds, a practice that easily could have developed some 500,000 years ago in Africa, a time when the size of the skull (and probably the brain) in early hominids increased in volume compared to what it was prior to that time and what it was afterwards (Allman, 2000). Our brains now are smaller than is indicated for early hominids who lived some 500,000 years ago. And the brain's control in such a use may have triggered changes, modifications, and alterations in the frontal lobes where all the cortical motor areas lie (representing the mouth cavity, larynx, limbs, eyes). Spoken language eventually became a better mode of communication than gestures and further adaptive changes had to take place in the brain (Carstairs-McCarthy, 2004; Holden, 2004; Pennisi, 2004). It has been suggested that spoken language evolved following facial and manual gestural language (Corballis, 2003). This may certainly have been a step in the sequence of human language evolution. Regardless, the initial fine control over the vocal cords could have originated with attempts to mimic animal sounds to perfection, and then to sing.

It is not implausible to speculate that early hominids and anatomically modern humans reacted to birds, and wished to do things as they did. Even nowadays humans are attracted by the regularity of bird courtship displays. Given their brain capabilities, early human ancestors, through learning from animals shaped the nature of their vocal utterances and thereby contributed somehow to their own adaptive evolution. Possibly, they shaped musical instruments to produce sounds similar to those that animals produced. While such "musical instruments" have not been unearthed yet, there is archaeological evidence from relatively recent times, for flutes shaped from bear bones by Neanderthals some 53,000 years ago (Fink, 2003; Gray et al., 2001), and they are not associated with the sophisticated language of the Homo sapiens. Humans are intrigued by animals, wanting to learn their "language", imitate their courage and physical strength, turn them into gods, and incorporate their movements into their own cultural dances. Many African dances, for example, utilize features that mimic the gait and strutting of certain animals (e.g., chicken flapping, ostrich walking, giraffe nodding). Indeed, religions with ancient origins represent their gods as animals or made their gods half-human, half-animal, and many cultures throughout the world, even until as recently as the ancient Greek culture, developed myths in which humans acquired fabulous animal skills or have made fools of themselves trying to be like them (e.g., the legend of Daedalus and Icarus who wished to fly like birds in order to escape their enemies). Relatively ancient figurines from Germany dated to be 32,000 years old (e.g., half-man, half-lion ivory figurine from the Hohle Fels Cave in the Ach Valley) attest to this interest (Conard, 2003), and wall paintings from Australia dated at 10,000 years old confirm the widespread use of this tendency (White, 2003b). Early on, before humans saw themselves as superior to animals, they might have considered themselves to be part of nature, and nature had animals. To this day, many non-Western societies have benevolent attitudes toward animals, seeing themselves and the animals as belonging to one ecosystem (even as they hunt animals down for food). Music may have developed and grown as early human ancestors wished to learn and mimic to their own advantage. This could have occurred in the pre-modern human stage, that is, in the early hominid period of brain development some 500,000 years ago in Africa, well before early hominids migrated out of that continent and before protospeech and protolanguage.

Innate reactions to music

Moreover, the biological nature of music can be seen in automatic reactions to the minor key. Why do sounds produced in this key sound sad? When and where did we learn to react with a feeling of sadness? Small toddlers, who can barely talk, react to music in the minor key with tears, the origin of which they themselves do not understand. The chief difference between the minor and major keys is the interval length; minor keys use a short interval while major keys use a long interval. It is not clear how interval length conspires to create sadness. Musical sounds are capable of triggering physiological and chemical reactions in the brain when the acoustic energy that enters the ears is translated into neuronal signals (Gray et al., 2001). The fact that this reaction happens without our conscious awareness, clearly indicates innate neuronal networks responsive to sounds of music. Currently, there is no agreement regarding neuroanatomical localization and how they operate. They must have been originally formed before hominid evolution, but as with all evolved brain structures, they became modified to match the brain of anatomically modern humans. Biologically old brain structures do not remain unchanged when the brain as a whole advances. Still, the very presence of those structures could explain automatic reactions to musical sounds, and many other environmental sounds, for that matter. Many babies react to loud sounds with extreme fright and many adults respond to unfamiliar loud noises with fright as well. Neuronal networks in our brain are modulating these responses and these reactions are possibly stimulating parts of the brain that evolved early in the formation of the mammalian brain. This is a general assumption and the exact localization is not agreed upon.

Symbolic nature of art and language

Language and art

Human language is made up of the mental lexicon, the words learned and known to the person, and grammar, the stored knowledge of rules. Single words themselves can stand for many meanings but the pairing of grammar and words together creates a highly powerful communication system. We know only a few of the equivalents of "words" and "grammar" in art although we are able to derive meaning from art without being aware of its words and grammar. In the visual arts, some of the words are based on the use of angles, perspective lines, convergence and vanishing points, overlap, light–dark manipulation, two-dimensional depth cues, canonical views, dis-embedding, texture, medium, and a few other principles. Keeping in mind that only humans have such a sophisticated language and only humans have art, it is tempting to associate the emergence of language with emergence of abundant art. The forms of expression, language on the one hand and art on the other, may have evolved through adaptation and selection pressures as forms of symbolic representations.

Evolution of language development: some issues and speculations

Several pivotal evolutionary and biological changes are currently considered and discussed in debates regarding what laid the neuronal underpinning for development of language (Holden, 2004; Pennisi, 2004). While the timing of language emergence in human evolution is a matter for debate and speculation, the several notions about its appearance now advocate a gradual development in which the neural and functional "seeds" were laid down (Aboitiz & Garcia, 1997); although the starting point of the development is not known, genetic research comparing several non-human primates proposes that a major turning point had begun sometime around 200,000 years ago (Enard et al., 2002). But this came after millions of years of anatomical brain structures evolving in non-human primates indicating growth of language-related areas in the left hemisphere (Holloway, Broadfield, & Yuan, 2004; Sherwood, Holloway, Erwin, & Hof, 2004). The functional adaptive factor considered to have made human language unique and powerful was the development of syntax (Nowak, Plotkin, & Jansen, 2000), which, in turn, is assumed to have conferred advantageous, competitive survival skills to early humans (Pinker, 2000; Pinker & Bloom, 1990). Single sounds, words, and concepts could now be combined infinitely through syntactic constructions, promoting and enhancing communication of ideas among people, which, in turn, enables thinking through ideas and significant planning (Deacon, 1997). By comparison, animals make multiple and varied single sounds, and even phrases, but together they appear to lack (as far as we know) the broadness and flexibility of syntactical communication.

Moreover, early humans living around 300,000 years ago already possessed a physiological prerequisite for enhanced range of speech sounds, namely a lower larynx in the throat cavity (the pharynx) than in non-human primates. But comparative neuroanatomical studies in non-human primates indicate that the neural precursors for oral-facial control have been laid down long before language fully developed in humans (Sherwood, Broadfield, Holloway, Gannon, & Hof, 2003a; Sherwood et al., 2003b; Sherwood, et al., 2004). In addition to the downward shifting of the larynx, space had been created that allowed more room for the tongue to move, and to create fine continuum of resonance in the vocal tract. Also, the shape of the chin and its movements had changed together with the larynx lowering. These anatomical changes could have been pivotal in language development according to some views (Deacon, 1997, 2000) since they allowed tremendous flexibility in vocal utterances. In gorillas or chimps, for example, the anatomy of the pharynx is too small and that places constraints on the movements of the tongue. Spoken language consists of refined oral and tongue praxis. Thus, coordinated rapid movements of the vocal cords, lips, and tongue with regulated breathing increased the range of possible emitted sounds. Speech is produced when the vocal cords, which sit within the larynx, vibrate selectively when air is pushed up from the lungs during voluntary exhalation. Neural control of these anatomical structures and speech processes in early humans might have triggered the critical turning-point.

There is more here. The essential step in the syntactical-related development could also have involved the recently discovered FOXP2 gene on chromosome 7 (Fisher, Vargha-Khadem, Watkins, Monaco, & Pembrey, 1998; Lai, Fisher, Hurst, Vargha-Khadem, & Monaco, 2001; Lai, Gerrelli, Monaco, Fisher, & Copp, 2003). This is inferred from the observation that disruption in this gene is linked specifically to developmental disorders in receptive and expressive language as well as in fine oral-facial movements. The genetic pinpointing was uncovered in several generations of one family known as the KE family (Vargha-Khadem et al., 1998). Affected members have effortful and sometimes unintelligible speech, grammatical errors, and difficulties in sequencing speech and fine facial movements. An MRI study (Watkins et al., 2002) revealed several abnormalities in the brains of the affected KE family members, bilaterally. The constellation of these abnormalities is presumed to be due in great part to mutation of the FOXP2 gene. Other genes, and yet unknown dynamic processes, could have contributed to the abnormalities as well (Marcus & Fisher, 2003; Newbury et al., 2002). For example, the severity of behavioral abnormalities was not equal across all affected family members (Harasty & Hodges, 2002; Watkins et al., 2002).

Two additional notions are debated in this evolutionary scenario: first, vital contributory mechanisms involve selective engagement of the motor pathway. Corballis (2003) has suggested that meaningful planned hand gestures and facial expressions provided the initial jumping board for speech development (see also McNeill, 2000). Lieberman has proposed that walking provided the essential adaptive change that promoted speech communication (Lieberman, 2002). Second, Arbib proposes that manual grasping, observing others, and imitation, together have prepared and readied the brain to accommodate syntactical language through development of mirror neuron mechanism (Mirror System Hypothesis), as inferred from neural circuitry in monkeys (reviewed in Arbib & Bota, 2003). Clearly, the precursors and readiness of the brain to develop combinatorial syntactical language were in place in monkeys, to say nothing of apes (Carstairs-McCarthy, 2004). This then needs to be linked to the brain readiness for art emergence.

When grammatical language "emerged", its format and components did not necessarily resemble most modern-day languages. First, it is assumed that language evolved gradually (Holden, 2004). What happened exactly during the evolved period is not clear at all. Second, not all the Homo sapiens lived in the same geographical spot: not all of them lived in Western Europe, for example. Suppose the language evolved in separated societies and was not uniform phonemically, morphologically, syntactically, and so on. What has not been studied is the relationship between the morphology, say, and the type of art that is produced by the people. Do societies with a morphologically complex language produce elaborate, sophisticated, symbolic, and abstract art? A clue lies in the current-day Piraha people of Brazil; they are a small hunter-gatherer society living in a few villages around the Amazon river. Their language has the fewest known phonemic arsenal, it has no color or number terms, and no perfect tense, but it is one of the most complex languages morphologically (Everett, 1986, 1988). Their art is practically non-existent; they produce the simplest looking drawings (child-like and resembling stick figures), make no sculptures, wear simple necklaces, and have no body decorations. Dan Everett (1988) proposes that their language is determined by their societal and cultural values. Regardless, the remarkable paucity of anything resembling art by the Piraha goes against the remarkable complexity of their linguistic morphology. The relationship between art making and at least one aspect of language, the morphology, can be tempered by cultural beliefs, and many other factors.

In sum, there is no unified consensus on the evolution of language since, basically, there is no direct fossil or archaeological evidence to indicate the precise time when human ancestors began to speak (Holden, 2004). There is also no obvious way to show how the emergence of language interplayed with early art practice. Still, as stated in preceding sections, language and art are assumed to have developed from adaptation and selection pressures as forms of symbolic representations.

Written pictures

Humans are unique in their use of symbolic notations. Even now humans use pictures, stylized or figurative, as symbols in order to economically communicate ideas. Marks and notches on cave walls and on old rocks suggest purposeful visual notations designed to communicate something through representation (White, 2003b). The visual notations were meant to convey an idea, concept, or actual words (which themselves are symbols, albeit consisting of sounds). With time, they later evolved to become the Egyptian hieroglyphs, and also logographs, as in Mayan writing glyphs, or Chinese characters. No such notational schemes are known to exist in other mammals. The evolution of this visual form of communication must have accompanied language development in the brain since writing is a form of language. Damage in the left hemisphere that results in aphasia can also disrupt writing. Moreover, writing is associated with the capacity to render graphically through manual control what is represented in the mind as well as the development of handedness. Such specialized manual ability (for writing) means having fine finger control, strong wrists, and bimanual coordination. The shape of the hand had to match the task; having strong hands and strong upper arm muscles cannot be essential for writing (Niewoehner, 2001). For example, the upper limb structures of the Neanderthals are biologically suitable to support heavy lifting and effort, consistent with the notion that they were very muscular. The hand remains of Neanderthals and early modern humans were compared through various imaging techniques and the results revealed differences that can explain why writing was possible in modern humans but not in the Neanderthals (Niewoehner, 2001).

Early modern human remains were found in the Near East, and good hand specimens have been uncovered in Israel, in Skhul and Qafzeh. They were dated to be between 80,000 and 100,100 years old. When those hand specimens were compared to European findings of Neanderthal hands, the early modern human hands showed a thumb in a particular opposition to the rest of the fingers that could support the holding of tools through their handles as well as facilitate fine finger movements. In other words, these hands could hold drawing, painting, and writing tools in order to execute delicate and fine finger motor movements. That is not to say that Neanderthal hands could not support tool making or tool handling, unimanually or bimanually (Conard et al., 2004). It is just that modern humans developed the kind of muscular strengths in their fingers, particularly in the strength of the thumb muscles and its mechanical agility. All of this could not have been accomplished had there not been a parallel adaptive development in the primary motor cortex.

Specific archaeological finds

Writing is a visual symbolic aspect of language and together with speech production, language comprehension, and reading, is specialized in the left hemisphere in the great majority of people. Earliest known writing systems include cuneiforms, hieroglyphs, and Indus river valley scripts (reviewed in Lawler, 2001). Scholars have dated the earliest recognizable writing system, cuneiforms, to 3200 BC, and to originate in Mesopotamia (modern-day Iraq). Archaeologists found them in the city of Uruk, approximately 200 miles south of Baghdad, written on hardened clay tablets. A little later in historical times, 3000 BC, the Egyptian hieroglyphs are believed to have developed (Oates & Oates, 2001). The earliest Chinese characters were dated to 1200 BC, to the Shang dynasty. It has been commonly believed that writing systems spread from Mesopotamia and Egypt to other parts of the world as humans migrated and cross-cultural exchanges took place.

However, recently discovered and analyzed finds from Iraq, Egypt, China, and South America suggest that the precursors of these writing systems existed earlier, and may have developed independently throughout the world. Finds in Iraq, in the same Uruk temple, as well as in Egypt, in the Abydos tomb, are now being redated to 3450 BC and 3320 BC respectively (Lawler, 2001). Even more revealing are new findings that suggest that writing precursors existed around 6600 BC in the form of markings, notations, and shapes. The shapes are called tokens and thousands of them have been discovered in the same ancient regions where the clear-cut writing systems existed. In China, for instance, archaeologists have discovered in graves located in the Huai river, in a site known as Jiahu, systematically marked tortoise shells dated to 6600 to 6200 BC (Lawler, 2003; Service, 2003). Some of the marks, consisting of geometrical shapes, have a great resemblance to the modern-day Chinese character for "eye" and to Chinese numbers. These marks could have functioned as systematic visual signs designed to mean something, they could have had a semantic content. In the Uruk site itself many clay tokens and spheres were also found and are now similarly interpreted; they may have served as early visual symbols, possibly with semantic content, before cuneiforms were written efficiently on wet clay tablets. In the Abydos site, in Egypt, fifty signs on bone and ivory objects are now interpreted to represent humans, animals, and a frontal view of a palace building. Although Egyptian hieroglyphs are supposed to have developed after the cuneiforms, these bone and ivory objects are dated to 3200 BC, the same time as the Mesopotamian cuneiforms. Additional cooking pot marks that appear to be deliberate, in the same Abydos site, were dated to 3500 BC. In Pakistan, archaeologists have dug up a site in Harapa, in the Indus river valley, where they found markings on artifacts that could also have been systematic and to predate the actual Indus river valley writing system dated to between 2800 and 1700 BC. The Harapa markings are being dated to 3500–3300 BC (Lawler, 2001).

Using realistic pictures is a good way to start notational systems because there is little room for ambiguity, and both young and old, in all levels of society, can understand messages conveyed in realistic pictures. The tendency to use pictorial symbols for representing ideas can be seen universally even today. The rough outline of a human moving, as in walking, is coupled with the green traffic light while an outline of a human figure standing still is coupled with the red light, both used for road traffic flow. Similarly, a stylized picture of an upright hand signals a road stop sign. Drawn symbols are another mode of human capacity to communicate.

Summary

Abundance of human art, of elaborate and detailed artifacts, appeared between 35,000 and 45,000 years ago in Western Europe, in an apparent sudden break from what was previously produced in that part of the world. However, evidence for production of some art goes as far back as 300,000 years ago (see Figure 1.2 in Chapter 1). Highly decorated handles in tools suggest a need to create something for symbolic reasons, over and above utilitarian use. The symbolic capability need not necessarily be tied up with linguistic capability. The latter could coexist without art production; in our current Western society few individuals produce art. Similarly, absence of archaeological evidence for elaborate visual art does not preclude presence of symbolic reasoning in the society (e.g., singing, music making, praying, beliefs, intentions). Nevertheless, art production has ancient origins and now appears to be universally ubiquitous. What is the biological purpose of art? Why do humans create art? These are some fundamental questions that anthropologists, biologists, archaeologists, and evolutionists have attempted to answer. One highly plausible explanation for how it all fits with the evolution and growth of the human brain is rooted in biology, that creating art is linked to its display, which in turn is associated with judgment by others, and the display together with the judgment hark back to biological mate selection strategies. In nature, animals display their prowess and physical appearance with the goal of exposing the quality of their genes and the potential of their progeny to survive. The better the genes, the more likely the survival. Art, in this sense, is an extension of this selection strategy – a production meant to show quality of physical strength plus intelligence, both of which are critical for survival of the species. This applies to all forms of the arts. With the visual arts, pictorial and visual symbols have led eventually to written symbols, and with music, mimicry of animal sounds have matured into language and music production, through the voice and instruments.

Further readings

Bickerton, D. (1998). Catastrophic evolution: The case for a single step from proto-language to full human language. In J. A. Hurford, M. Studdert-Kennedy, & C. Knight (Eds.), *Approaches to the evolution of language: Social and cognitive bases* (pp. 341–358). Cambridge: Cambridge University Press.

Christiansen, M. H., & Kirby, S. (Eds.). (2003). *Language evolution.* Oxford: Oxford University Press.

Conard, N. J., Grootes, P. M., & Smith, F. H. (2004). Unexpectedly recent dates for human remains from Vogelherd. *Nature, 430,* 198–201.

Cooke, B., & Turner, F. (Eds.). (1999). *Biopoetics: Evolutionary explorations in the arts.* St. Paul, MN: Paragon House.

Deacon, T. W. (1997). *The symbolic species: The co-evolution of language and the brain.* New York: W. W. Norton.

Dunbar, R. (1998). *Grooming, gossip, and the evolution of language.* Cambridge, MA: Harvard University Press.

Flinn, M. V., Geary, D. C., & Ward, C. V. (2005). Ecological dominance, social competition, and coalitionary arms races: Why humans evolved extraordinary intelligence. *Evolution and Human Behavior, 26,* 10–46.

Greenspan, S. I., & Shanker, S. (2004). *The first idea: How symbols, language, and intelligence evolved from our early primate ancestors to modern humans.* Boulder, CO: Perseus.

Hardy, B. L., Kay, M., Marks, A. E., & Monigal, K. (2001). Stone tool function at the paleolithic sites of Starosele and Buran Kaya III, Crimea: Behavioral implications. *Proceedings of the National Academy of Sciences, USA, 98,* 10,972–10,977.

Hauser, M. D., & Konishi, M. (Eds.). (2003). *The design of animal communication.* Cambridge, MA: MIT Press.

Hauser, M. D., Chomsky, N. & Fitch, W.T. (2002). The faculty of language: What is it, who has it, and how did it evolve? *Science, 298,* 1569–1579.

Holden, C. (2004). The origin of speech. *Science, 303,* 1316–1319.

Holloway, R. L., Broadfield, D. C., & Yuan, M. S. (Eds.). (2004). *The human fossil record, brain endocasts: The paleoneurological evidence.* Hoboken, NJ: Wiley-Liss.

Kuhn, S. L., Stiner, M. C., Reese, D. S., & Gulec, E. (2001). Ornaments of the earliest Upper Paleolithic: New insights from the Levant. *Proceedings of the National Academy of Sciences, USA, 98,* 7641–7646.

Lopes, D. M. M. (2000). From language of art to art in mind. *Journal of Aesthetics and Art Criticism, 58,* 227–231.

MacNeilage, P. F. (1998). The frame/content theory of evolution of speech production. *Behavioral and Brain Science, 21,* 511–546.

MacNeilage, P. F., & Davis, B. L. (2001). Motor mechanisms in speech ontogeny: Phylogenetic, neurobiological and linguistic implications. *Current Opinion in Neurobiology*, *11*, 696–700.

McNeill, D. (1992). *Hand and mind: What gestures reveal about thought*. Chicago: University of Chicago Press.

McNeill, D. (Ed.). (2000). *Language and Gesture: Window into thought and action*. Cambridge: Cambridge University Press.

Mellars, P. (2004). Neanderthals and the modern human colonization of Europe. *Nature*, *432*, 461–465.

Mithen, S. (2005). *The singing Neanderthals: The origins of music, language, mind and body*. London: Weidenfeld and Nicholson.

Pennisi, E. (2004). The first language? *Science*, *303*, 1319–1320.

Ridley, M. (1998). *The origins of virtue: Human instincts and the evolution of cooperation*. New York: Penguin.

Rogers, L. J., & Kaplan, G. (2000). *Songs, roars, and rituals: Communication in birds, mammals, and other animals*. Cambridge, MA: Harvard University Press.

Shlain, L. (2003). *Sex, time, and power: How women's sexuality shaped human evolution*. New York: Viking.

Smith, D. L. (2004). *Why we lie: The evolutionary roots of deception and the unconscious mind*. New York: St. Martin's Press.

Storaro, V. (2003). *Vittorio Storaro: Writing with light: Vol. 1. The light*. New York: Aperture.

Wallin, N. L., Merker, B. & Brown, S. (Eds.). (2001). *The origins of music*. New York: Bradford.

11 Further considerations in the neuropsychology of art

Introduction

A natural observational setting for neuropsychology and neuroscience is afforded in the artist's studio. Artists often produce on their own volition, their productions reflecting the mind in the brain outside carefully controlled conditions of a scientific laboratory. Yet no specific neuropsychological tests have been designed to assess art following brain damage in artists. This is largely due to the fact that only a few of the equivalents of "words" and "grammar" in art are known, and relatively few such artists can constitute the standardization sample. The alphabetical primitives in visual art consist of forms, shapes, and patterns represented with various angles, perspective lines, convergence, vanishing points, overlap, grayscale gradations, canonical views, disembedding, texture, medium, colors, shadows, and edges. These examples do not all have ready interpretations within existing neuropsychological tools or models. In addition, the significance of the whole composition lies in the culture in which the art is produced and is experienced. A method for separating this from alphabetical art primitives remains to be worked out.

Art expression is by and large unique to humans but there is no obvious direct relationship to language development and evolution. Although both art and language represent diverse communication forms, each with combinatorial powers, the neuropsychological evidence from brain-damaged artists suggests no or weak relationship between the two forms of communication. Complexity of linguistic components in human languages has never been studied in relation to complexity in art (see Chapter 10) but if studied with this in mind, it could reveal useful insights. The language of the Piraha people, a hunter-gatherer society in the Amazon basin of Brazil, has exceptionally few morphemes but a most complex word structure system (morphology), and yet their art is practically non-existent (Everett, 1986). At the dawn of human brain development, language and art may not have been closely intertwined. But since there is currently absence of fossil and archaeological evidence this still remains to be determined. In the evolutionary scheme of things, the neuronal support for abstraction and symbolism could have promoted art expression earlier than language. In any case, the emergence of both modes of communication likely relied on biological mechanisms that took millions of years to evolve (e.g., neuroanatomical asymmetries, frontal lobe enlargement).

Art's symbolic representations rely on the ability to use abstraction. The execution of this abstraction, in addition to its conception, depends on the interface of several neural systems, notably sensory systems of the eyes and ears, the motor system, and those processing cognitive, long-term memory, and emotions. Neuropsychology traditionally extracts interpretations from behavior following brain lesions. The alterations we see in artists' post-damage works open only a partial window into the neural substrates. The mental activity that goes into producing art encompasses additional factors (besides the culture within which it is created). Talent is one of those factors; its characteristics are unformulated at this point mostly because of debates regarding its nature versus nurture qualities (see general discussion of this issue in Howe et al., 1998). Yet, it, creativity, and imagery are part of art's formula as well. These topics and special complexities in art are further discussed in this chapter.

Talent and creativity

Creativity in art

Raw talent is considered to be abilities and skills with a strong innate basis. They are expressed through interaction with creativity in different forms of art, and in other fields of human endeavor (Guilford, 1950; Sternberg, 1988). Teasing these factors apart is no simple matter. The notion of talent is known to so-called primitive societies. In Papua New Guinea, people in the Sepik river region relegate the task of producing art works only to special individuals whose skills are admired. Similarly, the Gola people in Africa regard talented artists as being special people, inspired by unique forces (Dissanayake, 1988). In Western society, a great deal of respect, admiration, and appreciation is similarly directed to exceptional and successful artists. Still, if artistic talent is innate, it is still amenable to nurture, that is to shaping through experience and learning in normal individuals (see Amabile, 2001; Fein, Obler, & Gardner, 1988; Howe et al., 1998).

The practice of art allows experimentation and innovation, and the extent that the society allows this, the practice is a reflection of cognitive and emotional flexibility. Similarly, the extent to which artists in their work can rise above the conventional, established, familiar, stereotypical, accepted, and create something novel is a measure of their inventiveness. There is no agreement among researchers and theoreticians on "standardized tests" for measuring creativity (Sternberg, 1988). Writers, poets, dancers, scientists, film directors, and business people are creative individuals and their works have produced just as much awe and wonderment as the works of visual and musical artists. Although in the popular media and some textbooks the right hemisphere has been characterized as "creative" there has been no good evidence that this is so. If anything, as illustrated in this book, one could put up an argument in favor of left hemisphere cognition giving rise to creativity. Specialization in language draws on cognitive modes that support a combinatorial system with infinite possibilities of pairings that convey meaning. Such a broad range of pairings and conjoining could provide the basis for creativity. Attending to details in the environment, remembering details, cardinality, piecemeal approach to problems, all contribute to the cognitive ability of thinking deductively and logically. This, together with combinatorial cognition may give the left hemisphere an edge in the creative process. Language is not antithetical to creativity as evidenced by literary arts. Language is but a part of a cognitive system specialized in the left hemisphere. Imagery seems to be an essential element of the insight process, for instance, the realization moment of the long sought after solution to a scientific problem, and this is when the right hemisphere may be optimally involved (but see discussion on imagery below). But then, scientific and mathematical solutions have presented themselves in dreams, typically after spending days, weeks, and months on alternative solutions. Both the left and right hemispheres are active in dreaming (Buchsbaum, Hazlett, Wu, & Bunney, 2001; Hobson & Pace-Schott, 2003; McCormick et al., 1997, 2000). In general, it is highly likely that independently of the medium or mode of expression there is bilateral involvement of the two hemispheres in the creative process, albeit in asymmetric and complementary ways. In the context of this book, the most parsimonious substantial evidence is intactness of creativity in established artists with injury in the left or the right hemisphere.

The artist Georges Braque provides us with an additional insight into the thinking behind the creative process, particularly in visual art:

> In my paintings, if fantasy is non-existent, the effect of surprise nonetheless plays a role. Take my large canvas "In Full Flight", which is in the exhibition at the Louvre. So. It is finished, as harmonious as anyone could wish. At the end of four months, after seeing it every day, living with it, I noticed that I had become too used to it. Too comfortable for the eye. I therefore decided to create a disruption by painting in the lower left of the picture another bird confined in a sort of white rectangular frame, everything imposed there like a trademark, a stamp. By creating contradiction, and not disharmony, the entire picture comes to life in a more unexpected manner. Sometimes these effects of surprise are necessary. It prevents routine from setting in.
>
> (Braque, quoted in Wilkin, 1991, p. 103)

Imagery and imagination

Are imagination and imagery one and the same? Is mental visualization as in mental rotation equivalent to creativity in art? Imagery has sometimes been equated with insightful inventiveness in art and science (A. Miller, 2000, 2002). Scientists have described seeing in their mind's eye long-sought solutions to problems, reporting that the eureka moment consisted of some kind of a mental visual image. With artists, it has been assumed that imagery plays a critical role in the production process, in the visual and musical arts as well as in the literary or theater arts. This indeed may be the case and a topic of further research in the future (but see Chapter 7; see also Winner & Casey, 1992).

What is the evidence from neuroimaging techniques regarding brain activation during imagery tasks in non-artists? Such studies typically include verbal instructions to the subjects to imagine something specific. One fMRI study reports selective activation of the left inferior frontal and temporal lobes upon verbal imagery instructions (Yomogida et al., 2004). Another fMRI study involving playing piano in the mind's eye reports bilateral activation in the premotor areas as well as the fronto-parietal motor network and the precuneous (Meister et al., 2004; see also Figure 1.4). In subjects blind from birth, mental imagery instructions activated visual cortices bilaterally, including the occipital and parietal lobes, and similar visual networks were activated in sighted subjects (Lambert, Sampaio, Mauss, & Scheiber, 2004). When internally generated imagery was required in the context of deductive reasoning and spatial thinking, bilateral activation of several cortical regions was again observed (Knauff, Mulack, Kassubek, Salih, & Greenlee, 2002). Areas other than the V5 were found to be active bilaterally in mental rotation tasks, and the precuneous (located in the posterior parietal lobe: see Figure 3.3) was activated bilaterally (Barnes et al., 2000). The V5 complex (also known as the MT area, for motion cortex) is in the posterior bank of the superior temporal sulcus (Zeki, 2004); it contains motion sensitive neurons and one would expect this complex to be involved in mental rotations (see Figure 1.4). In all, V5 was active depending on the nature of the mental rotation task required thereby indicating that there are types of rotations and different neural substrates that are engaged selectively. Indeed, the Barnes et al. (2000) study found that Brodmann's area 19 (anterior portion of the occipital lobe) and the supplementary premotor area (anterior to the premotor gyrus in the frontal lobe) were active in the rotation tasks (see Figure 1.4).

Imagery, presumably, is one of the underpinning ingredients in creativity. The relationship between imagery and creativity was investigated in a meta-analytic study and the results indicated that the association is not at all strong, nor that it is obvious given individual differences and task paradigms (LeBoutillier & Marks, 2003). Overall, brain localization in imagery and the relationship with creativity are currently inconclusive.

Neuropsychology of creativity

Creativity is producing something new that did not exist previously, with positive, aesthetic appeal to society, whether in art, science, politics, or business. Obviously, there is a continuum of what can be considered to be creativity – some productions are more creative than others; the degree of "newness" is a sliding scale, albeit with defined limits. Importantly, creativity is a positive concept that implies an aesthetic and useful product for society. The basic principle in creativity is the ability to transcend the given, the known, the conventional and the established formula, by producing something new. Creativity in science, for example, may have a genetic basis (Shepard, 1997). That which is long known is entrenched in our long-term representation of experience, guiding our behavior, forming our concepts, directing accumulation of new information, and influencing what we remember and think. The truly creative individuals throughout human history were remarkable in that they created new associations in their minds despite entrenched concepts, and then worked through them relentlessly until the new product emerged. Einstein's theory of relativity is considered very creative and aesthetic. Newton's and Galileo's discoveries and theories are also considered very creative. Giotto, Michelangelo, Leonardo, Rembrandt, Bach, Mozart, Van Gogh, Cézanne, Picasso, and Magritte are all innovators in their art form. What part of their brains modulated the creativity? There is no easy answer to this question partly because problems with clear-cut definition notwithstanding, the creative time window, its instance of appearance in the mind of the creating person, is not known nor could ever be pinpointed, and thus could not be measured with, say, neuroimaging techniques in the same way that those techniques measure language or other cognitive processing in the brain. Even if the creator knows the time of a "creative window", it is a moment that reflects many hours, days, weeks, months, or years of previous work. For now it is worthwhile to speculate, discuss, and conduct experiments that potentially could tease apart some of the components of creativity and their control by the brain.

Language and creativity: clues from fronto-temporal dementia

In Chapter 4, the visual artistic work of patients with fronto-temporal dementia was described. Here, their cases are discussed from the perspective of creativity: we can obtain further clues to the neural substrates of creativity by considering dementia cases, particularly those with known pre-morbid accomplishments (Miller et al., 2000). As explained in Chapter 4, two remarkable inventors had fronto-temporal dementia, a neurodegenerative disease that gradually affected the frontal and temporal lobes and the connectivity between them, while sparing parietal and occipital regions. Widespread cortical atrophy eventually resulted in dementia. One case was an inventor who designed a chemical detector (Miller et al., 2000). Her progressive aphasia symptoms began at age 68 years; they became increasingly worse and extended to the inability to read. The remarkable feature in her condition was that despite the disease and until age 74 years she successfully worked on her inventions as evidenced by the fact that she obtained new patents. The parietal and occipital regions as well as frontal lobe regions were spared. The other case was an airplane designer who had patents for related inventions. At age 69 years he began to experience language and memory difficulties. Yet, his topographical navigation remained unimpaired as was his designing and engineering capabilities. All of this is post-disease diagnosis. He, too, had sparing of frontal, parietal, and occipital lobes.

What shall we make of these two cases as far as creativity is concerned? When everything is taken into account, the significance of the cases lies in demonstrating that inventions in pre-morbid intellectual areas of expertise – both patients did not invent in previously unpracticed fields – can proceed post-diagnosis despite brain deterioration in localized brain areas, including those that subserve language. However, they did not develop new inventive abilities. Post-diagnosis, the first case perfected her previous inventions. The report does not state that she went on to invent in brand new fields. The second case did not invent new patents or design brand new airplanes. The obvious inference is that intact parts of their brains contributed to their ability to work on what they already were proficient at doing (see neuro-anatomical basis in Chapter 4, in the section on slow brain changes and serial lesion effects). The fact that language was severely compromised, and in one case, memory was deteriorating, shows that professional expertise can proceed independently of the intactness of language – as was the case throughout most of their lives when their language was intact – and when language was deteriorating in the course of their disease. In other words, talent and excellence in specific skills are independent of language. Language and creativity do not have to be mutually exclusive, they could coexist or not.

These two exceptional individuals also demonstrate the notion of redundancy in storage of long-term experience. Had they gone on to invent brand new things in fields that they had not previously tackled, the meaning of creativity and its relationship to language would have to be drastically revised and reconsidered. The fact remains that when their language abilities were intact, in the long pre-morbid period of their lives, they created with originality and inventiveness all those products for which they received their first patents.

Left hemisphere creativity: clues from autistic savants

Further insight to the neuropsychology of creativity can also be obtained from exploring the productions of untypical artists (first described in Chapter 4). Let us consider the autistic visual arts savants; they have congenital brain dysfunction that prevents them from normal social and communication interaction with people and the world (Mottron et al., 2003; Sacks, 1995; Selfe, 1977; Treffert & Wallace, 2002). The evidence for specific brain damage in autism is not consistent (Rapin, 1999), and the nature of brain alterations are at present not fully explained in the literature (Sokol & Edwards-Brown, 2004). In autism there is reduced size of the vermis in the cerebellum (not a structure known to be important in high mental functions), in the medial temporal lobes bilaterally (DeLong, 1999); one study suggests that the left temporal lobe is more structurally affected than the right (Treffert & Wallace, 2002), and other evidence shows that levels of serotonin are particularly low in the left frontal, temporal, and parietal lobes (DeLong, 1999; Di Martino & Castellanos, 2003). Since autistic individuals suffer from severe language and communication problems, left hemisphere dysfunction is assumed to be mainly responsible for the disorder. There is scarcity of data on the brains of autistic visual artists but for the sake of discussion let us suppose that they, too, suffer from some form of left hemisphere dysfunction. However, if as some have claimed, their remarkable graphic skills are largely controlled by the right hemisphere (their left hemisphere being presumably dysfunctional, as deduced from the fact that their language skills are either non-existent or extremely poor), applying the logic of inferring function from brain damage, the absence of creativity in their works is due to lack of support from a poorly functioning left hemisphere. Their art displays great graphic skills, but it is a highly realistic kind of art, one with little abstraction, little signs of originality, or innovation. Nadia, EC, and Stephen Wiltshire have all received art instructions but benefited very little. If their art lacks creativity and their art does represent capacities of an intact right hemisphere then, by inference, the control of creativity in art comes mainly from the left hemisphere in the non-autistic person. While the right parietal lobe provides support for accurate depiction of reality including representations of three-dimensional space and good depictions of depth, something we see in the art of autistic artists, the contributions to creativity are doubtful. Thus, from the work of these untypical artists it is reasonable to suggest that the left hemisphere in the normal brain is more capable of reshaping existing concepts, giving rise to originality and innovation, than the right.

Neurotransmitters: clues from Parkinson's disease treatment

Talent may lie dormant until a particular neurological event uncovers its presence in the individual. Another neurological case in whom artistic expression emerged is that of a Parkinson's disease patient who developed Parkinson symptoms at age 40 and who eventually began to write high quality poetry for the first time in his life (Schrag & Trimble, 2001). Initially, the tremor and dystonia were lateralized to the left hand and leg, which implies greater right hemisphere dysfunction. In the course of four years the symptoms worsened and treatment in the form of dopamine agonist lisuride as well as levodopa was initiated. Within the first month symptoms improved and he began to produce poems for the very first time. An increase in libido was also a consequence of the drug treatment. In that same year, he wrote ten poems. Subsequently he published some poems and even won a prestigious poetry prize. He continued to write poems for many years despite progression of Parkinson symptoms and changes in levels of medication. The authors of the article note, however, that the patient's grandfather on his mother's side had written poetry. They speculate that dopaminergic and serotonergic stimulation (induced by drug treatment) together with loss of inhibition due to frontal lobe dysfunction allowed the emergence of new literary creativity. While their analysis may bear out as the best explanation, one has to wonder the extent to which elements of poetry conceptualization expressed themselves in his pre-morbid existence. But, then, one would still have to explain why such presumed conceptualization and cognition emerged only when drug treatment began and not when actual symptoms began. The implication is that neurotransmitter upheaval or imbalance together with specific structural brain alterations can go a long way to contribute to creative artistic production.

Complexities of visual art

While the neurological evidence indicates that the right parietal lobe is much more important for perceiving and rendering spatial relationships than the left, it is not so that all there is to visual art is spatial relationships (see Chapter 8). Consider the representation of light and its varying presence on different portions of the canvas. When Monet painted the same object under varying degrees of sunlight, it is hard to see how his understanding, analysis, and talent of execution of those effects were critically dependent on good spatial perception and mentation. Placing a dab of one color here and another color there to deliberately connote the interaction of light and object may only mildly require use of spatial relationship skills. Similarly, mixing of colors on a painter's palette to obtain just the desired pigment is not necessarily related to spatial knowledge. Other features in his paintings do indeed depend on spatial skills; the use of convergence and linear perspective would reflect such dependence.

   Another example is artists' ability to depict fast motion on canvas. Several graphic techniques are used to indicate that something is moving, including balance, partially overlapping frames denoting speed, and controlled patches of fuzziness and blurriness, to name but a few (Cutting, 2002). A famous example of motion depiction on canvas is by the Cubist artist, Marcel Duchamp, *Nude Descending a Staircase, No. 2*, which he painted in 1912. In modern times, it was the school of Futurism that showed particular interest in depicting fast motion, with the idea that art should look to the future and depict that instead of depicting the past (Shlain, 1991). The Futurist painter Giacomo Balla painted *Dynamism of a Dog on a Leash*, also in 1912, and illustrated in a most convincing way the very fast leg movements of a tiny walking dog. Other artists applied this difficult representation of changing time in planar work. The contemporary American artist Susan Rothenberg, depicts motion in several of her works, the most famous being *Vaulting* (Simon, 2000). The idea of motion on still surface may have been attempted as long ago as 30,000 years in the Chauvet cave in France. Such renditions require deliberate attention to minute details and logical analysis, which draw on left hemisphere cognition.

Some fMRI findings indicate that the brain region engaged in viewing real motion is also engaged in viewing apparent movement. The motion cortex in humans, V5, sits in the medial superior temporal cortex, in the zone of the posterior superior temporal sulcus (see Figure 1.4). This region becomes active upon viewing apparent movement as well as in pictures depicting humans in action (e.g., someone throwing a ball, a person about to hit a golf ball) and nature scenes depicting motion (e.g., a large rolling sea wave) (Kourtzi & Kanwisher, 2000). When seeing art works in which there is implied movement, this region is presumably activated as well (bilaterally). Damage to this area results in motion blindness, also known as akinetopsia, where moving objects appear frozen (Blanke, Landis, Mermoud, Spinelli, & Safran, 2003a; Zihl, von Cramon, & Mai, 1983). Visual perception of forms, shapes, and colors can remain intact in such cases. The problem lies specifically in motion perception. A stream of tea looks frozen in mid-air as it is being poured. Crossing the street may be dangerous because cars do not appear to be moving closer. What is particularly significant in the fMRI findings is that the brain region engaged in viewing real motion is the same one that is engaged in viewing *apparent* movement and *implied* motion in pictures.

Lessons from brain damage in artists

The study of neurological patients with focal brain damage has served as a reliable and valid source for understanding functional brain localization. We have seen throughout this book that art production continues in established artists despite the damage, its etiology or extent. This suggests a wide and diffuse representation of art talent and skill. The skill that produces art works appears to recruit several neuronal networks. Acquired damage to the right hemisphere or to the left hemisphere, in various focal areas, does not lead to disappearance, abolishment, or elimination of artistic production. Nor does the ability to draw objects from memory by non-artists disappear following similar damage. Talent, extensive lifelong practice, and skill preservation all suggest redundancy in functional representation and explain the spared artistic capacity.

In addition, what does not happen as a result of insult to the brain is a switch in mode of representation, where representation is what is meant by *art genre*, as in realism, Surrealism, abstract, and so on. So we do not see a shift from realistic to abstract depictions, and vice versa (see introduction to Chapter 2 where artistic style is defined). Importantly, whatever is different in the post-damage art is not unaesthetic or unartistic or uncreative. Indeed, artistic skill preservation is remarkable given extent of brain damage in a given artist.

The issue of skill preservation in the case of Edouard Manet (1832–1883) is also revealing: Manet was diagnosed around 1878 with severe locomotor problem in the left leg (inability to walk or move with the left leg), a symptom of cerebral neurosyphilis (Boime, 1996). Eventually, a gradual paralysis developed in the leg, greatly hampering his walking. He also experienced excessive fatigue and pain. All these symptoms interfered with his work to some extent and may explain, in part, increased creations in pastels. It is difficult to say when exactly he contracted the syphilis. The effect of his illness may be particularly evident in one of his large last paintings, completed in 1882, *A Bar at the Folies-Bergère* (Boime, 1996). In this painting, Manet depicts a central figure of a barmaid in the foreground. In the background is a huge mirror in which numerous objects and human figures are shown. The depictions in the mirror do not faithfully obey physical laws of light reflection. This in turn raises the tantalizing possibility that Manet's brain illness affected some of his spatial cognition (greater neural degeneration in the right hemisphere?) interfering somewhat with correct assessment of angles of sight in mirror reflections, without affecting his artistic skills to convey meaning and aesthetics. The painting is a subject of much debate and speculation by art historians with regards to what Manet intended to convey (Collins, 1996; Galligan, 1998).

Art in human existence

Art is ubiquitous throughout the world, appearing probably more than 300,000 years ago, with the greatest influx of artifacts emerging (surviving) in Western Europe around 35,000 to 45,000 years ago. The footprints of music from that long ago are now available only in flute-like musical instruments, including those made by the Neanderthals. It is highly likely that the beginnings of art were expressed by early hominids in both the visual and musical domains even before sophisticated syntactical language took hold in the brain. It is also not unreasonable to speculate that art expression preceded language development, possibly predicted its growth following prolonged use of symbolism and representation in art-related domains and then growing significantly together with language. We have seen in the artists with brain damage that art and language are dissociable but not antagonistic functions. In both there is reliance on pre-existing biological mechanisms and neuro-anatomical structures for supporting cognitive abstraction. Future experimental procedures can potentially unravel additional perspectives on how art and brain are related. Further unraveling of the neural substrates of art should shed light particularly when viewed through the lens of its communication value.

Summary

Art production by established artists represents the activities of several systems of neural substrates. There is no distinct "music center" nor "art center" in the brain but most likely dedicated neural networks. Artistic success stems from many factors including talent, lifelong practice, and creativity. Observable alterations in artists' work after brain damage do not embody the full gamut of the mental energy that goes into art. While the neurological evidence indicates that the right parietal lobe is much more important for perceiving and rendering spatial relationships than the left, it is not so that all there is to visual art is spatial relationships. Raw talent denotes abilities and skills that may be innate. They are expressed through interaction with creativity in different forms of art, and in other fields of human endeavors. Creativity is not confined to visual or musical art works. Writers, poets, dancers, scientists, and business people are creative as well. The role of each hemisphere in the creative process is not at all established. There is no evidence to support a binary hemispheric contribution to creativity; the notion that right hemisphere cognition gives rise to creativity and left hemisphere cognition does not is not parsimonious. Language, which is mainly specialized in the left cerebral hemisphere, is not a cognitive system that is antithetical to creativity. Language is but a part of a cognitive system in the left hemisphere. With artists, it has been assumed that imagery plays a critical role in the production process, but fMRI evidence suggests bilateral activation during imagery tasks. The best evidence that creativity is bilaterally controlled comes from intactness of creativity in established artists with damage in either the left or the right hemisphere. A further clue can be obtained from exploring the nature of productions by untypical artists. Autistic visual arts savants have severe language and social communication problems; left hemisphere dysfunction is assumed to be mainly responsible for the disorder. Their works are spatially correct but there is not much to see by way of creativity.

The evidence from artists with unilateral damage points to the involvement of several brain regions and to cooperation between the two hemispheres. Talent, extensive practice, and skill all suggest redundancy in functional representation and basis for spared artistic capacity following brain or sensory damage. Skill preservation is remarkable given extent of brain damage. We have seen in the established visual and musical artists that art and language are dissociable functions but are not antagonistic functions. Both have a reliance on pre-existing biological mechanisms.

The reliance of both art and language on abstraction invites the possibility of long evolving neural substrates to support both of these forms of communication. In the course of human brain evolution, art expression may have preceded language development, possibly even predicted language specialization following prolonged use of non-language forms of symbolism and representation, and then undergoing further modifications together with full-blown specific language development.

Further readings

Cassirer, E. (1965). *The philosophy of symbolic forms: Vol. 1. Language*. New Haven, CT: Yale University Press.

Crow, T. (1999). *The intelligence of art*. Chapel Hill, NC: University of North Carolina Press.

Dacey, J. S. (1998). *Understanding creativity: The interplay of biological, psychological, and social factors*. San Francisco, CA: Jossey-Bass.

Elgin, C. Z. (2000). Reorienting aesthetics, reconceiving cognition. *Journal of Aesthetics and Art Criticism, 58*, 219–225.

Eysenck, H. J. (1995). Creativity as a product of intelligence and personality. In D. Saklofske & M. Zeidner (Eds.), *International handbook of personality and intelligence: Perspectives on individual differences* (pp. 231–247). New York: Plenum Press.

Finke, R. A. (1990). *Creative imagery: Discoveries and inventions in visualization*. Hillsdale, NJ: Lawrence Erlbaum Associates, Inc.

Finke, R. A., Ward, T. M., & Smith, S. M. (1992). *Creative cognition: Theory, research, and applications*. Cambridge, MA: MIT Press.

Goodman, N. (1976). *Languages of art*. Indianapolis, IN: Hackett.

Gould, J. G., & Purcell, R. W. (2000). *Crossing over where art and science meet*. Three Rivers, MI: Three Rivers Press.

Hauser, M. D. (1997). *The evolution of communication*. Cambridge, MA: MIT Press.

Miller, A. I. (2002). *Einstein, Picasso: Space, time, and the beauty that causes havoc*. New York: Basic Books.

Simonton, D. K. (1999). *Origins of genius: Darwinian perspectives on creativity*. New York: Oxford University Press.

Winner, E. (1997). *Gifted children: Myths and realities*. New York: Basic Books.

12 Conclusion and the future of the neuropsychology of art

Convergent evidence coming from different experimental techniques and varied neurological etiologies has informed neuropsychology theories since the 1850s. Ideally, a theory or a model that captures the essence of the brain's control in art would emerge from the exploration of the cases described in this book as well. Such a collection of cases has not been assembled previously and the potential for a unified characterization is clearly present. A unitary formalization at this stage is hampered by several reasons: wide spectrum of personal artistic techniques, the relatively small sample size of artists, unmeasured factors of talent or creativity (innovation), cognitive abstraction, and variability in damage localization, laterality, and size of lesion area, to name but a few primary reasons. In other words, there would necessarily be a lack of uniformity in the way that artists adjust to the damage. Therein lies the difficulty in distilling an overarching neuropsychology theory that could predict how any given artist would produce his art following brain damage.

Although elucidation of the art–brain relationship is in its very early stages, some important insights and patterns have been discerned from the explorations in this book. A distinct recurrent type of artistic composition post-damage has not emerged across or within the different etiologies discussed here. For example, one visual artist with aphasia (ZB, described in Chapter 2) produced works that displayed left–right symmetry, reduced depth perspective, and muted colors. Such portrayals are not characteristic of the other artists with aphasia. Why? The myriad of approaches available to artists is so varied and diverse that individual artists can depict their art in nearly infinite ways; ultimately, they employ strategies reflecting their neuronal uniqueness. Moreover, the role of functional reorganization in producing variability in post-damage art behavior and production cannot be overlooked (see discussion of functional reorganization in Chapter 4).

At the same time, one clear recurrent outcome that did emerge post-damage, regardless of laterality or lesion localization, is the adherence to the pre-damage artistic style (mode of representation, the genre). What is meant by artistic style was defined in the introduction to Chapter 2. Techniques used to express the artistic style (if changed at all) were mildly, somewhat, or dramatically so; this could reflect the combined effects of the motoric, sensory, and cognitive consequences of the damage (plus neuronal factors such as reorganization). The combined effects, however, do not fit neatly into a specific neuropsychology theory. For example, the reasons for why the aphasia in artist ZB (and the brain damage) co-occurred with a particular artistic profile are not obvious at all. Nothing known about aphasia and its disorders would predict this profile. Nothing known about the functions lateralized to the left hemisphere would necessarily predict it. Again, the wealth of artistic techniques in each artist's arsenal seems to interfere with neat delineation of the post-damage artistic behavior. And, importantly, another recurrent outcome is the preservation of artistic skills in all the artists.

Furthermore, in non-artists with left hemisphere damage, we would expect absence of details in pictorial drawings but we would expect to see in the drawings an overall configuration, the gestalt (see Chapters 7 and 8). In artists, however, such dissociation is not observed. Similarly, with non-artists with right hemisphere damage we would expect to see disorders in depictions of convergent perspective and spatial organization, and yet such consistent dissociation is not seen in artists with right hemisphere damage. Even when we consider left hemi-neglect in some of the artists with right hemisphere damage, it is obvious that the artists continued to produce their artistry nevertheless. That is, whatever the neural underpinning of the phenomenon of neglect may turn out to be, that would not be an integral aspect of the neuroanatomy of art. Explanations for absence of such profiles lie with extensive pre-damage practice of skills and an artist's particular neural organization supporting talent (see Chapters 4 and 11).

How do we reconcile neuropsychological findings from non-artists with artistic productions post-damage? The answer requires careful examination of what is available by way of theory and model: a significant brain and behavior factor in neuropsychological formulations is hemispheric specialization. Characteristic cognitive and thinking styles of the left hemisphere, besides its main language specialization, includes detailed, attentive, piecemeal, analytic, and logical processes (see Chapter 1); right hemisphere computations are assumed to consist of global, wholistic, or gestalt strategies, and this includes facial processing (see Chapters 7 and 8). Somehow, asymmetry in artistic expression post-damage should have materialized according to laterality of damage. But this did not occur, save in one case (the fashion designer described in Chapter 2). The fact that the majority of the data did not fall neatly along hemispheric lines is not discouraging for neuropsychological elucidation of art. The future model or theory would have to be generated from empirical and observational data; it would accommodate what happens to art production (neuropsychologically) when established artists suffer unilateral, focal brain damage, and clearly would need to account for variability in functional reshaping and compensatory neural takeover. Importantly, assessment of cognitive abstraction would need to be performed. Neuroscientific elucidations of art and brain are currently at a very early stage.

Another recurrent pattern in the artists here is the preservation of creativity post-damage. Independently of damage laterality, neuropsychological profile, or etiology, the majority continued to develop and innovate within the boundaries of their chosen genre. Neuropsychology would not have predicted a priori what type of brain damage or its laterality could bring a halt to creativity. Neither right hemisphere nor left hemisphere damage seems to interfere with artistic creativity. The artists here demonstrated that creativity has diffuse functional representation in the brain (see Preface). In the future, creativity as a notion might need to be parsed further with an eye toward neuropsychological properties (Chapters 1 and 11).

No dramatic alteration in aesthetic preference emerged in the professional artists post-damage. This suggests that when dramatic alterations do emerge, as was documented in some non-artist neurological patients (described in Chapter 9), it does so as a result of extensive brain damage, much greater than in any of the artists assembled here. This type of tissue damage would be expected to disrupt several neuronal systems and to unbalance pathways supporting established preferences. Sorting them out, teasing them apart is a task for future empirical research in the neuropsychology of art. However, there is an additional clue here, namely that "obsessional" preferences could share only a few elements with aesthetic preferences. Intensity of seeking out preferred art needs to be understood in terms of a continuum; great intensity could be mediated by neural pathways not normally involved in the pleasure of aesthetic preference or in artistic formulations, whereas medium intensity might be involved in the pleasure. This tantalizing question could be resolved with empirical explorations of rare cases showing the dramatic alterations in aesthetic preference.

Observational science can contribute a great deal to the formation of a field of inquiry, as is the case with the artists described in this book. But empirical science can be more effective. This is still sorely missing in the elucidation of the brain and art relationship. Experimentation allows verification and testing of assumptions in a manner that can significantly contribute to theoretical formulation and predictions. Quantitative data analysis derived from experiments leads to the creation of further probes that can challenge theories and consequently lead to refinement by way of generalization and extrapolation. When such quantification is applied to a large series of neurological artists, we may see serious progress in a theoretical formulation of the neuropsychology of art.

I hope that this book will help create a swell in additional reports of neurological cases of established artists, for more cases are surely needed, and systematic studies could be launched. When this happens, documenting the artist's attempts at producing art work after the brain damage will help clarify the issues of functional reorganization and preservation of skills (something noted repeatedly in the cases described here). The immediate post-damage period, on the other hand, could reveal, for example, if artists with right hemisphere damage display spatial deficits (other than hemi-neglect);

we would expect such deficits from non-artists. In the immediate post-damage period, what type of skills decline the most, what type of creativity is expressed, what is the nature of the subject matter, are some of the questions that need to be addressed. The sequential progressive nature can prove most illuminating. There may emerge a strict order in the appearance of distinct artistic techniques and abilities and the order could be extremely useful to know particularly if those vary as function of etiology, laterality, or localization of damage. It would be equally interesting to determine if the order is invariant with respect to these factors.

The published reports on dementia patients displaying artistic skills for the first time only after the disease process set in can benefit a great deal from determination of art activity after a certain age in the general population. Let us consider that people with artistic talent put art activity on hold, art having a reputation for being financially unreliable; many are initially discouraged by family members from pursuing artistic careers. They opt instead to invest in professions with secure incomes. Their latent artistic talent lies dormant until retirement time. If we knew the percentage of normal retired people who paint and engage in various valid artistic activities upon ending their lifetime jobs, we might be better able to assess the significance of art production appearing seemingly for the first time in some dementia patients. If both groups have similar percentage rates, this would imply that art in old age, regardless of presence of dementia, is not that unusual and is not triggered by massive atrophy and pronounced white matter disconnection (as described in Chapter 4).

Even more intriguing, and not dependent on rarity of occurrence as with brain damage in established artists, is a type of quantitative analysis that could shed light on the relationship between language and art. Since we do not know the structure of the first language of the early humans, even of those who created abundant art between 45,000 and 35,000 years ago in Western Europe, perhaps we should consider the issue of language complexity as an influencing factor on the art that is produced. This is testable at the present time. That is, the emergence of art is associated with syntactical language development, but languages could vary in their complexity. Some linguistic variables may be small but their pairing system may yield large meaning possibilities. The idea is that the supposed relationship between art and language could vary along a complexity continuum. The complexity of art (the properties will have to be defined) expressed in a certain culture might co-vary in some correlational way with the complexity of the language, the latter being a particular linguistic dimension (the morphology, say). For example, the Piraha people of Brazil's Amazon region have a most complex morphology but practically no art (see Chapter 10); they do have a remarkably small number of phonemes. The art–language evolutionary relationship is far from being clear. It is certainly worth asking the question, for it may provide a handle on the evolutionary emergence of both.

Glossary

Agnosia: Loss of knowledge of previously known things such as objects (visual object agnosia), faces (prosopagnosia), topography or spatial layout (topographical agnosia), colors (color agnosia), and a few other categories of knowledge. The semantic or knowledge system may be relatively intact after the damage to the brain but inaccessible because of damage to connecting routes from perceptual centers.

Agraphia: The loss of the ability to write.

Alexia: The loss of the ability to read, typically due to damage in posterior regions of the left temporal and parietal lobes (in the angular gyrus).

Amusia: The loss of receptive knowledge of previously known components of music because of acquired brain damage. Also known as agnosia for music.

Anomia: A language disorder characterized by word finding difficulties; assumed to reflect the inability to retrieve single words from the mental lexicon. Nouns are the most affected.

Aphasia: Language disorder following brain injury. In the great majority of people the injury is in the left hemisphere. The common types are Broca's aphasia (also known as non-fluent, expressive, motor, anterior aphasia), Wernicke's aphasia (also known as fluent, receptive, sensory, posterior aphasia), global aphasia, and conduction aphasia (see individual entries in the Glossary).

Autism: Developmental disorder consisting of a severe communication disorder (linguistic and social), short attention span, and inability to treat others as people.

Autistic savant: A person with extraordinary unlearned skills, typically emerging in childhood, despite having low intelligence and severely compromised social and language abilities. "Savant" from the French skill.

Broca's aphasia: Symptoms of Broca's aphasia are labored, effortful, and halting, speech; absence of conjunctions, articles, and prepositions. Auditory comprehension is relatively better than speaking but there are problems in understanding syntax.

Commissurotomy: Neurosurgery in patients with intractable epilepsy; the surgery separates the two cerebral hemispheres on a cortical level by cutting the interhemispheric commissures (connections) down the midline. This prevents interhemispheric communication.

Conduction aphasia: Speech is fluent, comprehension is good, but patients are unable to repeat what they hear.

Cytoarchitecture: The particular cellular and neuronal organization of neurons in the brain.

Electroencephalogram (EEG): Recordings of the electrical activity in the brain through the measurement of electrical potentials on the skull. Fluctuations in potential are seen in the form of waves, which correlate well with different neurologic conditions and so are used as diagnostic criteria.

Flat-affect: Blunted affect, or blunted emotions, and the absence of facial expressions denoting emotions, or bodily expressions.

fMRI: Functional magnetic resonance imaging. A neuroimaging technique that shows increased blood flow in conjunction with neural activity during task performance. It is a non-invasive technique.

Gestalt: The whole configuration. The Gestalt school of psychology proposed that when we view visual patterns we automatically group the elements that make up those patterns into coherent wholes.

Hemi-neglect, hemi-inattention: Typically this is reflected in ignoring the left half of space. This most often occurs following right hemisphere damage. Patients do not paint or draw left half of objects, straighten their hair on the left side of the head, eat food on the left half of the plate, button the left sleeve, leave unlaced the left shoe. In formal testing, neglect patients bisect a straight line inaccurately, shifting the midpoint to the right half.

Hemiparessis: Weakness of muscles in one side of the body.

Hemiplegia: This can occur when there is paralysis of one side of the body.

Hemispherectomy: Neurosurgical removal of one cerebral hemisphere. Either the left or the right hemisphere is removed.

Hyperorality: Increased tendency to put objects (some inappropriate) in the mouth.

Magnetoencephalogram (MEG): Recordings of magnetic signals proportional to electroencephalographic (EEG) waves arising from electrical activity in the brain.

Mutism: Cessation of speech that occurs after stroke or other serious brain damage. The condition varies in duration depending on localization of damage.

PET (positron emission tomography) scan: A brain imaging technique that shows activation of brain areas during performance of a task; the scan detects concentrations of positron particles (injected into the bloodstream ahead of time) in the brain as function of the activity.

Simultanagnosia: The inability to provide the theme of a pictorial scene.

Stroke: A sudden loss of blood supply to a region (or regions) in the brain that leads to death of neurons in the affected area.

Wernicke's aphasia: Speech is generally fluent (rate and intonation are normal) but nonsensical and lacks meaning. Language comprehension is extremely poor.

References

Aalto, S., Naatanen, P., Wallius, E., Metsahonkala, L., Stenman, H., Niemi, P. M., & Karlsson, H. (2002). Neuroanatomical substrata of amusement and sadness: A PET activation study using film stimuli. *NeuroReport*, *13*, 67–73.

Aboitiz, F., & Garcia, V. R. (1997). The evolutionary origin of the language areas in the human brain. A neuroanatomical perspective. *Brain Research Reviews*, *25*, 381–396.

Aiken, N. E. (1998). *The biological origins of art*. Westport, CT: Praeger.

Alajouanine, T. (1948). Aphasia and artistic realization. *Brain*, *71*, 229–241.

Albert, M. L., Reches, A., & Silverberg, R. (1975). Hemianopic colour blindness. *Journal of Neurology*, *38*, 546–549.

Allman, J. M. (2000). *Evolving brains*. New York: Scientific American Library.

Alonso, R., & Pascuzzi, R. M. (1999). Ravel's neurological illness. *Seminars in Neurology*, *19*, 53–58.

Altenmuller, E. O. (2001). How many music centers are in the brain? *Annals of the New York Academy of Sciences*, *930*, 273–280.

Amabile, T. M. (2001). Beyond talent: John Irving and the passionate craft of creativity. *American Psychologist*, *56*, 333–336.

Amaducci, L., Grassi, E., & Boller, F. (2002). Maurice Ravel and right-hemisphere musical creativity: Influence of disease on his last musical works? *European Journal of Neurology*, *9*, 75–82.

Ambrose, S. H. (2001). Paleolithic technology and human evolution. *Science*, *291*, 1748–1753.

Amunts, K., Schlaug, G., Jaencke, L., Steinmetz, H., Schleicher, A., & Zilles, K. (1996). Hand motor skills covary with size of motor cortex: A macrostructural adaptation. *NeuroImage*, *3*, S365.

Annett, M. (2002). *Handedness and brain asymmetry: The right shift theory* (2nd ed.). Hove, UK: Psychology Press.

Appelle, S. (1972). Perception and discrimination as a function of orientation: The "oblique effect" in man and animals. *Psychological Bulletin*, *78*, 266–278.

Appenzeller, T. (1998). Art: Evolution or revolution? *Science*, *282*, 1451.

Arbib, M., & Bota, M. (2003). Language evolution: neural homologies and neuroinformatics. *Neural Networks*, *16*, 1237–1260.

Arnheim, R. (1958). *Film as art*. Berkeley, CA: University of California Press.

Arnheim, R. (1974). *Art and visual perception: A psychology of the creative eye*. Los Angeles: University of California Press.

Arnold, W. N. (1989). Absinth. *Scientific American, 260*, 112–117.

Arnold, W. N. (1992). *Vincent van Gogh: Chemicals, crises, and creativity*. Boston, MA: Birkhauser.

Assad, J. A. (2003). Neural coding of behavioral relevance in parietal cortex. *Current Opinion in Neurobiology, 13*, 194–197.

Ayotte, J., Peretz, I., & Hyde, K. (2002). Congenital amusia: A group study of adults afflicted with a music-specific disorder. *Brain, 125*, 238–251.

Baeck, E. (2002a). Maurice Ravel and right hemisphere creativity. *European Journal of Neurology, 9*, 315–322.

Baeck, E. (2002b). The neural networks of music. *European Journal of Neurology, 9*, 449–456.

Bahn, P. G. (1998). *The Cambridge illustrated history of prehistoric art*. Cambridge: Cambridge University Press.

Ball, P. (1999). *The self-made tapestry*. Oxford: Oxford University Press.

Balter, M. (2001). In search of the first Europeans. *Science, 291*, 1722–1725.

Banich, M. T., Heller, W., & Levy, J. (1989). Aesthetic preference and picture asymmetries. *Cortex, 25*, 187–196.

Baowang, L., Peterson, M. R., & Freeman, R. D. (2003). Oblique effect: A neural basis in the visual cortex. *Journal of Neurophysiology, 90*, 204–217.

Barnes, J., Howard, R. J., Senior, C., Brammer, M., Bullmore, E. T., Simmons, A., Woodruff, P., & David, A. S. (2000). Cortical activity during rotational and linear transformations. *Neuropsychologia, 38*, 1148–1156.

Barnhart, R. M. (1997). The five dynasties (907–960) and the Song period (960–1279). In R. M. Barnhart (Ed.), *Three thousand years of Chinese painting* (pp. 87–137). New Haven, CT: Yale University Press.

Basso, A. (1993). Amusia. In F. Boller & J. Grafman (Eds.), *Handbook of neuropsychology* (Vol. 8, pp. 391–409). New York: Elsevier Science Publishers.

Basso, A. (1999). The neuropsychology of music. In G. Denes & L. Pizzamiglio (Eds.), *Handbook of clinical and experimental neuropsychology* (pp. 409–418). Hove, UK: Psychology Press.

Basso, A., Faglioni, P., & Spinnler, H. (1976). Non-verbal color impairment in aphasics. *Neuropsychologia, 14*, 183–192.

Beardsworth, E. D., & Zaidel, D. W. (1994). Memory for faces in epileptic children before and after brain surgery. *Journal of Clinical and Experimental Neuropsychology, 16*, 589–596.

Beauchamp, M. S., Haxby, J. V., Rosen, A. C., & DeYoe, E. A. (2000). A functional MRI case study of acquired cerebral dyschomatopsia. *Neuropsychologia, 38*, 1170–1179.

Beaumont, J. G. (1985). Lateral organization and aesthetic preference: The importance of peripheral visual asymmetries. *Neuropsychologia, 23*, 103–113.

Behrmann, M., Geng, J. J., & Shomstein, S. (2004). Parietal cortex and attention. *Current Opinion in Neurobiology, 14*, 212–217.

Bellosi, L. (1981). *Giotto*. Florence: Scala Group SPA.

Bentivoglio, M. (2003). Musical skills and neural functions: The legacy of the brains of musicians. *Annals of the New York Academy of Science, 999*, 234–243.

Benton, A. L. (1977). The amusias. In M. Critchley & R. A. Henson (Eds.), *Music and the brain: Studies in the neurology of music* (pp. 378–397). London: William Heinemann Medical Books.

Benzon, W. L. (2001). *Beethoven's anvil: Music in mind and culture*. New York: Basic Books.

Bernat, E., Shevrin, H., & Snodgrass, M. (2001). Subliminal visual oddball stimuli evoke a P300 component. *Clinical Neurophysiology, 112*, 159–171.

Bever, T. G., & Chiarello, R. J. (1974). Cerebral dominance in musicians and non-musicians. *Science, 185*, 137–139.

Biederman, I. (1987). Recognition-by-components: A theory of human image understanding. *Psychological Review, 94*, 115–147.

Biederman, I., & Gerhardstein, P. C. (1993). Recognizing depth rotated objects: Evidence and conditions for three-dimensional viewpoint invariance. *Journal of Experimental Psychology: Human Perception and Performance, 19*, 1162–1182.

Birch, J. (2001). *Diagnosis of defective colour vision* (2nd ed.). Oxford: Butterworth Heinemann.

Blank, S. C., Scott, S. K., Murphy, K., Warburton, E., & Wise, R. J. (2002). Speech production: Wernicke, Broca and beyond. *Brain, 125*, 1829–1838.

Blanke, O., Landis, T., Mermoud, C., Spinelli, L., & Safran, A. B. (2003a). Direction-selective motion blindness after unilateral posterior brain damage. *European Journal of Neuroscience, 18*, 709–722.

Blanke, O., Ortigue, S., & Landis, T. (2003b). Colour neglect in an artist. *Lancet, 361*, 264.

Blood, A. J., & Zatorre, R. J. (2001). Intensely pleasurable responses to music correlate with activity in brain regions implicated in reward and emotion. *Proceedings of the National Academy of Sciences USA, 98*, 11,818–11,823.

Blum, H. P. (2001). Psychoanalysis and art, Freud and Leonardo. *Journal of the American Psychoanalytic Association, 49*, 1409–1425.

Blumer, D. (2002). The illness of Vincent van Gogh. *American Journal of Psychiatry, 159*, 519–526.

Boatman, D. (2004). Cortical bases of speech perception: Evidence from functional lesion studies. *Cognition, 92*, 47–65.

Boeve, B. F., & Geda, Y. E. (2001). Polka music and semantic dementia. *Neurology, 57*, 1485.

Bogen, J. E. (1992). The callosal syndromes. In K. M. Heilman & E. Valenstein (Eds.), *Clinical Neuropsychology* (4th ed., pp. 337–407). New York: Oxford University Press.

Bogen, J. E. (2000). Split-brain basics: Relevance for the concept of one's other mind. *Journal of the American Academy of Psychoanalysis, 28*, 341–369.

Bogen, J. E., & Bogen, G. M. (1976). Wernicke's area: Where is it? *Annals of the New York Academy of Sciences, 280*, 834–843.

Bogen, J. E., & Vogel, P. J. (1962). Cerebral commissurotomy in man: Preliminary case report. *Bulletin of the Los Angeles Neurological Society, 27*, 169–172.

Boime, A. (1996). Manet's Bar at the Folies-Bergère as an allegory of nostalgia. In B. R. Collins (Ed.), *12 views of Manet's Bar* (pp. 47–70). Princeton, NJ: Princeton University Press.

Borod, J. C. (1992). Interhemispheric and intrahemispheric control of emotion: A focus on unilateral brain damage. *Journal of Consulting and Clinical Psychology, 60*, 339–348.

Borod, J. C., Haywood, C. S., & Koff, E. (1997). Neuropsychological aspects of facial asymmetry during emotional expression: A review of the normal adult literature. *Neuropsychology Review, 7*, 41–60.

Bradshaw, J. L., & Rogers, L. (1993). *The evolution of lateral asymmetries, language, tool-use and intellect.* San Diego, CA: Academic Press.

Branch, D., Milner, B., & Rasmusssen, T. (1964). Intracarotid sodium amytal for the lateralization of cerebral speech dominance; observations in 123 patients. *Journal of Neurosurgery, 21,* 399–405.

Brown, D. A. (2001). *Virtue and beauty.* Princeton, NJ: Princeton University Press.

Brown, J. (1977). *Mind, brain, and consciousness.* New York: Academic Press.

Buchsbaum, M. S., Hazlett, E. A., Wu, J., & Bunney, W. E., Jr. (2001). Positron emission tomography with deoxyglucose-F18 imaging of sleep. *Neuropsychopharmacology, 25,* S50–S56.

Burgund, E. D., & Marsolek, C. J. (2000). Viewpoint-invariant and viewpoint-dependent object recognition in dissociable neural subsystems. *Psychonomic Bulletin and Review, 7,* 480–489.

Buss, D. M. (1998). *Evolutionary psychology: The new science of the mind.* Upper Saddle River, NJ: Allyn & Bacon.

Butts, B. (1996). Drawings, watercolours, prints. In P.-K. Schuster, C. Vitali, & B. Butts (Eds.), *Lovis Corinth* (pp. 324–378). Munich: Prestel-Verlag.

Cahill, J. (1997). Approaches to Chinese painting, Part II. In R. M. Barnhart (Ed.), *Three thousand years of Chinese painting* (pp. 5–12). New Haven, CT: Yale University Press.

Calabresi, P., Centonze, D., Pisani, A., Cupini, L., & Bernardi, G. (2003). Synaptic plasticity in the ischaemic brain. *Lancet Neurology, 2,* 622–629.

Calvin, W. H. (2003). *A brain for all seasons: Human evolution and abrupt climate change.* Chicago: University of Chicago Press.

Cantagallo, A., & Della Salla, S. (1998). Preserved insight in an artist with extrapersonal spatial neglect. *Cortex, 34,* 163–189.

Caplan, D. (1987). *Neurolinguistics and linguistic aphasiology: An introduction.* Cambridge: Cambridge University Press.

Carpenter, H. (1992). *Benjamin Britten: A biography.* New York: Charles Scribner's Sons.

Carstairs-McCarthy, A. (2004). Language: many perspectives, no consensus. *Science, 303,* 1299–1300.

Cela-Conde, C. J., Marty, G., Maestu, F., Ortiz, T., Munar, E., Fernandez, A., Roca, M., Rossello, J., & Quesney, F. (2004). Activation of the prefrontal cortex in the human visual aesthetic perception. *Proceedings of the National Academy of Sciences, USA, 101,* 6321–6325.

Chen, A. C., German, C., & Zaidel, D. W. (1997). Brain asymmetry and facial attractiveness: Beauty is not simply in the eye of the beholder. *Neuropsychologia, 35,* 471–476.

Chollet, F., & Weiller, C. (1994). Imaging recovery of function following brain injury. *Current Opinion in Neurobiology, 4,* 226–230.

Clark, G. A. (1999). Modern human origins: Highly visible, curiously intangible. *Science, 283,* 2029–2032.

Code, C. (1987). *Language, aphasia and the right hemisphere.* Chichester: Wiley.

Code, C. (1997). Can the right hemisphere speak? *Brain and Language, 57,* 38–59.

Coe, K. (2003). *The ancestress hypothesis: Visual arts as adaptation.* New Brunswick: Rutgers University Press.

Cole, G. G., Heywood, C., Kentridge, R., Fairholm, I., & Cowey, A. (2003). Attentional capture by colour and motion in cerebral achromatopsia. *Neuropsychologia, 41,* 1837–1846.

Collins, B. R. (Ed.). (1996). *12 views of Manet's Bar*. Princeton, NJ: Princeton University Press.

Collins, R. (1999). *Charles Meryon: A life*. Devizes, UK: Garton.

Conard, N. J. (2003). Paleolithic ivory sculptures from southwestern Germany and the origins of figurative art. *Nature, 426*, 830–832.

Conard, N. J., Grootes, P. M., & Smith, F. H. (2004). Unexpectedly recent dates for human remains from Vogelherd. *Nature, 430*, 198–201.

Cooke, J. B. (2001). CBA interview: A talk with Alex Toth. *Comic Book Artist, 11*, 3–8.

Cooper, L. A., & Shepard, R. N. (1984). Turning something over in the mind. *Scientific American, 251*, 106–114.

Cooper, M. (1985). *Beethoven: The last decade, 1817–1827*. Oxford: Oxford University Press.

Coppola, D. M., Purves, H. R., McCoy, A. N., & Purves, D. (1998). The distribution of oriented contours in the real world. *Proceedings of the National Academy of Science, USA, 95*, 4002–4006.

Corballis, M. C. (1994). Neuropsychology of perceptual functions. In D. W. Zaidel (Ed.), *Neuropsychology* (pp. 83–104). San Diego, CA: Academic Press.

Corballis, M. C. (2003). *From hand to mouth: The origins of language*. Princeton, NJ: Princeton University Press.

Cowey, A., & Heywood, C. A. (1995). There's more to colour than meets the eye. *Behavioral Brain Research, 71*, 89–100.

Critchley, E. M. R. (1987). *Hallucinations and their impact on art*. Preston, UK: Carnegie Press.

Critchley, M. (1953). *The parietal lobes*. New York: Hafner.

Critchley, M. (1965). Acquired anomalies of colour perception of central origin. *Brain, 88*, 711–724.

Critchley, M., & Henson, R. A. (Eds.). (1977). *Music and the brain: Studies in the neurology of music*. London: William Heinemann Medical Books.

Cronin, H. (1992). *The ant and the peacock*. Cambridge: Cambridge University Press.

Cronin-Golomb, A., Rizzo, J. F., Corkin, S., & Growdon, J. H. (1991). Visual function in Alzheimer's disease and normal aging. *Annals of the New York Academy of Science, 640*, 28–35.

Cronin-Golomb, A., Cronin-Golomb, M., Dunne, T. E., Brown, A. C., Jain, K., Cipolloni, P. B., & Auerbach, S. H. (2000). Facial frequency manipulation normalizes face discrimination in AD. *Neurology, 54*, 2316–2318.

Crutch, S. J., Isaacs, R., & Rosso, M. N. (2001). Some workmen can blame their tools: Artistic change in an individual with Alzheimer's disease. *Lancet, 357*, 2129–2133.

Crystal, H. A., Grober, E., & Masur, D. (1989). Preservation of musical memory in Alzheimer's disease. *Journal of Neurology, Neurosurgery, and Psychiatry, 52*, 1415–1416.

Cutting, J. E. (2002). Representing motion in a static image: Constraints and parallels in art, science, and popular culture. *Perception, 31*, 1165–1193.

Damasio, A. R., & Geschwind, N. (1985). Anatomic localization in clinical neuropsychology. In P. J. Vinken, G. W. Bruyn, H. L. Klawans, & J. A. M. Frederiks (Eds.), *Handbook of clinical neurology* (Revised ed., Vol. 45, pp. 7–22). Amsterdam: North-Holland.

Damasio, A., Yamada, T., Damasio, H., & McKee, J. (1980). Central achromatopsia: Behavioral, anatomic and physiologic aspects. *Neurology, 30*, 1064–1071.

Dan, N. G. (2003). Visual dysfunction in artists. *Journal of Clinical Neuroscience, 10,* 166–170.

Davidoff, J. (1991). *Cognition through color.* Cambridge, MA: MIT Press.

Davidoff, J. (1996). Lewandowsky's case of object-colour agnosia. In C. Code, C.-W. Wallesch, Y. Joanette, & A. R. Lecours (Eds.), *Classic cases in neuropsychology,* vol. 1 (pp. 145–158). Hove, UK: Psychology Press.

Deacon, T. W. (1997). *The symbolic species: The co-evolution of language and the brain.* New York: W. W. Norton.

Deacon, T. W. (2000). Evolutionary perspectives on language and brain plasticity. *Journal of Communication Disorders, 33,* 273–290.

Deeb, S. S. (2004). Molecular genetics of color-vision deficiencies. *Vision Neuroscience, 21,* 191–196.

De Leeuw, R. (Ed.). (1998). *The letters of Vincent Van Gogh.* New York: Penguin.

DeLong, G. R. (1999). Autism: New data suggest a new hypothesis. *Neurology, 52,* 911–916.

Dennell, R. (1997). The world's oldest spears. *Nature, 385,* 767.

De Renzi, E. (1982). *Disorders of space exploration and cognition.* New York: John Wiley.

De Renzi, E. (1999). Agnosia. In G. Denes & L. Pizzamiglio (Eds.), *Handbook of clinical and experimental neuropsychology* (pp. 371–407). Hove, UK: Psychology Press.

De Renzi, E., & Spinnler, H. (1966). Visual recognition in patients with unilateral cerebral disease. *Journal of Nervous and Mental Disease, 142,* 515–525.

De Renzi, E., & Spinnler, H. (1967). Impaired performance on color tasks in patients with hemispheric damage. *Cortex, 3,* 194–216.

De Renzi, E., Faglioni, P., & Scotti, G. (1969). Impairment of memory for position following brain damage. *Cortex, 5,* 274–284.

De Renzi, E., Faglioni, P., Scotti, G., & Spinnler, H. (1972). Impairment in associating colour to form, concomitant with aphasia. *Brain, 95,* 293–304.

d'Errico, F., & Nowell, A. (2000). A new look at the Berekhat Ram figurine: Implications for the origin of symbolism. *Cambridge Archaeological Journal, 10,* 123–167.

Devinsky, O. (2003). Temporal lobe epilepsy and auditory symptoms – Reply. *Journal of the American Medical Association, 290,* 2407.

Diamond, J. (1982). Rediscovery of the yellow-fronted gardener bowerbird. *Science, 216,* 431–434.

Di Martino, A., & Castellanos, F. X. (2003). Functional neuroimaging of social cognition in pervasive developmental disorders: A brief review. *Annals of the New York Academy of Sciences, 1008,* 256–260.

Dissanayake, E. (1988). *What is art for?* Seattle, WA: University of Washington Press.

Dissanayake, E. (1995). *Homo aestheticus: Where art comes from and why.* Seattle, WA: Washington University Press.

Djamgoz, M. B., Hankins, M. W., Hirano, J., & Archer, S. N. (1997). Neurobiology of retinal dopamine in relation to degenerative states of the tissue. *Vision Research, 37,* 3509–3529.

Dombovy, M. L. (2004). Understanding stroke recovery and rehabilitation: Current and emerging approaches. *Current Neurology and Neuroscience Reports, 4,* 31–35.

Dominy, N. J., & Lucas, P. W. (2004). Significance of color, calories and climate to the visual ecology of catarrhines. *American Journal of Primatology, 62,* 189–207.

Dronkers, N. F. (1996). A new brain region for coordinating speech articulation. *Nature, 384,* 159–161.

Duffau, H., Capelle, L., Denvil, D., Sichez, N., Gatignol, P., Lopes, M., Mitchell, M.-C., Sichez, J.-P., & Van Effenterre, R. (2003). Functional recovery after surgical resection of low grade gliomas in eloquent brain: Hypothesis of brain compensation. *Journal of Neurology, Neurosurgery, and Psychiatry, 74*, 901–907.

Ebert, R. (2002). *The great movies*. New York: Broadway Books.

Eco, U., & Bredin, H. (1988). *Art and beauty in the Middle Ages*. New Haven, CT: Yale University Press.

Efron, R. (1963). Temporal perception, aphasia, and deja vu. *Brain, 86*, 403–424.

Eiermann, W. (2000). Camille Pissarro 1830–1903: An artist's life. In C. Becker (Ed.), *Camille Pissarro* (pp. 1–34). Munich: Hatje Cantz.

Elbert, T., & Rockstroh, B. (2004). Reorganization of human cerebral cortex: The range of changes following use and injury. *Neuroscientist, 10*, 129–141.

Elbert, T., Pantev, C., Wienbruch, C., Rockstroh, B., & Taub, E. (1995). Increased cortical representation of the fingers of the left hand in string players. *Science, 270*, 305–307.

Enard, W., Przeworski, M., Fisher, S. E., Lai, C. S., Wiebe, V., Kitano, T., Monaco, A. P., & Paabo, S. (2002). Molecular evolution of FOXP2, a gene involved in speech and language. *Nature, 418*, 869–872.

Espinel, C. H. (1996). De Kooning's late colours and forms: Dementia, creativity, and the healing power of art. *Lancet, 347*, 1096–1098.

Everett, D. L. (1986). Piraha. In D. C. Derbyshire & G. K. Pullum (Eds.), *Handbook of Amazonia languages* (pp. 200–325). Berlin: Mouton de Gruyter.

Everett, D. L. (1988). On metrical constituent structure in Pirahá phonology. *Natural Language and Linguistic Theory, 6*, 207–246.

Evert, D. L., & Kmen, M. (2003). Hemispheric asymmetries for global and local processing as a function of stimulus exposure duration. *Brain and Cognition, 51*, 115–142.

Farah, M. J. (1990). *Visual agnosia: Disorders of object recognition and what they tell us about normal vision*. Cambridge, MA: MIT Press.

Fein, D., Obler, L. K., & Gardner, H. (Eds.). (1988). *The exceptional brain: Neuropsychology of talent and special abilities*. New York: Guilford Press.

Ferber, S., & Karnath, H.-O. (2003). Friedrich Best's case Z with misidentification of object orientation. In C. Code, C.-W. Wallesch, Y. Joanette, & A. R. Lecours (Eds.), *Classic cases in neuropsychology* (Vol. 2, pp. 191–198). Hove, UK: Psychology Press.

Fernandez-Carriba, S., Loeches, A., Morcillo, A., & Hopkins, W. D. (2002). Asymmetry in facial expression of emotions by chimpanzees. *Neuropsychologia, 40*, 1523–1533.

Ferrario, V. F., Sforza, C., Pogio, C. E., & Tartaglia, G. (1994). Distance from symmetry: A three-dimensional evaluation of facial asymmetry. *Journal of Oral Maxillofacial Surgery, 52*, 1126–1132.

Ferrario, V. F., Sforza, C., Ciusa, V., Dellavia, C., & Tartaglia, G. M. (2001). The effect of sex and age on facial asymmetry in healthy subjects: A cross-sectional study from adolescence to mid-adulthood. *Journal of Oral Maxillofacial Surgery, 59*, 382–388.

Finger, S. (1978). Lesion momentum and behavior. In S. Finger (Ed.), *Recovery from brain damage* (pp. 135–164). New York: Plenum Press.

Fink, R. (2003). *On the origin of music: An integrated overview of the origin and evolution of music*. Saskatoon, Sask: Greenwich Meridian.

Finlayson, C. (2004). *Neanderthals and modern humans: An ecological and evolutionary perspective*. London: Cambridge University Press.

Fisher, S. E., Vargha-Khadem, F., Watkins, K. E., Monaco, A. P., & Pembrey, M. E.

(1998). Localisation of a gene implicated in a severe speech and language disorder. *Nature Genetics, 18*, 168–170.

Flinn, M. V., Geary, D. C., & Ward, C. V. (2005). Ecological dominance, social competition, and coalitionary arms races: Why humans evolved extraordinary intelligence. *Evolution and Human Behavior, 26*, 10–46.

Franklin, S., Sommers, P. V., & Howard, D. (1992). Drawing without meaning? Dissociations in the graphic performance of an agnosic artist. In R. Campbell (Ed.), *Mental lives: Case studies in cognition* (pp. 179–198). Oxford: Blackwell.

Freimuth, M., & Wapner, S. (1979). The influence of lateral organization in the evaluation of paintings. *British Journal of Psychology, 70*, 211–218.

Freud, S. (1947). *Leonardo da Vinci: A study in psychosexuality*. New York: Random House.

Friederici, A. D., & Alter, K. (2004). Lateralization of auditory language functions: A dynamic dual pathway model. *Brain and Language, 89*, 267–276.

Fukushima, K. (2003). Frontal cortical control of smooth-pursuit. *Current Opinion in Neurobiology, 13*, 647–654.

Fuster, J. M. (1997). *The prefrontal cortex: Anatomy, physiology, and neuropsychology of the frontal lobe*. Philadelphia, PA: Lippincott-Raven.

Gablik, S. (1985). *Magritte*. New York: Thames & Hudson.

Gage, J. (1993). *Color and culture: Practice and meaning from antiquity to abstraction*. Berkeley, CA: University of California Press.

Gaillard, E. R., Zheng, L., Merriam, J. C., & Dillon, J. (2000). Age-related changes in the absorption characteristics of the primate lens. *Investigations in Ophthalmology and Visual Science, 41*, 1454–1459.

Gainotti, G. (1972). Emotional behavior and hemispheric side of lesion. *Cortex, 8*, 41–55.

Galligan, G. (1998). The self pictured: Manet, the mirror, and the occupation of realist painting. *The Art Bulletin, 80*, 139–171.

Gardner, H. (1974). *The shattered mind*. New York: Vintage.

Gernsbacher, M. A., & Kaschak, M. P. (2003). Neuroimaging studies of language production and comprehension. *Annual Review of Psychology, 54*, 91–114.

Geroldi, C., Metitieri, T., Binetti, G., Zanetti, O., Trabucchi, M., & Frisoni, G. B. (2000). Pop music and fronto-temporal dementia. *Neurology, 55*, 1935–1936.

Geschwind, N., & Fusillo, M. (1966). Color-naming defects in association with alexia. *Archives of Neurology, 15*, 137–146.

Gilot, F., & Lake, C. (1964). *Life with Picasso*. New York: McGraw-Hill.

Goldenberg, G., & Artner, C. (1991). Visual imagery and knowledge about the visual appearance of objects in patients with posterior cerebral artery lesions. *Brain and Cognition, 15*, 160–186.

Goldstein, E. B. (2001). *Sensation and perception* (6th ed.). New York: Wadsworth.

Gombrich, E. H. (1968). Meditations on a hobby horse, or the roots of artistic form. In L. L. Whyte (Ed.), *Aspects of form*. London: Lund Humphries.

Gordon, H. W., & Bogen, J. E. (1974). Hemispheric lateralization of singing after intracarotid sodium amylobarbitone. *Journal of Neurology, Neurosurgery, and Psychiatry, 37*, 727–738.

Gortais, B. (2003). Abstraction and art. *Philosophical Transactions of the Royal Society London, B, 358*, 1241–1249.

Gott, P. S. (1973). Language following dominant hemispherectomy. *Journal of Neurology, Neurosurgery, and Psychiatry, 36*, 1082–1088.

Gould, J. L., & Gould, C. G. (1989). *Sexual selection.* New York: Scientific American Library.

Gourevitch, G. (1967). Un aphasique s'exprime par le dessin. *L'Encephale, 56,* 52–68.

Gray, P. M., Krause, B., Atema, J., Payne, R., Krumhansl, C., & Baptista, L. (2001). The music of nature and the nature of music. *Science, 291,* 54–56.

Grill-Spector, K., Kushnir, T., Edelman, S., Avidan, G., Itzchak, Y., & Malach, R. (1999). Differential processing of objects under various viewing conditions in the human lateral occipital complex. *Neuron, 24,* 187–203.

Groot, J. C., Leeuw, F. E., Oudkerk, M., Gijn, J., Hofman, A., Jolles, J., & Breteler, M. M. B. (2000). Cerebral white matter lesions and cognitive function: The Rotterdam Scan Study. *Annals of Neurology, 47,* 145–151.

Grosbras, M.-H., & Paus, T. (2003). Transcranial magnetic stimulation of the human frontal eye field facilitates visual awareness. *European Journal of Neuroscience, 18,* 3121–3126.

Grosbras, M.-H., Lobel, E., Van de Moortele, P.-F., LeBihan, D., & Berthoz, A. (1999). An anatomical landmark for the supplementary eye fields in human revealed with functional magnetic resonance imaging. *Cerebral Cortex, 99,* 705–711.

Grusser, O.-J., Selke, T., & Zynda, T. (1988). Cerebral lateralization and some implications for art, aesthetic perception, and artistic creativity. In I. Rentschler, B. Herzberger, & D. Epstein (Eds.), *Beauty and the brain* (pp. 257–293). Basel: Birkhauser.

Guilford, J. P. (1950). Creativity. *American Psychologist, 5,* 444–454.

Gunning-Dixon, F. M., Gur, R. C., Perkins, A. C., Schroeder, L., Turner, T., Turetsky, B. I., Chan, R. M., Loughead, J. W., Alsop, D. C., Maldjian, J., & Gur, R. E. (2003). Age-related differences in brain activation during emotional face processing. *Neurobiology of Aging, 24,* 285–295.

Halligan, P. W., & Marshall, J. C. (1997). The art of visual neglect. *Lancet, 350,* 139–140.

Halpern, A. R. (2001). Cerebral substrates of musical imagery. *Annals of the New York Academy of Sciences, 930,* 179–192.

Hanley, J. R., & Kay, J. (2003). Monsieur C: Dejerine's case of alexia without agraphia. In C. Code, C.-W. Wallesch, Y. Joanette, & A. R. Lecours (Eds.), *Classic cases in neuropsychology* (Vol. 2, pp. 57–74). Hove, UK: Psychology Press.

Harasty, J., & Hodges, J. R. (2002). Towards the elucidation of the genetic and brain bases of developmental speech and language disorders. *Brain, 125,* 449–451.

Harris, J. C. (2002). The starry night (La nuit étoilée). *Archives of General Psychiatry, 59,* 978–979.

Hauser, M. D. (1993). Right hemisphere dominance for the production of facial expression in monkeys. *Science, 261,* 475–477.

Hauser, M. D., & McDermott, J. (2003). The evolution of the music faculty: A comparative perspective. *Nature Neuroscience, 6,* 663–668.

Hausser, C. O., Robert, F., & Giard, N. (1980). Balint's syndrome. *Canadian Journal of Neurological Science, 7,* 157–161.

Heaton, P., & Wallace, G. L. (2004). Annotation: The savant syndrome. *Journal of Child Psychology and Psychiatry, 45,* 899–911.

Hecaen, H. (1969). Aphasic, apraxic and agnosic syndromes in right and left hemisphere lesions. In P. J. Vinken & G. W. Bruyn (Eds.), *Handbook of clinical neurology* (Vol. 4, pp. 291–311). Amsterdam: North-Holland.

Hecaen, H., & Albert, M. L. (1978). *Human neuropsychology.* New York: John Wiley.

Heilman, K. M., & Valenstein, E. (Eds.). (2003). *Clinical neuropsychology.* Oxford: Oxford University Press.

Heiss, W. D. (2003). Editorial comment: Key role of the superior temporal gyrus for language performance and recovery from aphasia. *Stroke, 34*(12), 2906–2907.

Heiss, W. D., Thiel, A., Kessler, J., & Herholz, K. (2003). Disturbance and recovery of language function: Correlates in PET activation studies. *Neuroimage, 20,* S42–S49.

Heller, M. A. (2002). Tactile picture perception in sighted and blind people. *Behavioral Brain Research, 135,* 65–68.

Heller, W. (1994). Cognitive and emotional organization of the brain: influences on the creation and perception of art. In D. W. Zaidel (Ed.), *Neuropsychology* (pp. 271–292). San Diego, CA: Academic Press.

Henderson, V. W., Mack, W., & Williams, B. W. (1989). Spatial disorientation in Alzheimer's disease. *Archives of Neurology, 46,* 391–394.

Henke, K., Treyer, V., Nagy, E. T., Kneifel, S., Dursteler, M., Nitsch, R. M., & Buck, A. (2003). Active hippocampus during nonconscious memories. *Consciousness and Cognition, 12,* 31–48.

Henshilwood, C., d'Errico, F., Vanhaeren, M., van Niekerk, K., & Jacobs, Z. (2004). Middle Stone Age shell beads from South Africa. *Science, 304,* 404.

Hermelin, B., O'Connor, N., & Lee, S. (1987). Musical inventiveness of five idiots-savants. *Psychological Medicine, 17,* 685–694.

Hermelin, B., O'Connor, N., Lee, S., & Treffert, D. A. (1989). Intelligence and musical improvisation. *Psychological Medicine, 19,* 447–457.

Hetenyi, G. (1986). The terminal illness of Franz Schubert and the treatment of syphilis in Vienna in the eighteen hundred and twenties. *Bulletin of Canadian History of Medicine, 3,* 51–64.

Heywood, C. A., & Kentridge, R. W. (2003). Achromatopsia, color vision, and cortex. *Neurologic Clinics of North America, 21,* 483–500.

Heywood, C. A., Wilson, B., & Cowey, A. (1987). A case study of cortical colour "blindness" with relatively intact achromatic discrimination. *Journal of Neurology, Neurosurgery, and Psychiatry, 50,* 22–29.

Hillis, A. E., Work, M., Barker, P. B., Jacobs, M. A., Breese, E. L., & Maurer, K. (2004). Re-examining the brain regions crucial for orchestrating speech articulation. *Brain, 127,* 1479–1487.

Hiscock, M. & Kinsbourne, M. (1995). Phylogeny and ontogeny of cerebral lateralization. In R. J. Davidson & K. Hugdahl (Eds.), *Brain asymmetry* (pp. 535–578). Cambridge, MA: MIT Press.

Hobson, J. A., & Pace-Schott, E. F. (2003). The cognitive neuroscience of sleep: neural systems, consciousness and learning. *Nature Reviews Neuroscience, 3,* 679–693.

Hold, K. M., Sirisoma, N. S., Ikeda, T., Narahashi, T., & Casida, J. E. (2000). Alpha-thujone (the active component of absinthe): Gamma-aminobutyric acid type A receptor modulation and metabolic detoxification. *Proceedings of the National Academy of Sciences, USA, 97,* 3826–3831.

Holden, C. (2004). The origin of speech. *Science, 303,* 1316–1319.

Holloway, R. L., Broadfield, D. C., & Yuan, M. S. (Eds.). (2004). *The human fossil record, brain endocasts: The paleoneurological evidence.* Hoboken, NJ: Wiley-Liss.

Holmes, G. (1945). The organization of the visual cortex in man. *Proceedings of the Royal Society, 132,* 348–361.

Hook-Costigan, M. A., & Rogers, L. J. (1998). Lateralized use of the mouth in production of vocalizations by marmosets. *Neuropsychologia, 36,* 1265–1273.

Hovers, E., Ilani, S., Bar-Yosef, O., & Vandermeersch, B. (2003). An early case of color symbolism: Ochre use by modern humans in Qafzeh Cave. *Current Anthropology*, *44*, 491–522.

Howe, M. J. A., Davidson, J. W., & Sloboda, J. A. (1998). Innate talents: Reality or myth? *Behavioural and Brain Sciences*, *21*, 399–442.

Hughes, R. (2003). *Goya*. New York: Alfred A. Knopf.

Hui, A. C. F., & Wong, S. M. (2000). Deafness and liver disease in a 57-year-old man: A medical history of Beethoven. *Hong Kong Medical Journal*, *6*, 433–438.

Hummel, J. E., & Biederman, I. (1992). Dynamic binding in a neural network for shape recognition. *Psychological Review*, *99*, 480–517.

Husain, M., Parton, A., Hodgson, T. L., Mort, D., & Rees, G. (2003). Self-control during response conflict by human supplementary eye fields. *Nature Neuroscience*, *6*, 117–118.

Hutsler, J., & Galuske, R. A. (2003) Hemispheric asymmetries in cerebral cortical networks. *Trends in Neuroscience*, *26*, 429–435.

Jackson, G. R., & Owsley, C. (2003). Visual dysfunction, neurodegenerative diseases, and aging. *Neurologic Clinics of North America*, *21*, 709–728.

Janata, P., & Grafton, S. T. (2003). Swinging in the brain: Shared neural substrates for behaviors related to sequencing and music. *Nature Neuroscience*, *6*, 682–687.

Janata, P., Birk, J. L., Van Horn, J. D., Leman, M., Tillmann, B., & Bharucha, J. J. (2002). The cortical topography of tonal structures underlying Western music. *Science*, *298*, 2167–2179.

Jenkins, W. M., & Merzenich, M. M. (1987). Reorganization of neocortical representations after brain injury: A neurophysiological model of the bases of recovery from stroke. *Progress in Brain Research*, *71*, 249–266.

Jenkins, W. M., Merzenich, M. M., & Recanzone, G. (1990). Neocortical representational dynamics in adult primates: Implications for neuropsychology. *Neuropsychologia*, *28*, 573–584.

Johnson, A. W., & Earle, T. K. (2000). *The evolution of human societies: From foraging group to agrarian state*. Stanford, CA: Stanford University Press.

Judd, T., Gardner, H., & Geschwind, N. (1983). Alexia without agraphia in a composer. *Brain*, *106*, 435–457.

Jung, R. (1974). Neuropsychologie und neurophysiologie des kontur- und formschens in zeichnung und malerei. In H. H. Wieck (Ed.), *Psychopathologie musischer gestaltungen* (pp. 27–88). Stuttgart: FK Schattauer.

Just, M. A., Cherkassky, V. L., Keller, T. A., & Minshew, N. J. (2004). Cortical activation and synchronization during sentence comprehension in high-functioning autism: Evidence of underconnectivity. *Brain*, *127*, 1811–1821.

Kaczmarek, B. L. J. (1991). Aphasia in an artist: A disorder of symbolic processing. *Aphasiology*, *5*, 361–371.

Kaczmarek, B. L. J. (2003). The life of the brain. *Acta Neuropsychologica*, *1*, 56–86.

Kalat, J. W. (2002). *Introduction to psychology* (6th ed.). Pacific Grove, CA: Wadsworth Thomson Learning.

Kapur, N. (1996). Paradoxical functional facilitation in brain-behaviour research: A critical review. *Brain*, *119*, 1775–1790.

Karnath, H.-O., Ferber, S., & Bulthoff, H. H. (2000). Neuronal representation of object orientation. *Neuropsychologia*, *38*, 1235–1241.

Kaufman, L. (1974). *Sight and mind: An introduction to visual perception*. New York: Oxford University Press.

Kawabata, H., & Zeki, S. (2004). Neural correlates of beauty. *Journal of Neurophysiology, 91*, 1699–1705.

Kemp, M. (1990). *The science of art.* New Haven, CT: Yale University Press.

Kennard, C., Lawden, M., Morland, A. B., & Ruddock, K. H. (1995). Colour identification and colour constancy are impaired in a patient with incomplete achromatopsia associated with a prestriate cortical lesion. *Proceedings of the Royal Society, Series B, 260*, 169–175.

Kennedy, F., & Wolf, A. (1936). The relationship of intellect to speech defect in aphasic patients. *Journal of Nervous and Mental Disease, 84*, 125–145, 293–311.

Kennedy, J. M. (2003). Drawings from Gaia, a blind girl. *Perception, 32*, 321–340.

Kennedy, J. M., & Igor, J. (2003). Haptics and projection: Drawings by Tracy, a blind adult. *Perception, 32*, 1059–1071.

Keynes, M. (2002). The personality, deafness, and bad health of Ludwig van Beethoven. *Journal of Medical Biography, 10*, 46–57.

Kilts, C. D., Egan, G., Gideon, D. A., Ely, T. D., & Hoffman, J. M. (2003). Dissociable neural pathways are involved in the recognition of emotion in static and dynamic facial expressions. *NeuroImage, 18*, 156–168.

Kimura, D. (1963a). A note on cerebral dominance in hearing. *Acta Otolaryngology, 56*, 617–618.

Kimura, D. (1963b). Speech lateralization in young children as determined by an auditory test. *Journal of Comparative Physiological Psychology, 56*, 899–902.

Kimura, D. (1964). Left–right differences in the perception of melodies. *Quarterly Journal of Experimental Psychology, 16*, 355–358.

Kingdom, F. A. (2003). Color brings relief to human vision. *Nature Neuroscience, 6*, 641–644.

Kinsbourne, M., & Warrington, E. K. (1962). A disorder of simultaneous form perception. *Brain, 85*, 461–486.

Kirk, A., & Kertesz, A. (1991). On drawing impairment in Alzheimer's Disease. *Archives of Neurology, 48*, 73–77.

Kirk, A., & Kertesz, A. (1993). Subcortical contributions to drawing. *Brain and Cognition, 21*, 57–70.

Klarreich, E. (2004). Biography of Richard G. Klein. *Proceedings of the National Academy of Science USA, 101*, 5705–5707.

Klein, R. G., Avery, G., Cruz-Uribe, K., Halkett, D., Parkington, J. E., Steele, T., Volman, T. P., & Yates, R. (2004). The Ysterfontein 1 Middle Stone Age site, South Africa, and early human exploitation of coastal resources. *Proceedings of the National Academy of Sciences, USA, 101*, 5708–5715.

Kleiner-Fisman, G., Black, S. E., & Lang, A. E. (2003). Neurodegenerative disease and the evolution of art: The effects of presumed corticobasal degeneration in a professional artist. *Movement Disorders, 18*, 294–302.

Knauff, M., Mulack, T., Kassubek, J., Salih, H. R., & Greenlee, M. W. (2002). Spatial imagery in deductive reasoning: A functional MRI study. *Cognitive Brain Research, 13*, 203–212.

Knecht, S. (2004). Does language lateralization depend on the hippocampus? *Brain, 127*, 1217–1218.

Knecht, S., Dräger, B., Deppe, M., Bobe, L., Lohmann, H., Flöel, A., Ringelstein, E.-B., & Henningsen, H. (2000). Handedness and hemispheric language dominance in healthy humans. *Brain, 123*, 2512–2518.

Knecht, S., Flöel, A., Dräger, B., Breitenstein, C., Sommer, J., Henningsen, H.,

Ringelstein, E. B., & Pascual-Leone, A. (2002). Degree of language lateralization determines susceptibility to unilateral brain lesions. *Nature Neuroscience, 5*, 695–699.

Kohn, M. (2000). *As we know it.* London: Granta.

Koss, E. (1994). Neuropsychology of aging and dementia. In D. W. Zaidel (Ed.), *Neuropsychology* (pp. 247–270). San Diego, CA: Academic Press.

Kourtzi, Z., & Kanwisher, N. (2000). Activation in human MT/MST by static images with Implied motion. *Journal of Cognitive Neuroscience, 12*, 48–55.

Kubba, A. K., & Young, M. (1996). Ludwig van Beethoven: A medical biography. *Lancet, 347*, 167–170.

Kunst-Wilson, W. R., & Zajonc, R. B. (1980). Affective discrimination of stimuli that cannot be recognized. *Science, 207*, 557–558.

LaBar, K. S., Crupain, M. J., Voyvodic, J. T., & McCarthy, G. (2003). Dynamic perception of facial affect and identity in the human brain. *Cerebral Cortex, 13*, 1023–1033.

Labounsky, A. (2000). *Jean Langlais: The man and his music.* Portland, OR: Amadeus Press.

LaFrance, M., Hecht, M. A., & Paluck, E. L. (2003). The contingent smile: A meta-analysis of sex differences in smiling. *Psychological Bulletin, 129*, 305–334.

Lai, C. S., Fisher, S. E., Hurst, J. A., Vargha-Khadem, F., & Monaco, A. P. (2001). A forkhead-domain gene is mutated in a severe speech and language disorder. *Nature, 413*, 519–523.

Lai, C. S., Gerrelli, D., Monaco, A. P., Fisher, S. E., & Copp, A. J. (2003). FOXP2 expression during brain development coincides with adult sites of pathology in a severe speech and language disorder. *Brain, 126*, 2455–2462.

Lakke, J. P. (1999). Art and Parkinson's Disease. *Advances in Neurology, 80*, 471–479.

Lambert, S., Sampaio, E., Mauss, Y., & Scheiber, C. (2004). Blindness and brain plasticity: Contribution of mental imagery? An fMRI study. *Cognitive Brain Research, 20*, 1–11.

Landis, T., Cummings, J. L., Christen, L., Bogen, J. E., & Imhof, H. G. (1986). Are unilateral right posterior cerebral lesions sufficient to cause prosopagnosia? Clinical and radiological findings in six additional patients. *Cortex, 22*, 243–252.

Lang, P. J. (1994). The varieties of emotional experience: A meditation on James-Lange theory. *Psychological Review, 101*, 211–221.

Lanthony, P. (1995). Les peintres gauchers. *Revue Neurologie, 151*, 165–170.

Lanthony, P. (2001). Daltonism in painting. *Color Research and Application, 26*, S12–S16.

Latto, R. (1995). The brain of the beholder. In R. L. Gregory, J. Harris, & P. Heard (Eds.), *The artful eye* (pp. 66–94). Oxford: Oxford University Press.

Latto, R., & Russell-Duff, K. (2002). An oblique effect in the selection of line orientation by twentieth century painters. *Empirical Studies of the Arts, 20*, 49–60.

Latto, R., Brain, D., & Kelly, B. (2000). An oblique effect in aesthetics: Homage to Mondrian (1872–1944). *Perception, 29*, 981–987.

Lawler, A. (2001). Writing gets a rewrite. *Science, 292*, 2418–2420.

Lawler, A. (2003). Tortoise pace for the evolution of Chinese writing? *Science, 300*, 723.

Lawson, R. (1999). Achieving visual object constancy across plane rotation and depth rotation. *Acta Psychologica, 102*, 221–245.

Leader, D. (2002). *Stealing the Mona Lisa: What art stops us from seeing.* New York: Counterpoint.

LeBoutillier, N., & Marks, D. F. (2003). Mental imagery and creativity: A meta-analytic review study. *British Journal of Psychology, 94*(pt 1), 29–44.

Lederman, R. (1999). Robert Schumann. *Seminars in Neurology, 19,* 17–24.

Leff, A. (2004). A historical review of the representation of the visual field in primary visual cortex with special reference to the neural mechanisms underlying macular sparing. *Brain and Language, 88,* 268–278.

Leslie, K. R., Johnson-Frey, S. H., & Grafton, S. T. (2004). Functional imaging of face and hand imitation: Towards a motor theory of empathy. *NeuroImage, 21,* 601–607.

Levin, M. (2004). The embryonic origins of left–right asymmetry. *Critical Reviews in Oral and Biological Medicine, 15,* 197–206.

Levine, D. N., & Calvanio, R. (1978). A study of the visual defect in verbal alexia-simultanagnosia. *Brain, 101,* 65–81.

Levine, D. N., Warach, J., & Farah, M. (1985). Two visual systems in mental imagery: Dissociation of "what" and "where" in imagery disorders due to bilateral posterior cerebral lesions. *Neurology, 35,* 1010–1020.

Levitin, D. J., & Menon, V. (2003). Musical structure is processed in "language" areas of the brain: A possible role for Brodmann Area 47 in temporal coherence. *NeuroImage, 20,* 2142–2152.

Levy, J. (1976). Lateral dominance and aesthetic preference. *Neuropsychologia, 14,* 431–445.

Levy-Agresti, J., & Sperry, R. W. (1968). Differential perceptual capacities in major and minor hemispheres. *Proceedings of the National Academy of Science, 61,* 1151.

Lewandowsky, M. (1908). Uber Abspaltung des Farbensinnes. *Monatsschrift für Psychiatrie und Neurologie, 23,* 488–510.

Lewis, M. T. (2000). *Cezanne.* London: Phaidon Press.

Lewis-Williams, D. (2002). *The mind in the cave: Consciousness and the origins of art.* London: Thames & Hudson.

Lezak, M. D. (1995). *Neuropsychological assessment.* Oxford: Oxford University Press.

Lieberman, P. (2002). On the nature and evolution of the neural bases of human language. *American Journal of Physical Anthropology, 35,* 36–62.

Liegeois, F., Connelly, A., Cross, J. H., Boyd, S. G., Gadian, D. G., Vargha-Khadem, F., & Baldeweg, T. (2004). Language reorganization in children with early-onset lesions of the left hemisphere: An fMRI study. *Brain, 127,* 1229–1236.

Limosin, F., Loze, J. Y., Rouillon, F., Ades, J., & Gorwood, P. (2003). Association between dopamine receptor D1 gene DdeI polymorphism and sensation seeking in alcohol-dependent men. *Alcoholism, Clinical and Experimental Research, 27,* 1226–1228.

Liu, Z., Richmond, B. J., Murray, E. A., Saunders, R. C., Steenrod, S., Stubblefield, B. K., Montague, D. M., & Ginns, E. I. (2004). DNA targeting of rhinal cortex D2 receptor protein reversibly blocks learning of cues that predict reward. *Proceedings of the National Academy of Sciences USA, 101,* 12,336–12,341.

Livingstone, M. (2002). *Vision and art: The biology of seeing.* New York: Harry N. Abrams.

Loeffler, F. (1982). *Otto Dix: Life and work.* New York: Holmes & Meier.

Luria, A. R., Tsvetkova, L. S., & Futer, D. S. (1965). Aphasia in a composer (V. G. Shebalin). *Journal of the Neurological Sciences, 2,* 288–292.

McBrearty, S., & Brooks, A. S. (2000). The revolution that wasn't: A new interpretation of the origin of modern human behavior. *Journal of Human Evolution, 39,* 453–563.

McCarthy, R. A., & Warrington, E. K. (1990). *Cognitive neuropsychology: A clinical introduction*. San Diego, CA: Academic Press.

McCormick, L., Nielsen, T., Ptito, M., Hassainia, F., Ptito, A., Villemure, J. G., Vera, C., & Montplaisir, J. (1997). REM sleep dream mentation in right hemispherectomized patients. *Neuropsychologia, 35*, 695–701.

McCormick, L., Nielsen, T., Ptito, M., Ptito, A., Villemure, J. G., Vera, C., & Montplaisir, J. (2000). Sleep in right hemispherectomized patients: Evidence of electrophysiological compensation. *Clinical Neurophysiology, 111*, 1488–1497.

McFie, J., & Zangwill, O. L. (1960). Visual-constructive disabilities associated with lesions of the left cerebral hemisphere. *Brain, 83*, 243–260.

Mackay, G., & Dunlop, J. (1899). The cerebral lesions in a case of complete acquired colour-blindness. *Scott Medical Surgery Journal, 5*, 503–512.

McLaughlin, J. P., Dean, P., & Stanley, P. (1983). Aesthetic preference in dextrals and sinistrals. *Neuropsychologia, 21*, 147–153.

McMahon, M. J., & MacLeod, D. I. A. (2003). The origin of the oblique effect examined with pattern adaptation and masking. *Journal of Vision, 3*, 230–239.

McManus, I. C., & Humphrey, N. K. (1973). Turning the left cheek. *Nature, 243*, 271–272.

McNeill, D. (Ed.). (2000). *Language and gesture: Window into thought and action*. Cambridge: Cambridge University Press.

Madden, J. (2001). Sex, bowers and brains. *Proceedings of the Royal Society, London, B, 268*, 833–838.

Maguire, E. A., Gadian, D. G., Johnsrude, I. S., Good, C. D., Ashburner, J., Frackowiak, R. S. J., & Frith, C. D. (2000). Navigation-related structural change in the hippocampi of taxi drivers. *Proceedings of the National Academy of Sciences, USA, 97*, 4398–4403.

Maguire, E. A., Valentine, E. R., Wilding, J. M., & Kapur, N. (2003). Routes to remembering: The brains behind superior memory. *Nature Neuroscience, 6*, 90–95.

Marcus, G. F., & Fisher, S. E. (2003). FOXP2 in focus: What can genes tell us about speech and language? *Trends in Cognitive Sciences, 7*, 257–262.

Marins, E. M. (2002). Maurice Ravel and right hemisphere creativity. *European Journal of Neurology, 9*, 315–322.

Marmor, M. F., & Lanthony, P. (2001). The dilemma of color deficiency and art. *Survey of Ophthalmology, 45*, 407–415.

Marr, D. (1982). *Vision: A computational investigation into the human representation and processing of visual information*. San Francisco, CA: W. H. Freeman.

Marsh, G. G., & Philwin, B. (1987). Unilateral neglect and constructional apraxia in right-handed artist with a left posterior lesion. *Cortex, 23*, 149–155.

Marshack, A. (1997). The Berekhat Ram figurine: A late Acheulian carving from the Middle East. *Antiquity, 71*, 327–337.

Masure, M. C., & Tzavaras, A. (1976). Perception of superimposed figures by subjects with unilateral cortical lesions. *Neuropsychologia, 14*, 371–374.

Maurer, K., & Prvulovic, D. (2004). Paintings of an artist with Alzheimer's disease: Visuoconstructural deficits during dementia. *Journal of Neural Transmission, 111*, 235–245.

Meadows, J. C. (1974). Disturbed perception of colors associated with localised cerebral lesions. *Brain, 97*, 615–632.

Medin, D. L., Lynch, E. B., & Solomon, K. O. (2000). Are there kinds of concepts? *Annual Review of Psychology, 51*, 121–147.

Meister, I. G., Krings, T., Foltys, H., Boroojerdi, B., Muller, M., Topper, R., & Thron, A. (2004). Playing piano in the mind: An fMRI study on music imagery and performance in pianists. *Cognitive Brain Research, 19,* 219–228.

Mell, C. J., Howard, S. M., & Miller, B. L. (2003). Art and the brain: The influence of frontotemporal dementia on an accomplished artist. *Neurology, 60,* 1707–1710.

Mellars, P. (2004). Neanderthals and the modern human colonization of Europe. *Nature, 432,* 461–465.

Merker, B. (2000). Synchronous chorusing and human origins. In N. L. Wallin, B. Merker, & S. Brown (Eds.), *The origins of music* (pp. 315–328). Cambridge, MA: MIT Press.

Miall, R. C., & Tchalenko, J. (2001). A painter's eye movements: A study of eye and hand movement during portrait drawing. *Leonardo, 34,* 35–40.

Miller, A. I. (2000). *Insights of genius: Imagery and creativity in science and art.* Cambridge, MA: MIT Press.

Miller, A. I. (2002). *Einstein, Picasso: Space, time, and the beauty that causes havoc.* New York: Basic Books.

Miller, B. L., Ponton, M., Benson, D. F., Cummings, J. L., & Mena, I. (1996). Enhanced artistic creativity with temporal lobe degeneration. *Lancet, 348,* 1744–1745.

Miller, B. L., Cummings, J., Mishkin, F., Boone, K., Prince, F., Ponton, M., & Cotman, C. (1998). Emergence of artistic talent in frontotemporal dementia. *Neurology, 51,* 978–981.

Miller, B. L., Boone, K., Cummings, J. L., Read, S. L., & Mishkin, F. (2000). Functional correlates of musical and visual ability in frontotemporal dementia. *British Journal of Psychiatry, 176,* 458–463.

Miller, E. K., Li, L., & Desimone, R. (1991). A neural mechanism for working and recognition memory in inferior temporal cortex. *Science, 254,* 1377–1379.

Miller, G. (2000). *The mating mind: How sexual choice shaped the evolution of human nature.* New York: Doubleday.

Miller, G. (2001). Evolution of human music through sexual selection. In N. L. Wallin, B. Merker, & S. Brown (Eds.), *The origins of music* (pp. 329–360). Cambridge, MA: MIT Press.

Miller, L. K. (1989). *Musical savants: Exceptional skill in the mentally retarded.* Hillsdale, NJ: Lawrence Erlbaum Associates, Inc.

Mills, L. (1936). Peripheral vision in art. *Archives of Ophthalmology, 16,* 208–219.

Milner, B. (1958). Psychological defects produced by temporal-lobe excision. *Research Publication of the Association for Research of Nervous and Mental Diseases, 36,* 244–257.

Milner, B. (1962). Laterality effects in audition. In V. B. Mountcastle (Ed.), *Interhemispheric relations and cerebral dominance* (pp. 177–198). Baltimore, MD: Johns Hopkins University Press.

Milner, B. (1968). Visual recognition and recall after right temporal-lobe excision in man. *Neuropsychologia, 6,* 191–209.

Milner, P. M. (1991). Brain-stimulation reward: A review. *Canadian Journal of Psychology, 45,* 1–36.

Mirnikjoo, B., Brown, S. E., Kims, H. F. S., Marangell, L. B., Sweatt, J. D., & Weeber, E. J. (2001). Protein kinase inhibition by omega-3 fatty acids. *Journal of Biological Chemistry, 276,* 10,888–10,896.

Mithen, S. (1996). *The prehistory of the mind: The cognitive origins of art, religion, and science.* London: Thames & Hudson.

Mithen, S. (2004). *After the ice: A global human history, 20,000–5000 BC.* Cambridge, MA: Harvard University Press.

Mithen, S., & Reed, M. (2002). Stepping out: A computer simulation of hominid dispersal from Africa. *Journal of Human Evolution, 4,* 433 462.

Mohr, J. P. (2004). Historical observations on functional reorganization. *Cerebrovascular Disease, 18,* 258–259.

Moller, A. P., & Miller, A. P. (1994). *Sexual selection and the barn swallow.* Oxford: Oxford University Press.

Mottron, L., & Belleville, S. (1995). Perspective production in a savant autistic draughtsman. *Psychological Medicine, 25,* 639–648.

Mottron, L., Limoges, E., & Jelenic, P. (2003). Can a cognitive deficit elicit an exceptional ability? A case of savant syndrome in drawing abilities: Nadia. In C. Code, C.-W. Wallesch, Y. Joanette, & A. R. Lecours (Eds.), *Classic cases in neuropsychology* (Vol. 2, pp. 323–340). Hove, UK: Psychology Press.

Munsterberg, H. (1982). *The Japanese print: A historical guide.* New York: Weatherhill.

Nadel, L., & Bohbot, V. (2001). Consolidation of memory. *Hippocampus, 11,* 56–60.

Nadel, L., & Moscovitch, M. (2001). The hippocampal complex and long-term memory revisited. *Trends in Cognitive Science, 5,* 228–230.

Nathan, J. (2002). The painter and handicapped vision. *Clinical and Experimental Optometry, 85,* 309–314.

Navon, D. (1977). Forest before trees: The precedence of global features in visual perception. *Cognitive Psychology, 9,* 353–383.

Nebes, R. D. (1971). Superiority of the minor hemisphere in commissurotomized man for the perception of part–whole relations. *Cortex, 7,* 333–349.

Neill, D. B., Fenton, H., & Justice, J. B., Jr. (2002). Increase in accumbal dopaminergic transmission correlates with response cost not reward of hypothalamic stimulation. *Behavior and Brain Research, 137,* 129–138.

Newbury, D. F., Bonora, E., Lamb, J. A., Fisher, S. E., Lai, C. S., Baird, G., Jannoun, L., Slonims, V., Stott, C. M., Merricks, M. J., Bolton, P. F., Bailey, A. J., & Monaco, A. P. (2002). FOXP2 is not a major susceptibility gene for autism or specific language impairment. *American Journal of Human Genetics, 70,* 1318–1327.

Newell, F. A., & Findlay, J. M. (1997). The effect of depth rotation on object identification. *Perception, 26,* 1231–1257.

Niewoehner, W. A. (2001). Behavioral inferences from the Skhul/Qafzeh early modern human hand remains. *Proceedings of the National Academy of Sciences, USA, 98,* 2979–2984.

Nowak, M. A., Plotkin, J. B., & Jansen, V. A. (2000). The evolution of syntactic communication. *Nature, 404,* 495–498.

Nykvist, S. (2003). The director of photography. In IMAGO, The Federation of European Cinematographers (Eds.), *Making pictures: A century of European cinematography* (pp. 10–11). New York: Abrams.

Oates, J., & Oates, D. (2001) *Nimrud: An Assyrian imperial city revealed.* Cambridge: British School of Archaeology in Iraq.

Olds, J., & Milner, P. (1954). Positive reinforcement produced by electrical stimulation of septal area and other regions of rat brain. *Journal of Comparative and Physiological Psychology, 47,* 419–427.

Olivers, C. N. L., Humphrys, G. W., Heinke, D., & Cooper, A. C. G. (2002). Prioritization in visual search: Visual marking is not dependent on a mnemonic search. *Perception and Psychophysics, 64,* 540–560.

O'Shea, J. G. (1997). Franz Schubert's last illness. *Journal of the Royal Society of Medicine, 90,* 291–292.

O'Shea, J., & Walsh, V. (2004). Visual awareness: The eye fields have it? *Current Biology, 14,* R279–R281.

Otte, A., De Bondt, P., Van De Wiele, C., Audenaert, K., & Dierckx, R. (2003). The exceptional brain of Maurice Ravel. *Medical Science Monitor, 9,* RA133–RA138.

Ovsiew, F. (1997). Comment on paradoxical functional facilitation in brain-behavior research: A critical review. *Brain, 120,* 1261–1264.

Pachalska, M. (2003). Imagination lost and found in an aphasic artist: A case study. *Acta Neuropsychologica, 1,* 46–56.

Panofsky, E. (1991). *Perspective as symbolic form.* New York: Zone Books.

Paradiso, S. (1999). Minor depression after stroke: An initial validation of the DSM-IV construct. *American Journal of Geriatric Psychiatry, 7,* 244–251.

Patel, A. D. (2003). Language, music, syntax and the brain. *Nature Neuroscience, 6,* 674–681.

Paterson, A., & Zangwill, O. L. (1944). Disorders of visual space perception associated with lesions of the right cerebral hemisphere. *Brain, 67,* 331–358.

Paus, T. (1996). Location and function of the human frontal eye field: A selective review. *Neuropsychologia, 34,* 475–483.

Peck, S., Peck, L., & Kataia, M. (1991). Skeletal asymmetry in esthetically pleasing faces. *The Angle Orthodontist, 61,* 43–48.

Pennisi, E. (2004). The first language? *Science, 303,* 1319–1320.

Peretz, I. (2002). Brain specialization for music. *Neuroscientist, 8,* 372–380.

Peretz, I., & Coltheart, M. (2003). Modularity of music processing. *Nature Neuroscience, 6,* 688–691.

Peretz, I., Ayotte, J., Zatorre, R. J., Mehler, J., Ahad, P., Penhune, V. B., & Jutras, B. (2002). Congenital amusia: A disorder of fine-grained pitch discrimination. *Neuron, 33,* 185–191.

Peschel, E., & Peschel, R. (1992). Donizetti and the music of mental derangement: Anna Bolena, Lucia di Lammermoor, and the composer's neurobiological illness. *Yale Journal of Biological Medicine, 65,* 189–200.

Pickford, R. W. (1964). A deuteranomalous artist. *British Journal of Psychology, 55,* 469–476.

Pillon, B., Signoret, J. L., van Eeckhout, P., & Lhermitte, F. (1980). Le dessin chez un aphasique: Incidence possible sur le langage et sa reeduction. *Revue Neurologique, 136,* 699–710.

Pinker, S. (2000). Survival of the clearest. *Nature, 404,* 441–442.

Pinker, S., & Bloom, P. (1990). Natural language and natural selection. *Behavioral and Brain Sciences, 13,* 707–784.

Pitts, D. G. (1982). The effects of aging on selected visual functions: Dark adaptation, visual acuity, stereopsis, and brightness contrast. In R. Sekuler, D. Kline, & K. Dismukes (Eds.), *Aging and human visual function* (pp. 131–159). New York: Alan R. Liss.

Platel, H., Price, C., Baron, J.-C., Wise, R., Lambert, J., Frackowiak, R. S. J., Lechevalier, B., & Eustache, F. (1997). The structural components of music perception: a functional anatomical study. *Brain, 120,* 229–243.

Platt, M. L., & Glimcher, P. W. (1999). Neural correlates of decision variables in parietal cortex. *Nature, 400,* 233–238.

Polk, M., & Kertesz, A. (1993). Music and language in degenerative disease of the brain. *Brain and Cognition, 22,* 98–117.

Popescu, M., Otsuka, A., & Ioannides, A. A. (2004). Dynamics of brain activity in motor and frontal cortical areas during music listening: A magnetoencephalographic study. *NeuroImage, 21,* 1622–1638.

Poppelreuter, W. (1917). *Die psychischen Schadigungen durch Kopfschuss im Kriege 1914/16.* Leipzig: Leopold Voss.

Posamentier, M. T., & Abdi, H. (2003). Processing faces and facial expressions. *Neuropsychology Review, 13,* 113–143.

Preilowski, B. F. (1972). Possible contribution of the anterior forebrain commissures to bilateral motor coordination. *Neuropsychologia, 10,* 267–277.

Rapin, I. (1999). Autism in search of a home in the brain. *Neurology, 52,* 902–904.

Ravin, J. G. (1997a). Artistic vision in old age. In M. F. Marmor & J. G. Ravin (Eds.), *The eye of the artist* (pp. 168–180). St. Louis, MO: Mosby.

Ravin, J. G. (1997b). Pissarro, the tearful impressionist. In M. F. Marmor & J. G. Ravin (Eds.), *The eye of the artist* (pp. 187–192). St. Louis, MO: Mosby.

Ravin, J. G., & Kenyon, C. (1997). The blindness of Edgar Degas. In M. F. Marmor & J. G. Ravin (Eds.), *The eye of the artist* (pp. 193–203). St. Louis, MO: Mosby.

Ravin, J. G., & Ravin, R. B. (1999). What ailed Goya? *Survey of Ophthalmology, 44,* 163–170.

Ravin, J. G., Anderson, N., & Lanthony, P. (1995). An artist with a color vision defect: Charles Meryon. *Survey of Ophthalmology, 39,* 403–408.

Regard, M., & Landis, T. (1988). Beauty may differ in each half of the eye of the beholder. In I. Rentschler, B. Herzberger, & D. Epstein (Eds.), *Beauty and the brain* (pp. 243–256). Basel: Birkhauser.

Rizzo, M., Anderson, S. W., Dawson, J., & Nawrot, M. (2000). Vision and cognition in Alzheimer's disease. *Neuropsychologia, 38,* 1157–1169.

Rizzolatti, G., & Matelli, M. (2003). Two different streams form the dorsal visual system: Anatomy and functions. *Experimental Brain Research, 153,* 146–157.

Robertson, L., & Lamb, M. (1991). Neuropsychological contributions to theories of part/whole organisation. *Cognitive Psychology, 23,* 299–330.

Robertson, L., Treisman, A., Friedman-Hill, S., & Grabowecky, M. (1997). The interaction of spatial and object pathways: Evidence from Balint's syndrome. *Journal of Cognitive Neuroscience, 9,* 295–317.

Rondot, P., Tzavaras, A., & Garcin, R. (1967). Sur un cas de propagnosie persistant depuis quinze ans. *Revue Neurologie, 117,* 424–428.

Roos, K. L. (1999). Neurosyphilis in musicians and composers. *Seminars in Neurology, 19,* 35–40.

Rossini, P. M. (2001). Brain redundancy: Responsivity or plasticity? *Annals of Neurology, 48,* 128–129.

Roy, M., Roy, A., Williams, J., Weinberger, L., & Smelson, D. (1997). Reduced blue cone electroretinogram in cocaine-withdrawn patients. *Archives of General Psychiatry, 54,* 153–156.

Russo, M., & Vignolo, L. A. (1967). Visual figure–ground discrimination in patients with unilateral cerebral disease. *Cortex, 3,* 113–127.

Sabelli, H., & Abouzeid, A. (2003). Definition and empirical characterization of creative processes. *Nonlinear Dynamics in Psychological Life Science, 7,* 35–47.

Sacks, O. (1995). *An anthropologist on Mars.* New York: Alfred A. Knopf.

Saffran, E. (2000). Aphasia and the relationship of language and brain. *Seminars in Neurology*, *20*, 409–418.

Sahlas, D. J. (2003). Dementia with Lewy bodies and the neurobehavioral decline of Mervyn Peake. *Archives of Neurology*, *60*, 889–892.

Scheideman, G. B., Bell, W. H., Legan, H. L., Finn, R. A., & Reisch, J. S. (1980). Cephalometric analysis of dentofacial normals. *American Journal of Orthodontics and Dentofacial Orthopedics*, *78*, 404–420.

Schlag, J., & Schlag-Rey, M. (1987). Evidence for a supplementary eye field. *Journal of Neurophysiology*, *57*, 179–200.

Schlaug, G., Jancke, L., Huang, Y., & Steinmetz, H. (1995). In vivo evidence of structural brain asymmetry in musicians. *Science*, *267*, 699–701.

Schnider, A., Regard, M., Benson, F., & Landis, T. (1993). Effects of a right-hemispheric stroke on an artist's performance. *Neuropsychiatry, Neuropsychology, and Behavioral Neurology*, *6*, 249–255.

Schoental, R. (1990). The death of Schubert. *Journal of the Royal Society of Medicine*, *83*, 813.

Schrag, A., & Trimble, M. (2001). Poetic talent unmasked by treatment of Parkinson's Disease. *Movement Disorders*, *16*, 1175–1176.

Schultz, W. (2000). Multiple reward signals in the brain. *Nature Review Neuroscience*, *1*, 199–207.

Schultz, W. (2002). Getting formal with dopamine and reward. *Neuron*, *36*, 241–263.

Schultz, W. (2004). Neural coding of basic reward terms of animal learning theory, game theory, microeconomics and behavioural ecology. *Current Opinion in Neurobiology*, *14*, 139–147.

Schuppert, M., Munte, T. F., Wieringa, B. M., & Altenmuller, E. (2000). Receptive amusia: Evidence for cross-hemispheric neural networks underlying music processing strategies. *Brain*, *123*, 546–559.

Scott, S. K., Blank, C. C., Rosen, S., & Wise, R. J. (2000). Identification of a pathway for intelligible speech in the left temporal lobe. *Brain*, *123*, 2400–2406.

Seitz, A., & Watanabe, T. (2003). Is subliminal learning really passive? *Nature*, *422*, 36.

Selfe, L. (1977). *Nadia: A case of extraordinary drawing ability in an autistic child*. London: Academic Press.

Selfe, L. (1995). Nadia reconsidered. In C. Golomb (Ed.), *The development of gifted child artists: Selected case studies* (pp. 197–236). Hillsdale, NJ: Lawrence Erlbaum Associates, Inc.

Sellal, F., Andriantseheno, M., Vercueil, L., Hirsch, E., Kahane, P., & Pellat, J. (2003). Dramatic changes in artistic preference after left temporal lobectomy. *Epilepsy and Behavior*, *4*, 449–451.

Service, R. (2003). Tortoise pace for the evolution of Chinese writing? *Science*, *300*, 723.

Shafritz, K. M., Gore, J. C., & Marois, R. (2002). The role of the parietal cortex in visual feature binding. *Proceedings of the National Academy of Sciences, USA*, *99*, 10,917–10,922.

Sharpe, H. (2001). The star creators of Hollywood. In G. Peary & J. Lefcourt (Eds.), *John Ford: Interviews* (pp. 15–20). Jackson, MS: University Press of Mississippi.

Shepard, R. N. (1997). The genetic basis of human scientific knowledge. *Ciba Foundation Symposium*, *208*, 23–31, discussion 31–38.

Shepard, R. N., & Hurwitz, S. (1984). Upward direction, mental rotation, and discrimination of left and right turns in maps. *Cognition*, *18*, 161–193.

Shepard, R. N., & Sheenan, M. M. (1971). Mental rotation of three-dimensional objects. *Science, 171*, 701–703.

Sherwood, C. C., Broadfield, D. C., Holloway, R. L., Gannon, P. J., & Hof, P. R. (2003a). Variability of Broca's area homologue in African great apes: Implications for language evolution. *Anatomical Record, 271A*, 276–285.

Sherwood, C. C., Holloway, R. L., Gannon, P. J., Semendeferi, K., Erwin, J. M., Zilles, K., & Hof, P. R. (2003b). Neuroanatomical basis of facial expression in monkeys, apes, and humans. *Annals of the New York Academy of Science, 1000*, 99–103.

Sherwood, C. C., Holloway, R. L., Erwin, J. M., & Hof, P. R. (2004). Cortical orofacial motor representation in Old World monkeys, great apes, and humans. II. Stereologic analysis of chemoarchitecture. *Brain, Behavior and Evolution, 63*, 82–106.

Shevrin, H. (2001). Event-related markers of unconscious processes. *International Journal of Psychophysiology, 42*, 209–218.

Shipp, S. (2004). The brain circuitry of attention. *Trends in Cognitive Science, 8*, 223–230.

Shlain, L. (1991). *Art and physics: Parallel visions in space, time, and light*. New York: William Morrow.

Short, R. A., & Graff-Radford, N. R. (2001). Localization of hemiachromatopsia. *Neurocase, 7*, 331–337.

Shuwairi, S. M., Cronin-Golomb, A., McCarley, R. W., & O'Donnell, B. F. (2002). Color discrimination in schizophrenia. *Schizophrenia Research, 55*, 197–204.

Signoret, J. L., van Eeckhout, P., Poncet, M., & Castaigne, P. (1987). Aphasia without amusia in a blind organist: Verbal alexia-agraphia without musical alexia-agraphia. *Revue Neurologie, 143*, 172–181.

Silverstein, A. (1999). The brain tumor of George Gershwin and the legs of Cole Porter. *Seminars in Neurology, 19*, 3–9.

Simon, J. (2000). *Susan Rothenberg*. New York: Harry N. Abrams.

Slater, E., & Meyer, A. (1959). Contribution to a pathography of the musicians. 1. Robert Schumann. *Confinia Psychiatrica, 2*, 65–95.

Sloboda, J. A., Hermelin, B., & O'Connor, N. (1985). An exceptional musical memory. *Memory Perception, 3*, 155–170.

Sokol, D. K., & Edwards-Brown, M. (2004). Neuroimaging in autistic spectrum disorder (ASD). *Journal of Neuroimaging, 14*, 8–15.

Solms, M., Kaplan-Solms, K., Saling, M., & Miller, P. (1998). Rotated drawing: The range of performance and anatomical correlates in a series of 16 patients. *Brain and Cognition, 38*, 358–368.

Solomon, M. (2003). *Late Beethoven: Music, thought, imagination*. Berkeley, CA: University of California Press.

Somerville, L. H., Kim, H., Johnstone, T., Alexander, A. L., & Whalen, P. J. (2004). Human amygdala responses during presentation of happy and neutral faces: correlations with state anxiety. *Biological Psychiatry, 55*, 897–903.

Southall, G. (1979). *Blind Tom: The post-Civil War enslavement of a black musical genius*. Minneapolis, MN: Challenge Productions.

Sparr, S. A. (2002). Receptive amelodia in a trained musician. *Neurology, 59*, 1659–1660.

Sperry, R. W. (1968). Hemisphere deconnection and unity in conscious awareness. *American Psychologist, 23*, 723–733.

Sperry, R. W. (1974). Lateral specialization in the surgically separated hemispheres. In

F. Schmitt & F. Worden (Eds.), *Neurosciences Third Study Program* (Vol. 3, pp. 5–19). Cambridge, MA: MIT Press.

Sperry, R. W. (1980). Mind–brain interaction: Mentalism, yes; dualism, no. *Neuroscience, 5*, 195–206.

Spreen, O., & Benton, A. L. (1969). *Embedded Figure Test: Neuropsychology Laboratory*. Victoria, BC: University of Victoria.

Spreen, O., & Strauss, E. (1998). *A compendium of neuropsychological tests: Administration, norms, and commentary*. Oxford: Oxford University Press.

Stebbing, P. D. (2004). A universal grammar for visual composition? *Leonardo, 37*, 63–70.

Sternberg, R. J. (Ed.). (1988). *The nature of creativity: Contemporary psychological perspectives*. Cambridge: Cambridge University Press.

Stewart, L., Walsh, V., & Frith, U. (2004). Reading music modifies spatial mapping in pianists. *Perception and Psychophysics, 66*, 183–195.

Tattersall, I. (2001). *The human odyssey: Four million years of human evolution*. Lincoln, NE: iUniverse.

Teismann, I. K., Soros, P., Manemann, E., Ross, B., Pantev, C., & Knecht, S. (2004). Responsiveness to repeated speech stimuli persists in left but not right auditory cortex. *Neuroreport, 15*, 1267–1270.

Teuber, H. L., & Weinstein, S. (1956). Ability to discover hidden figures after cerebral lesions. *Archives of Neurology and Psychiatry, 76*, 369–379.

Thieme, H. (1997). Lower Paleolithic hunting spears from Germany. *Nature, 385*, 807–810.

Thomas Anterion, C., Honore-Masson, S., Dirson, S., & Laurent, B. (2002). Lonely cowboy's thoughts. *Neurology, 59*, 1812–1813.

Thomson, B. (2002). *The Post-impressionists*. London: Phaidon Press.

Thorp, R. L., & Ellis, R. (2001). *Chinese art and culture*. New York: Prentice-Hall.

Thurstone, L. L. (1944). *A factorial study of perception*. Chicago: University of Chicago Press.

Tootell, R. B. H., & Hadjikhani, N. (2001). Where is "Dorsal V4" in human visual cortex? Retinotopic, topographic and functional evidence. *Cerebral Cortex, 11*, 298–311.

Tramo, M. J. (2001). Biology and music: Music of the hemispheres. *Science, 291*, 54–56.

Treffert, D. A. (1989). *Extraordinary people: Understanding "idiot savants"*. New York: Harper & Row.

Treffert, D. A., & Wallace, G. L. (2002). Islands of genius: Artistic brilliance and a dazzling memory can sometimes accompany autism and other developmental disorders. *Scientific American, 286*, 76–85.

Trethowan, W. H. (1977). Music and mental disorder. In M. Critchley & R. A. Henson (Eds.), *Music and the brain: Studies in the neurology of music* (pp. 399–432). London: William Heinemann Medical Books.

Trevarthen, C. (1974). Functional relations of disconnected hemispheres with the brain stem and with each other: Monkey and man. In M. Kinsbourne & W. L. Smith (Eds.), *Hemispheric disconnection and cerebral function* (pp. 187–207). Springfield, IL: Thomas.

Trevarthen, C. (1999) Musicality and the Intrinsic Motive Pulse: Evidence from human psychobiology and infant communication. Rhythms, musical narrative, and the origins of human communication. In *Musicae Scientiae*, special issue, 1999–2000, European Society for the Cognitive Sciences of Music, Liège (pp. 157–213).

Trevor-Roper, P. (1970). *The world through blunted sight*. Indianapolis, IN: Bobbs-Merrill.

Trudo, E. W., & Stark, W. J. (1998). Cataracts: Lifting the clouds on an age-old problem. *Postgraduate Medicine, 103*, 114–126.

Tzortzis, C., Goldblum, M. C., Dang, M., Forette, F., & Boller, F. (2000). Absence of amusia and preserved naming of musical instruments in an aphasic composer. *Cortex, 36*, 227–242.

Ullman, M. T. (2001). A neurocognitive perspective on language: The declarative/procedural model. *Nature Reviews Neuroscience, 2*, 717–726.

Ullman, S. (1996). *High-level vision: Object recognition and visual cognition*. Cambridge, MA: MIT Press.

Ungerleider, L. G., & Mishkin, M. (1982). Two visual systems. In D. Ingle, M. A. Goodale, & R. J. W. Mansfield (Eds.), *Analysis of visual behavior* (pp. 549–586). Cambridge, MA: MIT Press.

Valentino, M. A., Brown, J. W., & Cronan-Hillix, W. A. (1988). Aesthetic preference and lateral dominance. *Perception and Motor Skills, 67*, 555–561.

Valladas, H., Clottes, J., Geneste, J.-M., Garcia, M. A., Arnold, M., Cachier, H., & Tisnerat-Laborde, N. (2001). Evolution of prehistoric cave art. *Nature, 413*, 479.

Vargas, L. M. (1995). The black paintings and the Vogt-Koyanagi-Harada syndrome. *Journal of the Florida Medical Association, 82*, 533–534.

Vargha-Khadem, F., Watkins, K. E., Price, C. J., Ashburner, J., Alcock, K. J., Connelly, A., Frackowiak, R. S., Friston, K. J., Pembrey, M. E., Mishkin, M., Gadian, D. G., & Passingham, R. E. (1998). Neural basis of an inherited speech and language disorder. *Proceedings of the National Academy of Sciences, USA, 95*, 12,695–12,700.

Varlet, I., & Robertson, E. J. (1997). Left–right asymmetry in vertebrates. *Current Opinion in Genetic Development, 7*, 519–523.

Vartanian, O., & Goel, V. (2004). Neuroanatomical correlates of aesthetic preference for paintings. *NeuroReport, 15*, 893–897.

Vig, P. S., & Hewitt, A. B. (1975). Asymmetry of the human facial skeleton. *The Angle Orthodontist, 45*, 125–129.

Vigouroux, R. A., Bonnefoi, B., & Khalil, R. (1990). Réalisations picturales chez un artiste peintre presentant une heminegligence gauche. *Revue Neurologie (Paris), 146*, 665–670.

Walker, F. (1968). *Hugo Wolf: A biography*. London: J. M. Dent & Sons.

Wallesch, C.-W., Johannsen-Horbach, H., Bartels, C., & Herrmann, M. (1997). Mechanisms of and misconceptions about subcortical aphasia. *Brain and Language, 58*, 403–409.

Warrington, E. K., & James, M. (1966). Drawing disability in relation to laterality of cerebral lesion. *Brain, 89*, 53–82.

Warrington, E. K., & Taylor, A. M. (1973). The contribution of the right parietal lobe to object recognition. *Cortex, 9*, 152–164.

Washburn, D. K. (2000). An interactive test of color and contour perception by artists and non-artists. *Leonardo, 33*, 197–202.

Wasserstein, J., Zappulla, R., Rosen, J., & Gerstman, L. (1984). Evidence for differentiation of right hemisphere visual-perceptual functions. *Brain and Cognition 3*, 51–56.

Wasserstein, J., Zappulla, R., Rosen, J., Gerstman, L., & Rock, D. (1987). In search of closure: Subjective contour illusions, Gestalt completion tests, and implications. *Brain and Cognition, 6*, 1–14.

Watkins, K. E., Vargha-Khadem, F., Ashburner, J., Passingham, R. E., Connelly, A., Friston, K. J., Frackowiak, R. S., Mishkin, M., & Gadian, D. G. (2002). MRI analysis of an inherited speech and language disorder: Structural brain abnormalities. *Brain, 125,* 465–478.

Weale, R. A. (1997). Age and art. In M. F. Marmor & J. G. Ravin (Eds.), *The eye of the artist* (pp. 26–37). St. Louis, MO: Mosby.

Weiller, C. (1998). Imaging recovery from stroke. *Experimental Brain Research, 123,* 13–17.

Westen, D. (2003). *Psychology: Brain, behavior, and culture.* New York: John Wiley.

Whitaker, H. A. (1996). Clinical and experimental research: Future directions in neurolinguistics in general and brain and language in particular. *Brain and Language, 52,* 1–2.

Whitaker, H. A., & Kahn, H. J. (1994). Brain and language. In D. W. Zaidel (Ed.), *Neuropsychology* (pp. 126–138). San Diego, CA: Academic Press.

Whitaker, H. A., & Selnes, O. (1976). Anatomic variations in the cortex: Individual differences and the problem of the localization of language functions. *Annals of the New York Academy of Sciences, 280,* 844–854.

White, M. (2003a). *De Stijl and Dutch modernism.* Manchester: Manchester University Press.

White, R. (2003b). *Prehistoric art: The symbolic journey of humankind.* New York: Harry N. Abrams.

Wieser, H. G. (2003). Music and the brain: Lessons from brain diseases and some reflections on the "emotional" brain. *Annals of the New York Academy of Sciences, 999,* 76–94.

Wijk, H., Berg, S., Sivik, L., & Steen, B. (1999a). Colour discrimination, colour naming and colour preferences among individuals with Alzheimer's disease. *International Journal of Geriatric Psychiatry, 14,* 1000–1005.

Wijk, H., Berg, S., Sivik, L., & Steen, B. (1999b). Colour discrimination, colour naming and colour preferences in 80-year-olds. *Aging and Clinical Experimental Research, 11,* 176–185.

Wilkin, K. (1991). *Georges Braque.* New York: Abbeville Press.

Winner, E., & Casey, M. B. (1992). Cognitive profiles of artists. In G. C. Cupchik & J. Laszlo (Eds.), *Emerging visions of the aesthetic process: Psychology, semiology, and philosophy* (pp. 154–170). Cambridge: Cambridge University Press.

Winston, J. S., Strange, B. A., O'Doherty, J., & Dolan, R. J. (2002). Automatic and intentional brain responses during evaluation of trustworthiness of faces. *Nature Neuroscience, 5,* 277–283.

Wise, R. A. (2002). Brain reward circuitry: Insights from unsensed incentives. *Neuron, 36,* 229–240.

Wise, R. J., Scott, S. K., Blank, S. C., Mummery, C. J., Murphy, K., & Warburton, E. A. (2001). Separate neural subsystems within "Wernicke's area". *Brain, 124,* 83–95.

Witkin, H. A., Moore, C. A., Goodenough, D. R., & Cox, P. W. (1977). Field-dependent and field-independent cognitive styles and their education implications: Cognitive styles and their educational implications. *Review of Educational Research, 47,* 1–64.

Wolfe, J. M. (1998). What do 1,000,000 trials tell us about visual search? *Psychological Science, 9,* 33–39.

Wolfe, J. M., Oliva, A., Horowitz, T. S., Butcher, S. J., & Bompas, A. (2002). Segmentation of objects from backgrounds in visual search tasks. *Vision Research, 42,* 2985–3004.

Wolpert, I. (1924). Die Simultanagnosie: Störung der Gesamtauffassung, *Zeitschrift für die Gesamte Neurologie und Psychiatrie, 93,* 397–415.

Wolpoff, M. H., Mannheim, B., Mann, A., Hawks, J., Caspari, R., Rosenberg, K. R., Frayer, D. W., Gill, G. W., & Clark, G. (2004). Why not the Neandertals? *Debates in World Archaeology, 36,* 527–546.

Woo, T. L. (1931). On the asymmetry of the human skull. *Biometrika, 22,* 324–352.

Yomogida, Y., Sugiura, M., Watanabe, J., Akitsuki, Y., Sassa, Y., Sato, T., Matsue, Y., & Kawashima, R. (2004). Mental visual synthesis is originated in the fronto-temporal network of the left hemisphere. *Cerebral Cortex, 14,* 1376–1383.

Young, R. L., & Nettelbeck, T. (1995). The abilities of a musical savant and his family. *Journal of Autism and Developmental Disorders, 25,* 231–248.

Yovel, G., Yovel, I., & Levy, J. (2001). Hemispheric asymmetries for global and local visual perception: Effects of stimulus and task factors. *Journal of Experimental Psychology: Human Perception and Performance, 27,* 1369–1385.

Zaidel, D. W. (1988a). Hemi-field asymmetries in memory for incongruous scenes. *Cortex, 24,* 231–244.

Zaidel, D. W. (1988b). Observations on right hemisphere language functions. In F. C. Rose, R. Whurr, & M. Wyke (Eds.), *Aphasia* (pp. 170–187). London: Whurr.

Zaidel, D. W. (1990a). Long-term semantic memory in the two cerebral hemispheres. In C. Trevarthen (Ed.), *Brain circuits and functions of the mind* (pp. 266–280). New York: Cambridge University Press.

Zaidel, D. W. (1990b). Memory and spatial cognition following commissurotomy. In F. Boller & J. Grafman (Eds.), *Handbook of neuropsychology* (Vol. 4, pp. 151–166). Amsterdam: Elsevier.

Zaidel, D. W. (1993). View of the world from a split-brain perspective. In E. M. R. Critchley (Ed.), *Neurological boundaries of reality* (pp. 161–174). London: Farrand Press.

Zaidel, D. W. (1994). Worlds apart: Pictorial semantics in the left and right cerebral hemispheres. *Current Directions in Psychological Science, 3,* 5–8.

Zaidel, D. W. (2000). Different concepts and meaning systems in the left and right hemispheres. *Psychology of Learning and Motivation, 40,* 1–21.

Zaidel, D. W., & FitzGerald, P. (1994). Sex of the face in Western art: Left and right in portraits. *Empirical Studies of the Arts, 12,* 9–18.

Zaidel, D. W., & Kasher, A. (1989). Hemispheric memory for surrealistic versus realistic paintings. *Cortex, 25,* 617–641.

Zaidel, D. W., & Kosta, A. (2001). Hemispheric effects of canonical views of category members with known typicality levels. *Brain and Cognition, 46,* 311–316.

Zaidel, D. W., & Sperry, R. W. (1973). Performance on the Raven's Colored Progressive Matrices test by subjects with cerebral commissurotomy. *Cortex, 9,* 34–39.

Zaidel, D. W., & Sperry, R. W. (1977). Some long-term motor effects of cerebral commissurotomy in man. *Neuropsychologia, 11,* 193–204.

Zaidel, D. W., Chen, A. C., & German, C. (1995a). She is not a beauty even when she smiles: Possible evolutionary basis for a relationship between facial attractiveness and hemispheric specialization. *Neuropsychologia, 33,* 649–655.

Zaidel, D. W., Hugdahl, K., & Johnsen, B. (1995b). Physiological responses to verbally inaccessible pictorial information in the left and right hemispheres. *Neuropsychology, 9,* 52–57.

Zaidel, D. W., Esiri, M. M., & Beardsworth, E. D. (1998). Observations on the relationship between verbal explicit and implicit memory and density of neurons in the hippocampus. *Neuropsychologia, 36*, 1049–1062.

Zaidel, E. (1975). A technique for presenting lateralized visual input with prolonged exposure. *Vision Research, 15*, 283–289.

Zaidel, E. (1976). Auditory vocabulary of the right hemisphere following brain bisection or hemidecortication. *Cortex, 12*, 191–211.

Zaidel, E. (1978). Concepts of cerebral dominance in the split brain. In P. A. Buser & A. Rougeul-Buser (Eds.), *Cerebral correlates of conscious experience* (pp. 263–284). Amsterdam: Elsevier.

Zaidel, E. (1979). Performance on the ITPA following cerebral commissurotomy and hemispherectomy. *Neuropsychologia, 17*, 259–280.

Zaimov, K., Kitov, D., & Kolev, N. (1969). Aphasie chez un peintre. *Encephale, 58*, 377–417.

Zatorre, R. J. (2003). Absolute pitch: A model for understanding the influence of genes and development on neural and cognitive functions. *Nature Neuroscience, 6*, 692–695.

Zeki, S. (1993). *A vision of the brain*. Oxford: Blackwell Scientific.

Zeki, S. (1999). *Inner vision: An exploration of art and the brain*. London: Oxford University Press.

Zeki, S. (2004). Thirty years of a very special visual area, Area V5. *Journal of Physiology, 557*, 1–2.

Zihl, J., von Cramon, D., & Mai, N. (1983). Selective disturbance of movement vision after bilateral brain damage. *Brain, 106*, 313–340.

Author index

Subject index

260   *Subject index*

M. M. 92–93
Mondrian, Piet 163
Monica 110
Monet, Claude 67–68, 73, 208
Monsieur C. 107–108
music 3–4, 9–10
  brain localization 9–10, 87–88,
    110–112, 119
  chords 96, 102
  early origin 9–10, 188–192
  fMRI 117–120
  innate reactions 191–192
  language commonality 108
  PET 117–120
  unilateral brain damage 87–120
  Wada test 114
  writing musical notes 89, 94–95,
    108
musicians 80, 107–120. *See also*
    composers
  singers with brain damage 104, 107,
    115
  performers 80, 88, 94, 100, 103, 104,
    107, 112, 116
  trained 107–109, 112–113, 119
musicians' hands brain representation
    115–116
movies; *see* film

Nadia 7, 76–78
Neanderthals 9, 13, 183–186, 191,
    195–196, 210
neglect; *see* hemi-neglect
neurotransmitters 10, 13, 67, 90, 173,
    207–208
  clues to art 207–208
  dopamine 67–68, 90, 173–174
  evolution (human brain) 13
Nykvist, Sven 64, 170–171, 177

oblique effect 162–163, 177
Ocean, Humphrey 7
optic nerve 62
optic pathway 53, 62

painters 29–36, 41–44, 50, 68–74,
    208–209
Paravincini, Derek 80
Parkinson's Disease; *see* artists with
    brain damage
Peake, Mervyn 46–47
perspective, convergent 7, 31, 38, 40,
    77–78, 142–143, 164, 192, 201, 214
  linear 77, 142–143, 208

views (three-dimensional) 7, 14, 60,
    74–78, 121, 125–126, 138–139,
    141–142, 157, 170, 185, 187
photography (still) 10, 63, 73, 171
Picasso, Pablo 63, 129–130, 149, 165
pictorial scenes; *see* scenes
Pissarro, Camille 68
pleasure 12, 14, 69, 89, 113, 162,
    172–174, 182, 190, 215
  loss, brain damage 113, 159
  reward (pleasure) system 172–174
Piraha people 194–195, 201, 216
poetry 46, 207–208
portraits (painted) 38, 147–149, 166–168,
    176–177
  asymmetry 166
  attractiveness 167
practicing (training) 78, 93–94, 112
preference (aesthetic) 158–160, 163–164,
    177, 215
preference change 158–160, 215
prefrontal cortex 117–119, 153–155, 160,
    173
Purdy, Donald 59

Raderscheidt, Anton 36
Ravel, Maurice 84, 88–91
recovery 24, 83–85, 94, 151. *See also*
    functional compensation
    (reorganization)
Rembrandt, van Rijn 70
Renaissance 142–145, 166, 170
Renoir, Pierre-Auguste 67, 70
retina 50, 52–53, 59–62, 65–67, 69,
    70–71, 121, 125, 162
right hemisphere language xv, 15–16
rods 61–62
Rothenberg, Susan 208

Sabadel 148
savant skills 75–85. *See also* autistic
    savants
scenes 11, 18, 44–45, 131, 152–155,
    163–164, 209
Schubert, Franz 102–103, 205
Schumann, Robert 100–101
semantic knowledge 58, 79–80, 153,
    196–197
sex differences 165–167, 177
Shebalin, Vissarion 93–94
simultanagnosia 18, 32, 152–155
singing 114–115
  loss 115
sketchbook practice 122–123